THE
ON-LINE REVOLUTION
IN LIBRARIES

BOOKS IN
LIBRARY AND INFORMATION SCIENCE

A Series of Monographs and Textbooks

EDITOR
ALLEN KENT

Director, Office of Communications Programs
University of Pittsburgh
Pittsburgh, Pennsylvania

Additional volumes in preparation

THE
ON-LINE REVOLUTION
IN LIBRARIES

Proceedings of the 1977 Conference
in Pittsburgh, Pennsylvania

Edited by

ALLEN KENT   THOMAS J. GALVIN

Graduate School of Library and Information Sciences
University of Pittsburgh
Pittsburgh, Pennsylvania

MARCEL DEKKER, INC.   New York and Basel

Library of Congress Cataloging in Publication Data

Main entry under title:

The On-line revolution in libraries.

    (Books in library and information science ; v. 23)
    "Convened . . under the auspices of the Graduate
School of Library and Information Sciences, University of
Pittsburgh. "
    Includes index.
    1. On-line bibliographic searching--Congresses.
2. Machine-readable bibliographic data--Congresses.
3. Information services--Congresses. I, Kent, Allen.
II. Galvin, Thomas J. III. Pittsburgh. University.
Graduate School of Library and Information Sciences.
IV. Series.
Z699.A1052   025.3'028'54   78-15800
ISBN 0-8247-6754-3

MARCEL DEKKER, INC.

270 Madison Avenue, New York, New York 10016

Current printing (last digit):

10 9 8 9 7 6 5 4 3

PRINTED IN THE UNITED STATES OF AMERICA

PREFACE

The ultimate impact of on-line information services on libraries and library users is today only dimly sensed. Yet, those vendors who market services to libraries report that the number of data bases available for on-line access continue to increase. The number of on-line terminals in use is also increasing about 20 per cent each year, and usage is increasing about 30 per cent each year.

Acronyms such as ORBIT, DIALOG, and BRS are becoming part of the everyday vocabulary of librarians and library users. Moreover, an increasing number of libraries are installing terminals. Both good and bad experiences are being reported, but the reasons are not understood. Do they relate to training? Do they relate to the skills of "intermediaries" or users who are directly on-line? Do they relate to the charging of fees vs. provision of services at no cost to the user?

Other questions raised concern whether or not the user derives any real benefit beyond that which can be obtained through use of more traditional information sources. How do the services affect the library "ecology"?--since the services alert users to much more than a given library holds. How do these services relate to the development of library resource-sharing networks?

This book represents the proceedings of a national conference on "The On-Line Revolution in Libraries" convened on November 14-16, 1977, under the auspices of the Graduate School of Library and Information Sciences, University of Pittsburgh, and attended by more than 700 persons from the United States and overseas.

The purpose of this national conference was to examine the potential of on-line information systems, placed within the context of other library services; to assess the various impacts--especially on the user; and to explore the critical issues that must be resolved--such as costs, fee vs. free services, training problems, standardization, quality control, and evaluation. It was the intent to provide a preview of some of the changes in the library world in the near future.

Five position papers prepared in advance were distributed to registrants prior to the conference to review:

1. The potential of on-line information systems (Chapter 1)
2. Impact on information policy (Chapter 8)
3. Impact on library functions (Chapter 10)
4. Impact on the clientele (Chapter 12)
5. Training and retraining librarians and users (Chapter 21)

The appropriate position paper was first summarized at each conference session; the principal speakers then reacted and discussion followed.

These proceedings are organized in four parts. The first three address the topics of the main sessions. A closing summary is given in Part Four.

ACKNOWLEDGMENTS

The conference was stimulated by developments supported by the Buhl Foundation and the National Science Foundation. The Buhl Foundation has provided substantial grants to the University of Pittsburgh; first for the study of library resource sharing, and currently for the development of an experimental resource-sharing network (WEBNET) as well as for the establishment of a training center for on-line information systems. The National Science Foundation, Division of Science Information, has provided grants for a study of the use of library materials (Grant Number DSI 75-11840 A02) and for the development of a campus-based information system (Grant Number G-27537).

Mrs. Priscilla Mercier, Office of Communications Programs, University of Pittsburgh, was responsible for the administration of the conference, starting with its organization, continuing with the hosting of the event, and concluding with the post-conference activities which led to the publication of these proceedings. It is clear that her efforts were of chief importance in bringing the enterprise to fruition.

Mrs. Karen Schirra was responsible for the typing of these proceedings for publication.

Allen Kent and Thomas J. Galvin

LIST OF CONTRIBUTORS

LEE G. BURCHINAL, Director, Division of Science Information, National Science Foundation, Washington, D.C.

ELAINE CARUSO, Assistant Research Professor, Interdisciplinary Department of Information Science, University of Pittsburgh, Pittsburgh, Pennsylvania.

EVALYN CLOUGH, Assistant to the Dean and Lecturer, Graduate School of Library and Information Sciences, University of Pittsburgh, Pittsburgh, Pennsylvania.

CARLOS A. CUADRA, President, Cuadra Associates, Inc., Santa Monica, California.

MELVIN S. DAY, Deputy Director, National Library of Medicine, Bethesda, Maryland.

RICHARD DE GENNARO, Director of Libraries, University of Pennsylvania, Philadelphia, Pennsylvania.

ELLEN GAY DETLEFSEN, Assistant Professor, Graduate School of Library and Information Sciences, University of Pittsburgh, Pittsburgh, Pennsylvania.

KEITH DOMS, Director, The Free Library of Philadelphia, Philadelphia, Pennsylvania.

MIRIAM A. DRAKE, Assistant Director, Administrative Services, Purdue University Libraries and Audio-Visual Center, West Lafayette, Indiana.

ELIZABETH E. DUNCAN, Office of Communications Programs, University of Pittsburgh, Pittsburgh, Pennsylvania.

THOMAS J. GALVIN, Dean, Graduate School of Library and Information Sciences, University of Pittsburgh, Pittsburgh, Pennsylvania.

ALLEN KENT, Director, Office of Communications Programs, University of Pittsburgh, Pittsburgh, Pennsylvania.

JOHN G. LORENZ, Executive Director, Association of Research Libraries, Washington, D.C.

ANTHONY A. MARTIN, Director, Carnegie Library of Pittsburgh, Pittsburgh, Pennsylvania.

SUSAN K. MARTIN, Head, Library Systems Office, University of California-Berkeley, Berkeley, California.

JAMES M. MATARAZZO, Assistant Dean for Student Affairs and Associate Professor, School of Library Science, Simmons College, Boston, Massachusetts.

PAUL EVAN PETERS, Manager, Social Science Information Utilization Laboratory, University of Pittsburgh, Pittsburgh, Pennsylvania.

MARTIN D. ROBBINS, Director, Colorado Energy Research Institute, Golden, Colorado.

ANITA R. SCHILLER, Data Services Librarian/Bibliographer, University of California, San Diego, La Jolla, California

JOSEPH F. SHUBERT, State Librarian and Assistant Commissioner for Libraries, State of New York, Albany, New York.

SALLY BACHELDER STANLEY, Vice President, The Information Bank, New York, New York.

ROGER K. SUMMIT, Manager, Lockheed Information Systems, Palo Alto Research Laboratory, Palo Alto, California.

ALPHONSE F. TREZZA, Executive Director, National Commission on Libraries and Information Science, Washington, D.C.

JUDITH WANGER, Vice-President, Cuadra Associates, Inc., Santa Monica, California.

JAMES G. WILLIAMS, Associate Professor, Interdisciplinary Department of Information Science, University of Pittsburgh, Pittsburgh, Pennsylvania.

MARTHA E. WILLIAMS, Director, Information Retrieval Research Laboratory, University of Illinois, Urbana, Illinois.

SAMUEL A. WOLPERT, President, Predicasts, Inc., Cleveland, Ohio.

CONTENTS

Part One
THE POTENTIAL OF ON-LINE INFORMATION SYSTEMS

Part Two
IMPACT OF ON-LINE SYSTEMS

Part Three
TRAINING AND RETRAINING OF LIBRARIANS AND USERS

Part Four
CLOSING SUMMARY

INTRODUCTION

Thomas J. Galvin

Dean
Graduate School of Library and Information Sciences
University of Pittsburgh
Pittsburgh, Pennsylvania

In October 1976, some four hundred librarians and information specialists gathered in Pittsburgh for a national conference, the first of its kind to
be sponsored by the University of Pittsburgh's Graduate School of Library
and Information Sciences. The subject of that first conference was resource-
sharing in libraries, and the Proceedings were published a few months later
by Marcel Dekker, Inc. of New York and Basel in a volume titled Library
Resource Sharing. One year later, in November 1977, nearly seven hundred
fifty librarians, information specialists, administrators and representatives
of the information industry, from almost every state of the union and many
foreign countries, assembled at the William Penn Hotel for the second annual
Pittsburgh Conference, titled "The On-Line Revolution in Libraries." The
present volume incorporates the papers presented at that second Pittsburgh
Conference, along with extensive excerpts from the discussion sessions that
followed each group of formal papers. The Proceedings volume has been
compiled in order to provide those who participated in the second Pittsburgh
Conference with a full record of its content, to make the conference papers
and related discussion available to the large number of those who, while
unable to attend the conference, have expressed a deep interest in its subject
matter, and to respond to the needs of both students and practitioners for a
current review of the present status and future prospects in the application
of on-line technology to library functions and services.

That the subject matter of the second Pittsburgh Conference is highly
significant is clearly demonstrated by the size of the roster of participants
alone. Not only was the number of attendees unprecedented for a conference
of this kind, but the composition of the audience reflected a rich mix of both
a wide range of types and sizes of libraries, as well as a strong representa-

tion from various sectors of the "information industry." The result was to provide producers and consumers of the products of this new electronic technology with an unusual (and all-too-infrequent) opportunity for interaction. The outcome, as reflected chiefly in the discussion sessions which concluded each of the four major segments of the conference program, was a kind and level of dialogue characterized by an unusually constructive approach to the identification and resolution of problems of urgent mutual concern to both the information industry and its librarian clients. It is clear from the results of this conference that both groups would benefit from more opportunities of this kind.

The title of the conference, "The On-Line Revolution in Libraries," might, at first glance, appear more rhetorical than substantive. If so, it is a shared rhetoric where the impact of on-line technology on library services is concerned. In a collection of essays commissioned by the Association of College and Research Libraries in conjunction with the Centennial of the American Library Association, David C. Weber, Director of Libraries at Stanford University, wrote:

> American academic libraries have reached a watershed that is almost as significant as the change from block printing to printing with movable type. This conclusion is based on the assumption that on-line computer-based operational programs constitute a radical and permanent change in cooperative style. When one is freed from most of the constraints of the card catalog, of the U.S. mail, and of locally prepared cataloging data, this adoption of sophisticated on-line computer-based programs may well be by far the most significant change ever achieved in library operations. It is a permanent change in the mode of library operations which should be accomplished during the period from 1965 to 1990.
>
> (David C. Weber, "A Century of Cooperative Programs Among Academic Libraries," in Libraries for Teaching, Libraries for Research: Essays for a Century, ed. Richard D. Johnson. Chicago: American Library Association, 1977.)

The problem with revolutions, of course, is always to recognize one when we are living in the middle of, and through it. And the thing about revolutions is that they sometimes happen either before we know it, or without knowing it, or without our really having intended it. A very basic question about on-line technology and libraries is, do we really have a revolution --actual, potential, or both--on our hands? If so, what is the true dimension of the on-line revolution and the ultimate scope and range of its impact? Is the on-line technology just a means to achieve, for those who can afford it, a quantitative upgrading of existing library and information services? Will the on-line technology merely enable us to offer our clienteles more of the same, but to do traditional kinds of things faster and, hopefully, better? Is it simply, in this sense, a quantitative, evolutionary phenomenon, or does it actually have the capacity to bring about a true qualitative change in the character of information delivery in libraries?

While these fundamental questions permeated the entire conference program, the opening session, titled "The Potential of On-Line Information Systems," was directed specifically at a description and assessment of the power of on-line technology. Allen Kent's position paper (Chapter 1), distributed in advance to both panelists and conference registrants, addresses the issue squarely and unequivocally. If exploited to its maximum potential, the on-line technology, Professor Kent asserts with confidence, does indeed offer a "qualitative advantage" in realizing the opportunity to achieve a new service level, to move to a new and higher plane in facilitating human interaction with knowledge records. The ability to conduct multi-dimensional searches, thus overcoming the monodimensional limitations of both manual and computer approaches to subject analysis of documents, the capacity to update files on a daily basis, and the capability to modify search strategies while a search is in progress combine to make possible a customized, individualized product substantially beyond the reach of traditional literature searching. To realize that advantage to the fullest, however, Kent points out that librarians have to free themselves from the constraints of established approaches to literature searching, and the cost issue, which he elucidates in detail, has to be resolved.

Each of the five panelists responding to Professor Kent's paper approaches the "revolutionary" character of on-line access to remote data bases from a slightly different point of view. Samuel A. Wolpert, President of Predicasts, Inc. (Chapter 2), emphasizes multiple-postings, the capacity of the computer to make a document accessible from many points of view, as well as the potential of the on-line system to generate customized output. Noting that "the historical division--that of librarians pushing documents around and research departments pushing information around--can no longer exist," Wolpert sees only two alternatives for librarians: "They can move up and become information specialists, or they can move out."

Anita R. Schiller of the University of California, San Diego (Chapter 3), examines the impact of on-line technology in the broader context of a social and economic, rather than merely a technological, revolution. Citing the dangers inherent in the "commoditization of information," Schiller warns of the potential erosion of the concept of information as a national resource and a "public good," which may, in turn, require government intervention and oversight to protect citizen access.

Another aspect of "revolution" is the focus for the comments of Martin D. Robbins, Vice President of EDUCOM (Chapter 4). Recognizing the growing trend in social science research to utilize data files and archives as an alternative to laboratory experiment and natural observation, Robbins stresses the need to integrate these data files with traditional library resources, as well as to bring them under control through creation of a "standardized, machine-readable national union catalog that can be searched interactively. "

Pursuing the theme of the capability of on-line technology to provide access to a vastly enlarged body of knowledge records, Joseph F. Shubert, State Librarian and Assistant Commissioner for Libraries of the State of New York (Chapter 5), directs attention to the potential disturbance in the library and user "ecology" that may result unless we can achieve a corresponding gain in the capacity of both librarians and clients to utilize and control the contents of an expanded body of literature and data. Shubert is the first of several speakers to address the cost issue in terms of the potential price spiral that could result if libraries engage in wholesale substitution of on-line access for subscriptions to the printed indexes that form the basic input for the on-line data bases. Elaborating on an implied theme in Schiller's remarks, Shubert notes the urgent need to assure that the clienteles of smaller public libraries and school media centers are not excluded from participation in the benefits of the new technology.

Concluding the opening session's formal papers, Carlos Cuadra, representing System Development Corporation, and a member, as well, of the National Commission on Libraries and Information Science (Chapter 6), joins with those who view the advent of on-line technology as "the most important innovation in the field of library and information science in the past decade. " Examining the converse of Shubert's argument, Cuadra demonstrates that on-line systems offer the potential to equalize access to recorded knowledge, and to reduce the present resource inequity between smaller and larger libraries. Costs of on-line searching, he predicts, will decline if the free market is preserved, but the question remains as to the extent of governmental responsibility to make high technology information systems available without charge to all citizens.

The second general session of the 1977 Pittsburgh Conference provided a day-long opportunity to address the complex matter of the actual current impact of on-line systems on library operations. Underlying the day's discussions were two basic questions: first, whether librarians will control the new technology or be controlled by it; and second, the distinction between what this technology makes it possible to do, by contrast with what librarians and information specialists, as professionals, judge it desirable to do.

Initially, the focus is on the implications of the on-line revolution for national information policy and for local, state and regional library planning.

At the national level, Lee G. Burchinal of the National Science Foundation
(Chapter 8), sees in the growth of on-line systems a further example of the
general shift toward alternatives to "paper dominated" systems of information transfer and away from a reliance on local holdings to meet user information needs. In turn, he relates these trends to the overall growth of the
U. S. information industry, characterized by the replacement of labor-
intensive operations with capital-intensive technologies. Like Schiller,
Burchinal notes expansion of fee-based services, and the current ferment
at the federal level in the regulatory area.

Responding to Burchinal's overview, Melvin S. Day, Deputy Director
of the National Library of Medicine (Chapter 9), emphasizes the impact of
on-line systems on the governmental decision-making process at both federal
and state levels. While recognizing the potential need for coordinated policy
planning at the national level, Day cites the limitations of this approach,
reminding us of H. L. Mencken's observation that "for every complex problem there is a solution that is neat, plausible and wrong." He asserts that
American pre-eminence in information science and technology has been
achieved without centralized planning, in the context of a diversified, pluralistic, competitive information environment.

In the second of three position papers prepared for this session,
Miriam A. Drake, Assistant Director of Libraries at Purdue University
(Chapter 10), assesses the impact of on-line technology on library operations.
"Traditional library systems," she concludes, "are being gradually overthrown without violence" in the context of a controlled technological revolution
affecting every functional area of library service. Citing attitudinal barriers
among librarians as a major impediment to realizing the potential of the new
information technology, Drake postulates a changing professional climate as
"many librarians are learning that active participation is more rewarding
than static resistance."

For John G. Lorenz, Executive Director of the Association of Research
Libraries (Chapter 11), however, the obstacles to realization are not primarily attitudinal, but fiscal. In a sharp rejoinder to Drake's stance, Lorenz
focuses on the economic constraints under which all types of libraries currently labor, and looks to the federal level to provide new capital through
full funding of Title IIC of the Higher Education Act and Title III of the Library
Services and Construction Act.

Paul E. Peters and Ellen Gay Detlefsen of the University of Pittsburgh
(Chapter 12), conclude the session with an examination of on-line systems
in their ultimate impact on reference and information service. They elaborate
on the capability of the new technology to provide individualized, personalized
search services, and to vastly enrich the information environment of the
library's clientele. Recognizing the limitations of broad generalizations with

respect to users as a class, they offer a four-part taxonomy of clients, distinguishing carefully between "first-order clients, those who use the system or who use the information from it," and "second-order clients--those who manage first-order clients," and whose decisions ultimately determine the character and quality of information services to be provided. In a thoughtful response, Martha E. Williams of the University of Illinois (Chapter 13), elucidates in greater detail the major research priorities in relation to users and their interactions with on-line systems. Given the phenomenal growth in on-line activity detailed by Professor Williams, the need for applied research to enhance what she terms "the user-orientedness" of systems becomes readily apparent. Her paper concludes with a forecast of both quantitative and qualitative changes likely to affect the future of on-line information transfer.

From a consideration of these three individual elements, the conference next moved to a full afternoon devoted to an attempt to reassemble the parts of the impact question into a coherent whole. A panel of five, comprising Alphonse F. Trezza, Executive Director of the National Commission on Libraries and Information Science; Roger K. Summit, Manager of the Dialog Information Retrieval Service of Lockheed Information Systems; Richard De Gennaro, Director of Libraries, University of Pennsylvania; Keith Doms, Director of the Free Library of Philadelphia; and Ellen Gay Detlefsen collectively probes a wide range of complex problems, assisted by Mr. Day, Mr. Lorenz, Dr. Williams and by trenchant questions and comments from the audience (Chapters 15-20).

The panel stresses the importance of obtaining new monies from the state and federal levels to create the "full service network" that is the goal of NCLIS, and to assure full access to it through individual libraries. The potential of on-line technology to bring a higher order of information delivery to all citizens is identified, as are critical issues of service philosophy, quality control and funding that must be resolved in order for that potential to be realized. Summit offers the opinion that "no longer is the feasibility of on-line retrieval being discussed, rather problems reflecting the maturity of the process and the problems resulting from its rather rapid development and acceptance are given consideration." Among these, the panel identifies the unresolved question of the optimal balance between the public and private sectors, the issue of indirect as contrasted with direct costs, and the desirability of integrating local and regional data bases with national systems. A detailed statement, incorporated in the summary of audience discussion, considers user fees from an economist's point of view.

Because of the complex and critical character of the training problem, and because the University of Pittsburgh has had a special concern for the training needs of both librarians and users, this was chosen as the topic for the concluding session of the conference. Dr. Elaine Caruso, who has been deeply involved in research and development work in this area at the University of Pittsburgh, prepared the position paper which serves as a basis for reaction and discussion by a panel and the audience (Chapter 21). Extending the notion of revolutionary change stated at the opening session, Caruso cites the need for a new approach to training "not just because the data base files are different in structure and invisible to us, but because use is so different; the strategy for searching a machine-stored file is qualitatively and quantitatively different...." She stresses the importance of "understanding the content and structure" of the machine-stored files as a key to reducing "the expense of inefficient and ineffective searches," a theme repeated by her respondents.

Sally Bachelder Stanley, Regional Manager of The Information Bank (Chapter 22), views the training experience as having inherent value in itself in terms of developing the ability to utilize a data base to the fullest. Pursuing a central question of training priorities, Judith Wanger of System Development Corporation (Chapter 23), identifies what she views as a false dichotomy between the training of intermediaries and training of end-users. Susan K. Martin of the University of California-Berkeley's Library Systems Office (Chapter 24), alerts us to the importance of "training for the negatives," particularly in the orientation of end-users. Anthony A. Martin, Director of the Carnegie Library of Pittsburgh (Chapter 25), identifies needed types of training materials, examines the phenomenon of the "period of latency" between the beginning and advanced stages of training, and emphasizes Caruso's conclusion that there is, at present, a lack of "a coherent, comprehensive learning experience." Concluding the formal panel presentations, Dr. Elizabeth E. Duncan, Coordinator of the University of Pittsburgh's model Campus-Based Information System (Chapter 26), discusses the complexity of the training problem in light of variations in patterns of on-line searching among different types of libraries, while at the same time identifying practice on the terminal as a vital element in the achievement of search proficiency.

As will be evident from the foregoing, the 1977 Pittsburgh Conference participants addressed a wide range of complex questions and closely related issues. The concluding chapter (Chapter 28), constitutes an attempt at summary and synthesis, and is presented here in full as was not possible at the conference itself because of time constraints. Omitted from this Proceedings volume was a most engaging dinner address delivered on the second evening of the conference by Dr. Joseph C. R. Licklider of the Massachusetts Institute of Technology on the broad topic "New Initiatives and New Technology." This presentation, which centered around a series of visuals, regrettably did not lend itself to replication in the printed volume, and could not be summarized without gross injustice to the character of the talk. Included as an appendix, however, is a summary of the participants' evaluation of the

conference prepared by James M. Matarazzo of the School of Library Science,
Simmons College, Evalyn Clough and James G. Williams of the University of
Pittsburgh.

The participants' own evaluations of the conference experience make
clear that they view on-line systems as highly significant for the future of
library and information services, and that they consider the problem of
training and retraining staff as one of high priority. As a professional school
in a large urban university dedicated to research, teaching and service, the
Graduate School of Library and Information Sciences of the University of
Pittsburgh recognizes a twofold obligation: first, to contribute to the continued growth of knowledge, and second, to facilitate the effective dissemination of new knowledge, with special concern for the continuing education
needs of library and information professionals.

In response to these obligations, the School announced at this conference
its intention, with the generous support of the Buhl Foundation, to open in the
Spring of 1978 a national on-line training center. Through the use of unique
training materials and emulations developed and tested at the University of
Pittsburgh, an intensive, highly individualized training experience can be
provided which will be responsive to many of the special training concerns
expressed by participants in this conference.

Beyond this, the annual Pittsburgh Conferences themselves constitute
a major vehicle through which the School and the University seek to advance
knowledge and its dissemination in library and information services. Through
future conferences of this kind, as well as through the publication of this
Proceedings volume, we hope to make a significant continuing contribution to
the professional growth of the library and information communities.

THE
ON-LINE REVOLUTION
IN LIBRARIES

Part One

THE POTENTIAL OF ON-LINE INFORMATION SYSTEMS

The on-line revolution has different potential for various libraries. The ways in which conventional and on-line functions are performed have similarities and differences based on type of library and form of materials. On-line activities will not have come of age until there is common understanding of the fundamental services that such systems have been designed to produce, and until they are integrated with traditional services. Lack of understanding and insufficient competency in using the new tools is widespread among librarians who have not learned to exploit such systems to their benefit and to the benefit of library users in a cost-effective way. The state of the art suggests that the on-line revolution will facilitate a major reallocation of the responsibilities of librarians and provide opportunities for greater use of their professional talents.

The position paper distributed in advance of the conference is given in Chapter 1. Chapters 2-6 present reactions from the panelists. Chapter 7 presents the discussion at the conference.

Chapter 1

THE POTENTIAL OF ON-LINE INFORMATION SYSTEMS

Allen Kent

Director
Office of Communications Programs
University of Pittsburgh
Pittsburgh, Pennsylvania

PROLOGUE

.... Our ineptitude in getting at the record is largely caused by the artificiality of systems of indexing. When data of any sort are placed in storage, they are filed alphabetically or numerically, and information is found (when it is) by tracing it down from subclass to subclass. It can be in only one place, unless duplicates are used; one has to have rules as to which path will locate it, and the rules are cumbersome. Having found one item, moreover, one has to emerge from the system and re-enter on a new path.

The human mind does not work that way. It operates by association. With one item in its grasp, it snaps instantly to the next that is suggested by the association of thoughts, in accordance with some intricate web of trails carried by the cells of the brain. It has other characteristics, of course; trails that are not frequently followed are prone to fade, items are not fully permanent, memory is transitory. Yet the speed of action, the intricacy of trails, the detail of mental pictures, is awe-inspiring beyond all else in nature.

-- from Vannevar Bush

"As We May Think," Atlantic Monthly,
Vol. 176, July 1945, pp. 101-108.

INTRODUCTION

Vannevar Bush, in his widely read and frequently cited article, "As We May Think," identified more than thirty years ago a fundamental problem--perhaps the critical one, the solution of which has eluded those who serve information seekers by acquiring, organizing, retrieving, and disseminating the record of our society. Selection, or retrieval from human memory, is not oriented to alphabetical or numerical sequences, and yet many or most conventional catalogs and indexes are arrayed in that way. Vannevar Bush was not optimistic that one could even hope that the associations and their trails which permit man to conceptualize could be duplicated artifically.

But it is thirty-two years since the Bush article appeared in print. During that time the computer has emerged as a powerful tool for processing information. Associations can now indeed be made artificially; results of such associations can be displayed faster than they can be read. And so scenes (or "screens") such as in Figure 1 are becoming more familiar as more and more librarians hop on a bandwagon which some have called an "on-line revolution in libraries."

SEARCH PROFILE:

ANY ONE OF:

    ENVIRONMENT OR POLLUTION

ANY ONE OF:

    ENERGY

AND ONE OF:

    FUEL*

TIME	0 MINS.	45.88 SECS.
NUMBER OF DOCUMENTS:		9,585
TOTAL HITS FOR SEARCH:		5

Figure 1

Many are attracted to on-line systems because of the lure of technology--the symbiosis of people and machines, involving a computer terminal, a distant computer, and a communication system that brings the power of the remote computer to one's fingertips--to a typewriter keyboard in one's customary work environment. Others are attracted by the automation of functions which have been tedious and redundant (cataloging) or extraordinarily laborious and expensive (literature searching). Some perceive the ability to produce a bibliography on any topic, on demand, simply by "pushing a button," with no need to instruct library users on the intricacies of how to use indexes. And then there are those who react defensively, recognizing that a portion of the library clientele is becoming increasingly oriented to on-line information systems and will, more and more, bypass the library which is not on the bandwagon; particularly worrisome is that this often represents the business community--the prize clients of many libraries.

In the forefront of the on-line revolution is the issue of costs, particularly those which were never overt, but which now mount with each tick of the clock as computer and communications time become explicit--and are invoiced in a businesslike manner by the vendors. The issue is twofold: first, the magnitude of the now explicit costs, which are viewed as alarming and/or prohibitive by the non-profit sector; and second, the question of how and by whom the costs are to be paid.

Many librarians and information specialists perceive on-line information systems merely in terms of substitution of functions currently performed manually. But few, if any, systems can be "installed" beneficially without rethinking current functions with the purpose of optimizing service objectives. And those who engage in this process find the cost-effective attainment of objectives inhibited by conventional staffing patterns and the heavy hand of tradition. Most difficult of all is achievement of the qualitative advantage of enhanced information delivery capability--which is the rationale for an on-line information system.

This advantage is achieved by the ability of a computer to "correlate" aspects of a search. There are two problems confronting this author in attempting to make this ability clear in this paper. First, it is exceptionally difficult to describe a process or an "experience," especially since it appears deceptively simple to those who have not had the "experience." Nevertheless, it seems important to try to put the process into words, since the behavior of many who believe it to be self-evident belies their comprehension. Second, a description of process is tutorial in nature and not needed by those readers who have experienced the on-line process. These readers may wish merely to scan, or even skip, the next dozen or so pages.

THE FUNDAMENTALS

As with many bandwagons, some fall off, or climb off. The reasons vary, but this author suspects that many climbed on for the wrong reasons, while others became disillusioned or frustrated because they never understood what these systems can produce (and what they cannot produce) and accordingly never understood how to exploit the systems effectively. The blurb for a recent workshop in this field tried to provide an alert in this regard:

We need to orient ourselves in a new way to the study of this new resource. We need a new approach, not just because the data base files are different in structure, and invisible to us, but because use is so different; the strategy for searching a machine-stored file is qualitatively and quantitatively different; it is different in a purely physical mechanical sense. Searchers of mechanized systems need to think, not just of the best first approach to file contents, but of all possible approaches, and how to combine them in a kind of simultaneous combing of the whole file. One doesn't thread a path--except at great expense!

But it is my thesis that man has been so conditioned by arrays and displays in alphabetic and numeric sequence, that the promise of the emerging systems is not realized. The challenge is how to recondition those who would use these systems so that they are indeed effective supplements to their own memory.

Alphabetic thinking is hard to avoid, since alphabetic artifacts are all around us: telephone directories, dictionaries, library card catalogs, book indexes; and alphabetic thinking (and consequent searching) is frequently efficient. As we all know, the telephone directory provides a listing of names, followed by addresses and finally the telephone numbers. This alphabetic array of names is a highly efficient display and searching mechanism if one is seeking the phone number of an individual whose name is known. But sometimes there are listings for more than one person with identical names. Then the address must be known to be able to select the correct one. A problem develops when the given name is not known and the correct spelling of the surname is not known. If one heard a name pronounced "bràun" it might be listed in several ways (September 1976 directory for Greater Pittsburgh):

BROWN	(1800 entries)
BROWNE	(40 entries)
BRAUN	(160 entries)
BRAUNE	(2 entries)

Other examples are:

SMITH	(3500 entries)
SMYTH	(16 entries)
SMYTHE	(12 entries)

Perhaps the most exasperating example is:

COHEN, COEN, COHN, KOHEN, KOHN,
COHAN, KOHAN

If one wished to locate a gynecologist (name unknown) with offices in the Oakland area of Pittsburgh, one would have to review thirteen pages of the classified directory to locate the several dozen who meet these criteria. It would be so nice to be able to pose a question to the classified directory which would make it unnecessary to review the names of physicians, but rather to specify only those criteria which are desired (and known): specialty (gynecology), and location (Oakland).

Even with these few examples, it is clear that for some requirements, the displays provided in published telephone directories are inadequate, and inefficient to use. The key lesson here is that printed alphabetic arrays work well for "monodimensional" searches (one name, one subject, etc., to be searched at a time), but only when the precise spelling of the desired item is known.

Let us then move on to an "on-line system, to illustrate the types of problems they are designed to solve. In preparing to write this paper, I wished to conduct some searches which might be useful as examples. So I decided to examine some output from ERIC (Educational Resources Information Center), one of the data bases maintained "on-line" at the University of Pittsburgh. The starting point was a "monodimensional" search, on ENVIRONMENT. I searched a sample of the ERIC file, consisting of the index entries (and abstracts) of some 10,000 documents. Not knowing what to expect, I merely requested a report of how many items (or "hits") I would receive as a result of this search, and the abstracts of the first 10 responses. Within 17 seconds the search was completed, and 501 hits were identified.

Upon reading the first few abstracts, I discovered that there are at least two contexts for "environment" in this file:

(1) The environment which influences student learning
     (e.g., classroom)

(2) The external environment which is a subject taught in
the classroom (e.g., pollution, nuclear energy, noise)

I decided to pursue the latter context in further searches. The next probe
was a search for documents on ENVIRONMENT and ENERGY (both must be
present in a single document). Nine documents satisfied my request (within
26 seconds). It was noted that the words I sought were identified regardless of whether they appeared in the title, the index-entries (keywords), or
the abstract.

It then occurred to me that I was missing some articles of interest
when terms such as ENVIRONMENTAL EDUCATION appeared. In order to
catch these as well, I would need to employ the truncation technique,
searching for ENVIRONMENT*, the asterisk calling for any word starting
with "environment," regardless of the word ending.

The next step was to explore the term POLLUTION together with
ENERGY, which yielded 7 hits, leading me to decide that what I really
wanted was only those documents discussing either ENVIRONMENT* or
POLLUTION and ENERGY. The search produced 14 hits from diverse
sources (e.g., Science Teacher, Environmental Quality Magazine, and
Science). I then decided to constrain the search even more, requiring
FUEL* to be added to the previous search, leading to 4 hits. But then I
went too far, wanting to add "ethical problems" (ETHIC*) as well, and
received the report: SORRY NO HITS FOUND.

There are a number of lessons to be learned from the examples provided above:

(1) It is important to understand the contents of a data base
before conducting a search (relevant background information is obtained by: (a) familiarity with the paper
copy index or abstracts related to the data base; (b)
knowledge of the differences between the paper edition
and the magnetic edition that have been introduced by
the developer of the data base; (c) knowledge of special
features that have been added by the system staff who
make it available on a particular computer installation;
and (d) familiarity with the printed search aids written
either by the data base developer or the system staff).

(2) The terms (keywords) used in search strategies must
be selected carefully, checking vocabulary control aids
(e.g., thesauri) and/or truncating words to take variant
forms into account.

(3) The effectiveness of a search strategy can be evaluated
     quickly by:

     (a) determining number of hits for different
          configurations (i.e., search strategies);

     (b) obtaining sample results to be used as a
          basis for refinement of search strategies.

(4) The strategy of logical sum (term A or term B) tends to
     increase output.

(5) The strategy of logical product (term A and term B) tends
     to decrease output; adding too many terms to the logical
     product eventually results in no output.

(6) Interactive searching, on-line, permits the above lessons
     (and others) to be learned effectively in relation to a given
     problem.

The examples developed above are typical of what can be accomplished with most bibliographic data bases. But several data bases provide
additional computational capabilities. Thus access can be provided to
statistical series which can be used for on-line analysis and forecasting.
In the Predicasts service, users may also enter their own data, perform
econometric programs for forecasting and plot graphs. From these examples I can move on to the fundamentals of information retrieval by computer,
which will set the stage for the on-line systems.

Information retrieval relates to the identification of material based
on the matching of a question against an index to documents in a collection.
Although distinctions are often made in the literature among data retrieval,
information retrieval, and document retrieval, there are some fundamental
principles that are common to all three types of retrieval.

Retrieval assumes the availability of an "index" which purports to
identify the important contents of documents. The index entries may include such aspects as author, source, and date of publication, as well as
subjects which describe concepts discussed in documents. The index
entries may be recorded on various media, the most familiar of which is
the printed page, and displayed in alphabetic array. Searches directed to
the index have typically been monodimensional in nature; that is, a question is posed in terms of a single index entry. The search is conducted by
consulting the printed index and locating the desired entry in an alphabetical array in order to determine the desired reference. Thus, in Figure 2,

a search for

"Card-actuated cameras"

provides the reference

(2) 664

which means that the article in Volume 2, on page 664, contains material relevant to that topic.

Canticum Canticorum (2)643
Card-actuated cameras (2)664
Card catalogs (2)660; (3)411; (4)277
Card punch, automatic data processing
    (2)195
Card reader, automatic data processing
    (2)195
Cards-with-Books-Program (4)287
The Carl H. Pforzheimer Library:
    English Literature 1475-1700 (2)417
Carnegie, Andrew (2)252; (3)347, 375,
    392; (4)192-200, 200
Carnegie Corporation of New York
    (4)200-207

Figure 2. Portion of an Alphabet Index

Indexes to large collections frequently contain many references to single entries--more than one might wish to consult. For example,

Catalogs and Cataloging, (1) 356,

(1) 426, (1) 436, (1) 471,
(1) 517, (1) 600, (2) 131,
(2) 210, (2) 409, (2) 664,
(3) 288, (3) 548, (3) 661,
(4) 242-305, (4) 393, (4) 642

Modifications, or subheadings, may then be provided, listed under the "main" entry, as in Figure 3. Thus one can select a more specific aspect of the main entry, reducing the number of references to be traced and examined.

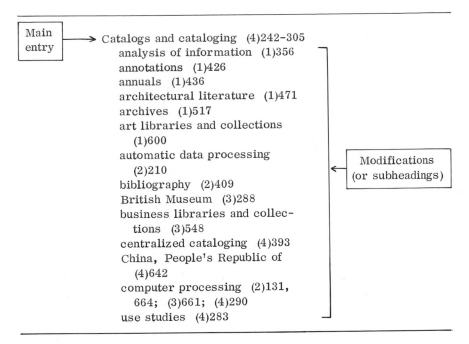

Figure 3. Portion of Index Showing Main Entry
and Modifications, or Subheadings

Question: Find all references to: (1) catalogs and
cataloging of (2) nonprint materials

Index entries:

1. Catalogs and cataloging, (1) 356,
      (1) 426,   (1) 436,   (1) 471,
      (1) 517,   (1) 600,   (2) 131,
      (2) 210,   (2) 409,   (2) 664,
      (3) 288,   (3) 548,   (3) 661,
      (4) 242-305, (4) 393, (4) 642

2. Nonprint materials, (2) 234,
      (2) 594,   (3) 112,   (3) 288,
      (4) 163,   (4) 342,   (4) 395,
      (4) 602,   (4) 629

Figure 4. Multidimensional Question:
The Common Reference Is (3) 288

   Some questions entail searches for two or more main entries, all of
which must refer to the identical references (see Figure 4), i.e., "multidimensional" searches which cannot be performed conveniently by using a
printed or a card index. The difficulty is in visually correlating references
listed under all the desired entries to discover which are common (that is,
refer to the same "document"), especially when the entries appear on
different pages of a printed index or in different catalog trays.

   The information explosion has mandated a change in the nature of
search requirements as a consequence of the exponential growth of recorded
knowledge. When it was possible for an individual to read substantially all
of the materials of potential interest on a given field or topic prior to their
being filed, searches were frequently based on recall from memory. Thus
the individual might remember the author, source, date or main subjects
of documents that had been perused in the past. A search of an index, monodimensional in nature, could be conducted without too many uninteresting
references being identified. But as the quantity of material of potential
interest increased to the point at which the individual could no longer read
or scan all of it, a question based on recall from memory was no longer
possible. The nature of questions began to change. Questions were posed
more frequently in terms of characteristics of a problem or area of interest.
For example, a mechanical engineer who earlier might have read about a
new material of interest might have posed a question asking for all documents which discussed that material. Later, the same engineer, not
previously having read about the new material, might pose a question which
described the properties of a material of interest.

> I am interested in developing a diaphragm for a valve
> which is to be used under nuclear conditions. I would
> like to have all documents which describe materials
> (names unknown to me) which might be used for the
> diaphragm. The desired material must exhibit the
> following properties:
>
>> corrosion resistance
>> flexibility
>> ductility
>> good fatigue life
>> usable at temperatures of 800-900°F

In order to be able to respond to such questions, there was an increasing
demand for "in-depth" indexing to provide mutliple reference points that
could be coordinated retrospectively for searches from many, perhaps
unexpected, points of view.

Given the requirement to search multidimensionally, with many index entries available for search, a printed index became less and less convenient to exploit. As computers became increasingly available, they were employed to conduct searches. It was convenient to record index entries on magnetic tape. A suitable program could then be written to search more conveniently for references which had several index entries in common.

Once this opportunity existed, more complicated search strategies were possible:

(1) The search for alternative index entries:

> An individual could specify several (or many) entries, any one of which might produce useful references. For example: I am interested in documents which discuss "Watergate" or "Haldeman" or "Erlichman" or "Mitchell" or "Stans." This strategy is called a logical sum.

(2) The search for sets of alternative index entries, with one or more of each set required to be present:

> For example: I am interested in documents which discuss "Nixon" or "Watergate" and "Haldeman" or "Erlichman" and "Mitchell" or "Stans." This strategy is called the logical product of logical sums.

(3) The search for index entries if others are absent:

> For example: I am interested in documents which discuss "Haldeman" and "Erlichman," if "Mitchell" and "Stans" are not mentioned. This strategy is called the logical difference.

(4) The search for index entries, one weighted more than the other:

> For example: I am interested in documents which discuss "Haldeman" and "Erlichman"; if none are available, I will review those which discuss "Mitchell" or "Stans."

The next step came with the introduction of interactive computing, with searching performed "on-line." A user operating a terminal establishes direct contact with the computer where the data base is stored.

Strategies can be altered midway in a search as references uncovered indicate a need for a change.

The use of computers for retrieval has highlighted the problems of
indexing which twenty years ago were recognized mainly by librarians and
compilers of indexes. If indexes are prepared without standardization or
control, using the words of authors (keywords selected from the title, for
example), the indexes are easily and cheaply produced, a condition made
even easier and cheaper by the computer.

But the emergence of "keyword" indexes based on titles of documents,
while cost-effective to produce by computer, placed a burden on the retrieval function. Searchers could not rely on standard index entries, since
no control of vocabulary was introduced during the production of such indexes. Thus a search for an entry such as "advertise" would miss references to entries under all other variant forms such as:

ADVERTISE	and	ADVERTIZE
ADVERTISING	and	ADVERTIZING
ADVERTISER	and	ADVERTIZER
ADVERTISERS	and	ADVERTIZERS
ADVERTISEMENT	and	ADVERTIZEMENT
ADVERTISEMENTS	and	ADVERTIZEMENTS
ADVERTISABLE	and	ADVERTIZABLE

If such a search were to be performed by computer, then it might be expe-
ditious to conduct the search for all words starting with the characters

ADVERTI

regardless of what the word endings might be. In other words, all characters following the "i" are arbitrarily truncated. Serious difficulties also
emerge when synonymous terms widely separated alphabetically are allowed
to become primary index terms.

The problem of control of vocabulary used for indexing has led to the
reemergence of the thesaurus. It is used as a guide to input (to control the
entries used) or as a guide to strategy preparation (to obviate the need for
the searcher to remember all words that are probably related).

Mechanized information retrieval has necessitated the formalization
of search processes that have traditionally been used in human searching,
but had not been made explicit previously. But when they are made explicit,
when symbols are used to represent index entries, when "search operators"
(and, or, not) are used to represent desired logical interactions, and when
special characters are used to represent functions, the resulting repre-

sentation of a "complex" search strategy can become frustrating to one who is accustomed to descriptive statements of problems or questions in natural language.

An example of a statement may make my point clear:

$$(A_1 + A_2 + A_3 + A_4 + A_5 + A_6 + A_7 + A_8 + A_9 + A_{10}) *$$

$$(B_1 + B_2 + B_3 + B_4 + B_5 + B_6) * (C_1 + C_2)$$

which in "natural" language would be:

I am interested in only those documents which discuss all three of the following subjects:

Blood coagulation disorders
Heart disease
Children

Further, the cross reference structure suggests that one should also consider the following (see also) subject headings:

Blood coagulation disorders (A_1)
See also
Blood coagulation (A_2)
Anticoagulants (A_3)
Thrombocytes (A_4)
Blood platelets (A_5)
Hemmagglutination (A_6)
Blood viscosity (A_7)
Blood diseases (A_8)
Hemostatics (A_9)
Hematologic diseases (A_{10})

Heart disease (B_1)
See also
Ausculation (B_2)
Cardiovascular disease (B_3)
Cardiology (B_4)
Cardiac arrest (B_5)
Heart ausculation (B_6)

Children (C_1)
See also
Infants (C_2)

To accomplish such a search using conventional printed indexes, one would have to consult 18 subject headings (A_1 to A_{10}, B_1 to B_6, C_1, and C_2) and determine whether any documents had been referenced under any one of the following combinations of headings:

A_1 and B_1 and C_1
A_2 and B_1 and C_1
A_3 and B_1 and C_1
A_4 and B_1 and C_1
A_5 and B_1 and C_1
A_6 and B_1 and C_1
A_7 and B_1 and C_1
A_8 and B_1 and C_1
A_9 and B_1 and C_1
A_{10} and B_1 and C_1
A_1 and B_2 and C_1
A_2 and B_2 and C_1
A_3 and B_2 and C_1
etc. for 120 such combinations.

It is no wonder that such searches would not be conducted using conventional alphabetic indexes. It also suggests the rationale for using computers to conduct such searches. Looking back to the formal, symbolic representation of the search strategy, it is no wonder that the uninitiated user, who is oriented to monodimensional searches in printed indexes, might become frustrated. Some would also see the formal representation as a "mathematical equation," a field of study that many avoided during their schooling.

ON-LINE INFORMATION RETRIEVAL

The dimension added to information retrieval by being "on-line" is communication among (1) a user, (2) a computer, and (3) a file. A user can enter a question at a terminal by "typing" a formal statement of the search "strategy"; the statement is transmitted to a remotely located computer; the computer, using a search program, then accesses (searches) a file; and transmits back to the user at the terminal the responses to the question. All this can occur in "real-time"--that is, quickly enough so that the user may either utilize the results (output) immediately, or adjust the search strategy if the initial output is not relevant. (This may be akin to browsing.) Depending upon the type of terminal employed, the results may be displayed on a screen (of a cathode ray tube) or in hard copy (printed out as from a conventional typewriter). Depending upon the options offered by a given system, the output may be a document number, a bibliographic citation, an abstract, or any other evidence of the results of the search.

The computer program may offer additional features, such as tutorial messages to help the user enter a question, suggestions as to aids (e.g., a thesaurus) to formulating a question, or admonitions when a mistake has been made. These features are related to "interactivity." They provide the opportunity for user refinement of search strategies in response to immediate feedback from the system, and can increase the probability of success in the retrieval of useful material.

The major advantages accrued by being on-line are that access to data bases is now convenient regardless of geographic location, and that the searcher and the system can interact, make changes--and thus achieve good results quickly.

THE LIBRARY CONTEXT

Providing access to library materials requires the development and provision of locator tools to aid library patrons or reference librarians in determining what is available and where it is stored. Traditionally, those books and monographs held in a given library are cataloged, so that these materials can be accessed from a subject (and author) point of view. As libraries band together to share their resources, it is necessary to develop a union catalog, which "interfiles" the catalogs of individual libraries and also provides location information so that delivery of the materials from remote sites can be initiated.

The current situation is quite different for journals and technical and research reports that are held in most individual libraries. In this case, only the journal titles are "cataloged," but such cataloging does not provide either author or subject access to individual articles for the library patron. * Mostly, librarians rely instead on indexing services which market the tools necessary for locating specific journal articles or documents from a subject point of view. These services typically prepare indexes for the articles published in a given specialty or discipline. Since any given library acquires only a portion of these articles, the library patron who uses the index is frequently alerted to materials that are held elsewhere. The local library will usually be able to arrange for the desired articles to be copied or borrowed for the local patron.

There are many indexing services, which cover different collections of journals and reports. But it is difficult for the patrons to wend their

---

* In the 19th century most general libraries did catalog individual journal articles; some special libraries currently do so.

way through these indexes; even when they do learn to use the various
indexes, it is extremely time consuming to do so, frequently resulting in
searches not being conducted at all, or being done ineffectively.

Traditionally, the indexing services have been provided in printed
form, cumulated annually, and sometimes with five or ten year accumula-
tions. It is difficult to use these printed indexes, especially when a subject
search requires location of articles which have several concepts in common
("multidimensional" searches). The printed indexes, usually arranged
alphabetically, are not amenable to such searches. Also the more current
articles are not available for search until the printed index appears months
or, in some instances, years later, making these articles inaccessible
during the time when interest in them is greatest.

More recently, many indexing services began to consider the use of
computers for searching, with the indexes made available on magnetic
tapes, which could be leased to libraries. These tapes (sometimes called
"bibliographic data bases") were provided quarterly, monthly or even
weekly, so that searches of more current materials could be conducted. *
As mentioned earlier, the development of computerized bibliographic data
bases has resulted from a subtle change in the "recall" mechanism of those
who must deal with the increasing quantity of information of possible relevance to the solution of problems and to support decision processes. The
ability to correlate diverse points of view is made possible by using the
logical capabilities of computers. The traditional printed index can be
used substantially in a monodimensional manner--that is, through consultation of entries only one at a time and from single points of view. The
ability to conduct "multidimensional" searches of indexes presents an
opportunity to achieve an unparalleled qualitative advance that has not been
experienced before computers could augment the human mind in the correlation process. But few libraries had the facilities or expertise to handle
the indexes on magnetic tapes. The number of individuals who were
trained to exploit this growing resource was very small.

Meanwhile, the computer/bibliographic data base world outside of
the library was growing rapidly. More and more magnetic data bases were
being generated, some in fields not previously having files (e.g., history,
art). The annual price of many individual data bases was so high ($1,000
to $10,000 per year) that libraries could not consider acquiring the files.

---

* Some individual (chiefly small, special) libraries have created their own
  data bases in-house by local indexing and inputing the results into the
  computer in the context of a local information retrieval system.

At the same time, two commercial organizations* recognized the opportunity to develop "wholesaler" relationships with the manufacturers of data bases and to offer "on-line" searches through time-sharing terminals to their computers. But many libraries could not finance free access to all the large files available through these organizations. Even if fees are charged to cover line costs, there are other cost factors to consider: if a librarian and/or a patron spends two hours with printed indexes trying to locate material on a particular subject, there is no overt cost; only the "hidden costs" of the librarian's and/or the patron's salary. A computer search has entirely different costs. Over and above any hidden costs, there are the very overt, relatively high costs of communication, computer usage (calculated as a fixed cost per second per data base), and, frequently, a royalty charge per document identified during a search. This latter condition is true whether or not the document is relevant to the user's need. Thus, whether the costs for a particular search are nominal or relatively high can depend very much on the skills of the person doing the search.

Another factor which exacerbates the problem is that training of librarians and patrons by external organizations has been quite expensive. The training is episodic, frequently arranged away from the local environment, and not necessarily coincident with the initiation of local services. The cost of the services inhibit substantial practice sessions, so that the effects of training may be lost quickly. The consequence is that many searches of the data bases are not performed adequately, and frustration and loss of interest result, especially with the fees involved.

COSTS AND FEES

The presentation of costs and fees by the eager salesperson is a bit like the story of the optometrist in presenting a fee for a new set of spectacles: "The cost is $50," he says. If the client does not flinch, he continues, "...for each glass." If the customer still does not flinch, he concludes, "Of course, the frames are extra."

The basic cost of on-line service can be presented as $1,500 for the terminal. To connect a terminal to the service, there is, often, an annual membership fee--but of course "connect" time is extra--for both communication costs and per hour charge of accessing a particular data base. Then, there are "royalties" to be paid to many of the data base suppliers for each

---

* These are Lockheed and System Development Corporation; more recently Bibliographic Reference Service entered the field.

"hit"--but training is extra, beyond the initial period. This type of fee
structure entails a small down payment and incremental and continuing
costs.

Fees for on-line services pay for services which are, in a sense,
consumed immediately, and a fee must be paid even if useful results are
not obtained. It is difficult to relate the fee to a physical item, as when
purchasing an automobile. Although the notion of "fee for service" is not
unfamiliar to librarians (viz. the service basis method of charge has been
employed by H. W. Wilson for many years), typically a library buys something that will be available forever. The binding might wear out, but the
information will not. The item will be paid for once, and can be used as
many times as desired, without the user having to pay for leafing through
the pages, for stopping to read something (whether or not it turned out to
be interesting). The data bases now require a fee each time they are accessed, even though the same information is scanned over and over again--
and one even has to pay to learn how to use it.

The overt costs of such services have raised the question of how to
pay for them. Many suggest that the user should pay some or all of the
fees involved. But there is also considerable sentiment against this practice. For example, the Social Responsibilities Round Table of the American Library Association organized a meeting (Detroit, June 19, 1977)
entitled "The Prostitution of Information: Fees for Service." The announcement of this meeting stated, in part*:

> The practice of FREE library service is being challenged
> again. This time, computer-based services priced beyond
> the hard-times budgets of free libraries today are being
> offered as lure. And 'intellectual freedom' free-traders
> bite hard: 'How,' they ask, 'can we deprive those users
> who will pay extra for these services?' The IF free-
> traders are shocked, as if librarians would be denying
> people's primal urge to pay; and they are myopic, as if
> ignorant of the free-trade fact that these services cannot
> make profit without substantial subsidization from the
> general public monies or libraries would never have been
> approached as a market.
>
> Who pays? Who profits? When new fee services are added,
> are any free practices curtailed in libraries? Nowadays,

---

* SSRT, ALA Newsletter, No. 45, June 1977.

when most folks have trouble paying overdue fines, can we
pretend that fee charges for services will not deny service
to many? Can libraries that charge fees for service con-
fidently continue to rely on good will and tax support from
the public? Do service fees constitute double taxation on
an already overburdened taxpayer? Will the push for federal funding guarantee free services?

Subsequently, the ALA Council adopted a policy on equal access to
information:

The American Library Association supports the principle
of equal access to information through the maintenance of
publicly funded institutions providing library and information services. The charging of fees and levies for information services, including those services utilizing the
latest information technology, is discriminatory in publicly
funded institutions providing library and information
services.

The American Library Association through its membership
will promote the concept of equal access to information in
a free society. The Association calls upon all concerned
citizens to join in developing the kind of public support for
libraries and information agencies which will insure the
utilization of latest technological developments in information delivery without placing additional fees and levies upon
the individual seeking access.

The question remains whether libraries can find a way to avoid fees to
users by augmenting budgets.

One might question whether the on-line services are really as expensive as the overt costs make them seem to be. For example, if one were
to spread the true cost of conventional materials over the number of uses,
one might find that these are beyond ordinary expectations, especially for
expensive materials that are little used. But since these latter costs are
frequently not known, and since the economic value of saving the time of
librarians and users is seldom made explicit, it is no wonder that the
explicit fees (which must take all costs into account) are shocking to many.
It is no wonder that these services are therefore labeled "sophisticated"
and "specialized," and therefore the fees must be passed on--in whole or
in part--to the "sophisticated" and "specialized" user; all this while other
users may incur much greater costs to libraries when they demand the
acquisition of expensive items that are little if ever used.

The data base searches are frequently seen as useful only to the elite, who can find a way to cover the costs. The assumption is made, tacitly or explicitly, that these services merely provide mechanisms for conducting searches which can be performed as well, but less quickly, using the alphabetic, printed index. And this is the most pervasive misconception, and perhaps the most difficult to correct, since computer searching of indexes in a way that "correlates" aspects of a search, is not a part of common experience, and cannot be described by analogy.

REPRISE

The on-line revolution in libraries is addressing the issues raised by Vannevar Bush, in his 1945 look into the future. The logical capabilities of the computer are permitting correlation of concepts derived from published materials, facilitating the identification of those materials which are more likely to be related to the problems or interest of the end user. The speed of computers, together with appropriate file organization, is permitting such identification from very large collections of material. Interactive computing is permitting convenient changes in search strategies, based on review of initial search results. Time sharing is permitting groups of individuals to conduct such searches at the same time. Communication facilities permit all this to happen from locations which are convenient for users--remote from the files and from the computers.

The issue of delivery of primary source materials still remains, in that the user is alerted to many materials which are not held locally. The provision of abstracts or other "surrogates" helps to reveal more about the contents of these materials than the bibliographic citations alone, making it easier to select those which are interesting; but the technology for transmission of images of the full source materials is still not cost effective, nor are the mails a suitable mechanism for rapid delivery.

But this issue is not faced alone by on-line information systems; the conventional indexes do not solve the problem either. Some services do attempt to cope with the problem, providing:

(1) an "electronic mailbox" for recording orders for source
    materials to be delivered within 24 hours

(2) source materials recorded on microfilm, with depositories
    in many geographic locations.

One vendor offers access to non-bibliographic files, with capabilities for statistical analysis and for graphing--making it unnecessary to have the source materials.

EPILOGUE

A New Kind of Power. On-line retrieval has been characterized in terms of "document retrieval" and "information retrieval." The former is said to produce references to full documents; the latter is said to produce answers to questions. As early as 1911, long before the introduction of computers, it was said that for some purposes "...we do not want books, we want information, and although this information is contained in books, it should be looked upon as quite a different material and must be treated differently from books. Information taken away from literature can be organized more compactly, more homogeneously, and above all it gives us an opportunity to select better what we want, to reject what is of no use to us. As long as we have the information required, we can get on quite well without any books at all."*

Once computers were introduced into the retrieval arena, it became convenient to search the contents of documents in a penetrating way. Whatever is recorded in computer-readable form can be searched, and correlated, to produce references to the full documents, or to specific sections of the document. It is of course possible to print out whatever sections of the document contain the desired information.

Currently, many data bases record document citations, index entries, and abstracts. Any word or combination of words can be reference points for searches; printouts of some or all of the recorded material can be printed out and provided to the user. It is even possible, although not yet economically feasible, to record the entire text of a document, to search the entire text, and to print out all or parts of the text.

On-line retrieval makes it convenient to exercise a new kind of power in bibliographical control, which may be termed "exploitative control."** Such control permits as much penetration into the contents of source materials as one is willing to invest in recording in computer-sensible form and in expending computer time to search and correlate. The supplementation of conventional bibliographic elements by abstracts and even texts provides an enhanced basis for selection or exploitative control. Such control can even go as far as dealing with specific data which can be exploited further through computer analysis.

---

* J. Kaiser, Systematic Indexing, London, 1911.

**Patrick Wilson, Two Kinds of Power: An Essay on Bibliographic Control, Berkeley: University of California Press, 1968, pp. 23 ff.

As with any kind of power, both evil as well as good can result. The enhanced capabilities, if used indiscriminately and without skill, can produce results which are too voluminous, irrelevant and even misleading.

But used appropriately, the new kind of power will become relevant both to the library clientele and to the librarian, both released from many unwanted, uninteresting and time-consuming tasks in locating information, and able to spend more time in creatively dealing with professional decisions.

Chapter 2

POTENTIAL: REACTION

Samuel A. Wolpert

President
Predicasts, Inc.
Cleveland, Ohio

PREFACE

Allow me to make a few personal comments as prelude to my response to Mr. Kent's presentation. One must be cautious when making a critique of Allen Kent. In 1960, I had the temerity to criticize him. As a result, Predicasts, Inc. was born. We can therefore estimate that my last criticism of this gentleman cost me and the members of my staff some where in the range of one and a half million hours of work. Perhaps I ought to sit down right now. If the past is a guide, future work will multiply with every word I speak. All jokes aside. Allen Kent is one of the seminal thinkers in the field of information science. The paper he has just presented fully supports this thesis.

CURRENT CAPABILITIES

In his paper, Allen Kent makes the point that on-line systems are not merely a low-cost substitute for the printed index. They do in fact offer many new features, and these should be stressed. First is the tremendous increase in the number of postings. In a printed index, by virtue of space limitations, a citation may be listed under one, two or possibly three subjects. In on-line systems, citations can be listed under hundreds of subjects, which increases the user's ability to access this information by an extremely high multiple. Having more index terms is the equivalent of having more information. For example, consider the difference between filing an article which gives polyethylene capacity by producer, by process, and by country only once under polyethylene or filing it under each term mentioned. In the first case, the Union Carbide file will not contain the article nor will the Canadian file.

Another capability of on-line systems is their provision of abstracts or data rather than bibliographic citations. This feature, combined with the correlation of data mentioned by Allen, permits the on-line report to stand as an end product in and of itself. Abstracts insure that it will be substantive, while correlation assures the reader that it will contain relevant information only. Many studies have indicated that the prime cost involved in obtaining information lies in the time it takes to read. Consequently, a system which can sharply reduce this cost and yet provide quality information is indeed valuable. In fact large scale usage of information in decision making depends upon the availability of such a system. From an analyst's point of view, not only is reading time cut, but the sorting capability of the on-line system eases his job considerably. This sorting feature permits, for example, the user to receive all his production figures or all his new technology information together. As the analyst's time spent in searching, sorting, and reading diminishes, time available for creative problem solving increases.

POTENTIAL FOR ON-LINE SYSTEMS

Let us turn to the potential for on-line systems. Currently, Predicasts Terminal System is computational and can produce graphic displays, and I believe the demand for this type of graphic capability illustrates an obvious truth: the world is becoming increasingly visually oriented. While people may hesitate to read or study tables, they do not have to be coerced to look at pictures, graphs or maps. This thesis should lead logically to the advent of on-line decision-making modeling systems. Currently, one of the problems of in-depth research reports is their static nature. While reading the report, the decision maker cannot easily conceptualize the effects of alternative decisions. In the future, we can place the literature, data and equations on-line. The decision maker can then hypothesize various alternatives and, almost simultaneously, tables, graphs and pictures would dramatize the results of the various options.

Also awaiting on-line systems is the development of SDI, the selective dissemination of information. SDI would work as follows. Each decision maker would be interviewed by a systems user and an interest profile constructed from that interview. One or two paragraphs summarizing both internal and external developments which might be of interest to any and all executives would then be keyboarded and coded. The computer would match codes and/or words from the information bank to those of the decision makers' profiles. In this manner, custom reports could be generated for each and every decision maker. We foresee the day when the executive and the researcher, upon arrival at the office, will turn on the terminal, execute commands representing their profiles, and sit back to read of yesterday's events and ideas which may vitally affect today.

On another front, we expect significant developments within the next decade in document delivery systems. An increasing percentage of the world's literature will be stored in a form from which it could be rapidly retrieved for long distance telecommunication. Material used frequently will be stored in computer memories. Less frequently used material will be stored in automated microfilm systems; from these systems, documents could be mechanically retrieved, converted to digital characteristics, and eventually transmitted by means of telecommunication. Thus vital documents would be displayed on demand. It is becoming increasingly clear that the historical division--that of librarians pushing documents around and research departments pushing information around--can no longer exist.

THE NEW INFORMATION SPECIALIST

We've looked at the current capabilities of on-line systems. We've discussed a few futuristic visions. Underlying all of these concepts is how --and why--the boundary between research departments and librarians is being radically realigned. Where will the librarian stand in the face of such rapid change? The role of librarians is going to alter, and alter drastically. Information centers will become decentralized and far more numerous while the demand for specialization will continue to grow. The old world, one which found the $12,000-a-year female librarian serving the $75,000-a-year male executive, will cease. Frankly, today's librarians have two alternatives: they can move up and become information specialists or they can move out.

Such an ominous statement deserves some elaboration. The search for and manipulation of information requires a great deal of academic knowledge, substantive knowledge, and information technology. At Predicasts, we joke that the ideal systems operator should know his or her industry, know the data bases, know the DIALOG search system, know Predicasts' codes, and know our computational system. And then there are the small matters such as a thorough knowledge of market research and economics. Obviously we have not found such a person--and I hesitate to guess at what that individual's salary demands would be. In other words, the systems are outrunning human capabilities.

Some people maintain that this is a temporary phenomenon, that future gains in hardware and software will make the system simpler to operate. We do not agree. What makes the system complicated is neither hardware nor software, but the complexity of the information itself. The world is a complex place, and if systems are going to produce realistic results, they must in fact be complex systems. Simpleton systems will yield simpleton answers. Consequently, the retrieval and manipulation of information has not been, is not, and will never be the task of the layman.

On-line systems demand that someone act as intermediary between the machine, on one hand, and the person requiring information, on the other. Whereas executives, sales managers, and other decision makers would probably be poor candidates for the job, librarians are excellent candidates. The intermediary must know the data bases, the system, and the end user well. Librarians will have to spend more time with customers rather than documents. Their main role will be information exchange rather than information itself. If they refuse to accept the challenge of on-line systems, others will be more than willing to assume that position. In other words, refusal to accept this new role might trigger the disappearance of the profession.

COSTS

I'd like now to address some of the social implications which will arise when librarians emerge from their cocoon to become information specialists. As information specialists, a considerably increased value will be imputed to their job functions. Pay scales and benefits will rise correspondingly, reaching levels far beyond the historic wage of librarians. This leads to an important question first raised by Allen--who should pay?

I propose that the answer to this question depends upon the nature of the systems work done for the information specialist's end user and the purpose that work serves. Certainly, if the work is done for market research purposes or serves as input for executive decision making, the end user should pay. One can claim that librarians are already devoting too much time to the concerns of the privileged members of this society and too little to those of the underprivileged. However, public librarians have other customers: the student, the retired person, the job seeker, and just plain citizens. These people who desire information for purposes other than profit must be served. The provision of on-line services to these people can greatly enrich both society and their individual lives.

One can propose many extremely useful services tailored to the needs of these customers--for example, an on-line social agency referral service

or the voting patterns of their congressmen.   Money for these on-line
services will have to come from public funds as additional financial burdens
cannot be placed upon this type of end user.   Total fee for service will
serve only to increase the gap between the haves and the have-nots.   We
need a two-tier pricing system in our libraries--full cost for the haves and
free for the have-nots.

Chapter 3

THE POTENTIAL OF ON-LINE SYSTEMS:
THE LIBRARIAN'S ROLE

Anita R. Schiller

Data Services Librarian/Bibliographer
University of California, San Diego
La Jolla, California

Professor Kent has opened up a wide range of issues. His emphasis
on multidimensionality is important. On-line searching is not simply an
electronic substitute for manual techniques. It offers capabilities of a different order. Yet, as has also been suggested, we are not dealing only with
a new technology. It comes to us embedded within a much larger set of
social and economic forces. And it is these forces, as much as the technology itself, which are creating the "on-line revolution in libraries." As we
consider its impact, and explore its potential, it is crucial to examine the
new configurations which are emerging in the information delivery chain
between the private and public sectors; for despite the library's historically
marginal position, it has suddenly been catapulted into a pivotal role between
advanced technology in the private sector, and the American public.

The introduction of on-line services in libraries results from developments originating far outside the library environment, but acting with
great intensity to change it. Spurred nationally by advances in computer/
communications technology, and growing investment in the information
sector of the economy; and using a technology developed initially for reasons
which had nothing to do with the needs of library users, the implementation
of on-line search services in libraries is only one element in a rapidly
developing national pattern of information costing, pricing, and charging.
The growing commoditization of information is made visible in libraries by
the new charges being levied for search services. These charges stand out
in a particularly striking way because the library has been identified with
information as a "public good," freely available at no charge.

Ironically, and significantly, it is largely due to its public character that the library has been sought out by the information industry to introduce the new service to the public, and institute fees for service. Considered within the context of expanding investment in the computer/communications industries in the national economy, what seems to be emerging is a major shift from public and institutional support to the financing of individual information services by those who can afford to pay for them. It can also be stated that libraries are further subsidizing this transformation, although this may well lead to the library's own demise.

I would like briefly to explore this rapidly developing movement away from public to private financing in libraries, and to show how libraries are being utilized to accomplish this shift. Also, and more important, I want to emphasize that the privatizing of support for information activities will have a profound impact on the role of information in a democratic society. Finally, I would like to suggest why librarians should attempt to have some impact on changing these directions, to increase public knowledge and awareness of what is occurring, and to begin to consider such questions as public oversight in the information sector.

THE SHIFT FROM PUBLIC TO PRIVATE FINANCING

In his widely acclaimed recent study entitled The Information Economy, Marc Porat attempts to define and measure "information activity" in the U.S. economy. He classifies industries and occupations in primary and secondary information sectors. The occupational class for librarians is designated as "public information disseminators," and carries the following explanation:

> Whether these people work in public libraries or in
> privately financed (corporate) libraries, their services
> are in the provision of a 'free good' to the user com-
> munity--distribution of knowledge. Whether society
> allocates sufficient resources for this public good is a
> matter of much public debate.[1]

Porat's statement calls attention to what librarians are engaged in--"the provision of a 'free good' to the user community." Yet Porat's study, although published in 1977, was begun a few years earlier, and with every passing day, the concept of "free goods" in the information area comes under sharper attack. Librarians have been so heavily bombarded with the idea that information is not free, that it seems no longer possible even to encounter this word in library literature without quotation marks around it.

Professor Kent has characterized some of the central issues. He notes that costs are in the forefront of the on-line revolution. "The issue," he points out, "is twofold: first, the magnitude of the now explicit costs...; and second, the question of how and by whom the costs are to be paid."[2] He emphasizes the magnitude of the explicit costs--those that are billed directly to libraries for computer and communications time, and for the print-outs that generally result.

Yet quite apart from these explicit costs, the implementation of on-line services requires additional institutional support for information delivery, and a substantial portion of this has been borne by libraries. Costs for terminals, for the training workshops offered by the commercial vendors and data base suppliers, for staffing the services and the attendant record keeping activities, for purchases of manuals and search-aids, etc., and for library overhead. All of these costs together are rarely acknowledged as part of the search costs.

As to "how and by whom the costs" are to be paid, despite the attention to direct costs, and fees for service, libraries in fact are subsidizing the on-line systems and assisting to underwrite their market development.

If the current period is indeed what has been advertised as "the era of the $5.00 search," who is paying the rest of the bill? And here it is worth noting additionally, that just as libraries subsidize the costs of search delivery, the federal government subsidizes the costs of some of the data bases.

A recent ranking of charge rates for 64 data bases shows a range of $15 to $150 per hour.[3] This is a wide range. In the lower portion, it is federally supported data bases that predominate. When costs for searches are tabulated, the inclusion of these data bases has the effect of lowering the average cost.

Criticized by the information industry as traditionalists who are ill-equipped to provide effective information delivery, librarians have nonetheless been wooed and called upon by this same industry. Explicitly, they are enjoined to link the products and services of the information industry to end users for a fee. Implicitly, libraries are assisting in other ways as well; accustoming individuals to the use of the new services, marketing them during this initial test period as they undergo further development, and preparing the way for a national distribution system selling search services to the American public.

Ultimately, the signs point to a technology offering search capability at home or office terminals without the aid of the librarian intermediaries who now perform the searches. But libraries are now serving to lay the groundwork for future use on an expanded scale outside their own institutional setting.

Whether or not this eventuality occurs, I think we are justified in asking if present arrangements are the best solution that can be found for bearing the cost of introducing the new technology.

Overall, in this developmental period, the commercial vendors appear to have it both ways--fees and subsidies, for both are used to support their on-line services. The For-Profit sector view is that "while publicly supported library functions providing free information should not be abolished, it should be recognized that there is no such thing as <u>free</u> information. "[4] The statement is ironic. As for the first part, if current trends continue, and if libraries divert staff from publicly supported library functions to income producing functions, the overall character of the public information function will be affected. The principle of "who pays the piper..." will become an operational and determining fact of life.

The concept of information as a "national resource" seems to be eroding. A recent government report of national significance refers, for example, to information as a "resource for public good and private gain. " Are the authors of this report so out of touch with recent events in our country that they do not recognize some possibility for conflict between public good and private gain? The report clarifies this as follows: "This is not to say that commercial considerations are or ought to be paramount in the determination of these issues. Certainly there are other values which must be served by public policy. "[5] My point here however, is that the public good ought to be paramount. These "other values" are not the concern of the commercial sector. The provision of a "free good" to the user community, equal access to information, and equitable distribution of information resources are not the business or the interest of the commercial sector. And there is no reason to expect that they should be. They are however, the concern of libraries.

THE LIBRARIAN'S ROLE

The introduction of on-line systems raises a basic question about the librarian's role. In their present intermediary position between the commercial vendors and end users, libraries have been described as "channels, " "linking agents, " "brokers, " and "retailers. " What does this terminology tell us about the librarians' involvement in the new service? Although these terms suggest various interpretations, such as a neutral role, or a possible advisory role, or an implicit association with the pricing of services and products, in general they convey the notion that librarians will pass on to library consumers whatever comes down the pike. Yet there are many areas for improvement, and these range from the initial data base production through the completion of the search print-out. A basic problem is the lack of consistency and lack of standarization within and among the individual data bases. Another is the different command languages which must be learned for each of the separate vendor services. Poor indexing quality, poor data base formatting, uncontrolled vocabularies, overlap between files, and incomplete or defective tapes are also problems which have been noted.

These are most often encountered at the operational level, where ongoing work with users, developing search strategies, performing the searches, reviewing the results, etc., become an all-engrossing job. When immediate and specific problems become apparent, they are rarely perceived as part of a broader set of policy issues. I believe however that professional responsibility for effective and equal access requires us to examine and define these issues which concern the profession and the public it serves. It is professional policy or its lack, which will determine what occurs at the operational level, and how user needs ultimately will be met. For librarians, user needs are paramount. For commercial vendors, other interests take precedence. If libraries have been assigned as "linking agents" between the service suppliers and the public, librarians are not thereby the sales representatives of the suppliers. They have, or should have, an independent professional role.

During the present period, end users scarcely know what to expect from on-line services. They are unfamiliar with the capabilities and limitations of the new services, and librarians who do the searching for them, serve in a sense as consumer surrogates. Yet despite the weaknesses which searchers may encounter in their day to day work, up to now they have paid scant attention to the need for on-line service standards. They have turned instead to the commercial vendors for advice on operational problems, or have made recommendations to suppliers on an ad hoc basis.

As a result of suggestions from searchers, certain technical improvements have been made, and several of these have been important. The sense of commitment on the part of librarians who have requested them is exceptional, as is the initiative some have taken to establish various user groups. But the way the library market is now structured, librarians most often deal with suppliers through individual search centers. Librarians are not a cohesive force. Suggestions which they offer for operational improvements may be acceptable or even welcome to the commercial vendors where they add to the effectiveness of the system and are relatively inexpensive to implement. But if they conflict with proprietary interests, suggestions are less likely to be incorporated.

As proprietary interests take a firmer hold in the information economy at large, the library perspective needs to be identified more sharply with public access to information. Standards need to be established and policy issues need to be identified and addressed. How, for example, do data rights, royalties, exclusives and other proprietary arrangements set forth in the contracts between data base producers and the commercial vendors affect public access ? These are murky areas, and they are filled with legal uncertainties. The present period is still formative and developmental. But as we can see, economic pressures to own information resources are growing, and the next step on the way from ownership is private control of these resources.

A recent report from the National Bureau of Standards refers to this issue and cites an example in the on-line services industry. The report is entitled <u>Copyright in Computer-Readable Works: Policy Impacts of Technological Change</u>.

> In some instances, publishers of data bases have leased them exclusively for use in one computerized information service system... Exclusive licensing of data bases may tend to foster the monopolization of data base search services by one or two giant systems. Whether the prevention of such a monopoly or the regulatory control of a permitted monopoly as a public service organization would be preferable is an open question.[6]

While exclusives are only one aspect of the issue, they are illustrative. Examining a potential for market monopoly, the report also states: "A question that may be asked is what form of intervention should be pursued by consumers collectively or by the Government ?"[7] It seems to me that this is a question that librarians collectively must also begin to consider.

During the current period, the character of information as a "public good" is being transformed. There are growing economic pressures to extract national information resources, and to process them for market development and distribution for private gain. Ultimately, this will require some form of public intervention and public oversight.

These are large and complex issues. They affect the very core of a democratic society. Yet up to now, they have remained in the background. As librarians whose primary mission is public information access, it is up to us to raise them for the widest possible public discussion throughout the nation.

The introduction of on-line services in libraries has engaged librarians in the new technology and the opportunities it offers for a new form of information delivery. At the same time, as the important debates on the "free or fee" issue demonstrate, the new services have also raised crucial national issues of library policy. While librarians may choose to allow this policy to be forged entirely by outside forces, or turn implicitly to the service vendors as technical experts for their direction, or even leave the profession for greater rewards as information managers elsewhere, it seems to me that as a profession, librarians are responsible for defining other alternatives.

This is not an easy task. But no one else can do it for us. Let us hope that the recently established ALA Ad Hoc Committee on National Information Policy and the ensuing preparations for the White House Conference will begin to establish the directions.

REFERENCES

1. Marc U. Porat. The Information Economy, OT Special Publication 77-12(1), (Washington, D.C.: Department of Commerce, Office of Telecommunications, 1977), p. 109.

2. Allen Kent. "The Potential of On-Line Systems," Pittsburgh Conference on the On-Line Revolution in Libraries," November 14-16, 1977.

3. Gordon L. Monsen, Jr. "Computer Terminals and Minicomputers in On-Line Retrieval," On-Line Review 1:221 (September 1977).

4. Quincy Rodgers. National Information Policy; Report to the President of the United States, Domestic Council Committee on the Right of Privacy, (Washington, D.C.: National Commission on Libraries and Information Science, 1977), p. 76.

5. Ibid., p. 60.

6. Roy Saltman. Copyright in Computer-Readable Works: Policy Impacts of Technological Change, NBS Special Publication 500-17, (Washington, D.C.: National Bureau of Standards, October 1977), pp. 57-58.

7. Ibid., p. 56.

Chapter 4

A NEW POTENTIAL FOR NUMERIC
AND STATISTICAL DATA FILES

Martin D. Robbins

Director
Colorado Energy Research Institute
Golden, Colorado
(At the time of the conference, Mr. Robbins was Vice-President,
EDUCOM, Princeton, New Jersey)

INTRODUCTION

I would like to use one of the main points in Allen Kent's presentation, as a point of departure for my remarks. Kent said that on-line retrieval makes it convenient to exercise a new kind of power, which he called exploitative control. "Such control," Kent claimed, "permits as much penetration into the contents of source materials as one is willing to invest in recording in computer sensible form and in expending computer time to search and correlate." I want to discuss one such area of source materials, to which I believe we will continue to have random access at best, without the application of on-line computer based retrieval systems. Specifically, I am talking about numeric and statistical information of all kinds that are stored in machine-readable data files. The kinds of on-line bibliographic services that are the subject of much of this conference have the potential of opening up this vast and important body of information to a large number of users.

One of the most significant trends in scientific methodology today is the shift away from sole reliance on typical laboratory experimentation and natural observation toward access to and manipulation of existing data bases. The Committee on Scientific and Technical Information (COSATI), early in 1968, first recognized the potential impact that such data systems would eventually have on science and technology. It commissioned a report describing these emerging systems and provided an inventory of them by type, size and location.[1]

With the widespread availability of computers, numeric and statistical information of all kinds is being stored and processed by machine. Unfortunately, these data resources are not fully utilized because potential users are unaware of the existence and accessibility of the statistical data files.

Historically, the library has served as a reservoir for our nation's information resources. These resources have taken the form of books, journals, documents, and more recently audio and visual materials which may be stored on magnetic tape, punched cards, disc packs, or other media suitable for computer interpretation. Unfortunately, machine-readable data files (MRDF) are not yet recognized or accepted as valuable additions to library holdings.

As a result, MRDF are not routinely acquired, stored, cataloged, or processed. These activities have been relegated to the various special data libraries or archives that have emerged to handle the recent proliferation of data files. Individual data archives have developed their own procedures for handling MRDF. There are no standard procedures. Accordingly, a comprehensive MRDF reference system does not exist and MRDF as a source of information are not fully employed by researchers, administrators, or decision makers.

The types of files I am talking about include, by way of example, those represented by the Louis Harris Data Center, Roper Public Opinion Research Center, National Opinion Research Center, International Data Library and Reference Service (Berkeley), Data Program Library Service (Madison), Inter-University Consortium for Political and Social Research, U.S. Bureau of the Census, the National Archive, the Urban Institute, and numerous other data files resulting from ongoing research projects. These type of files are a relatively new phenomenon, in terms of their application to research and teaching. They developed out of the need by many social scientists to exploit the masses of governmental, academic, and commercial data produced and accumulated over the past three decades.

The importance of such files and their relationship to libraries was stated in 1970 by the late Ralph L. Bisco, who at one time was on the faculty here at the University of Pittsburgh. Bisco said:

> In the future, social science data archives can be
> expected to play an especially important role in
> storing, maintaining, and distributing the many
> computer usable materials that are increasingly
> a by-product of the printing process. For the same
> reasons that libraries were invented to preserve
> books, it will be more and more necessary to have
> libraries of the future--organizations that can

> service the journalistic, academic, commercial, and
> statistical products of society for computer use as
> well as "hand use" by human beings. Social science
> data archives of today are developing experience and
> procedures for acquisitions, data maintenance, con-
> trol, documentation, and services to users. Some of
> the knowledge obtained will be important for the
> development of libraries of the future.[2]

At the present time, information relating to machine-readable data
files, such as those cited earlier, is fragmented among varying archives,
institutions, and data centers. Among these archives, there is no common
format of information on the existence of data files, nor is there any standardized structure that would facilitate retrieval of information from many
different sources. Existing information on computerized files is available
to some but not to all. I believe what is needed is a central source of information within the public domain that will provide equal access to all interested users.

Current access to such data files is generally limited to those scholars
and students who know of them and know the right resource person(s). This
places great constraints on the use of such data files. Since these materials
are not under any bibliographic control, it is rare when librarians know
what is available in their own institutions, let alone at other institutions.
The problems users face have been described in the following manner by one
author:

> The foremost difficulty...is that users have no efficient
> means of determining the sources of specifically needed
> machine-processable information. Users are now
> confronted with a time-consuming, inefficient, and
> costly means for determining what specific data hold-
> ings match their immediate research needs.
>
> They must first identify which of several score archival
> organizations are likely to maintain the kinds of data
> they might need, and then they must call, visit, or
> write each of the likely sources to determine whether
> these specific organizations have individual collections
> that meet their present requirements.[3]

This same author went on to say that in dealing with such data files:

> ...we should be able to benefit from the experiences of
> the traditional library network, which has uniform
> systems for cataloging, indexing, and the like.[4]

Therefore, what appears to be most needed to overcome the barriers and increase user access is the development of a standardized machine-readable national union catalog that can be searched interactively over a computer network by remote users. That is why I believe the subject of this conference--on-line services--is so crucial to the issue of access to numerical and statistical data files. The scenario we can envision with such a system would allow a user--be it a student, scholar or librarian--to sit down at a computer terminal and through a simplified language, specify the information desired by means of an appropriate set of keywords (e.g., female, rural, voting, national elections). The computer would then search the data base and respond with a series of citations and abstracts of machine-readable data files that might meet the users needs. In addition to the citation and abstract, information might include: sample size; citations to journal articles, books and reports that grew out of the original development and use of the data file; and, most importantly, how to gain access to the file itself.

This scenario is not too different from that which presently exists with the on-line bibliographic retrieval services, which are the subject of so much of this conference. The difference is that most of the bibliographic services are based upon well-established files, such as Psychological Abstracts and ERIC. The research data files that are the subject of my presentation are presently not under bibliographic control and therefore not available for searching by potential users--no matter whether a manual search through a card catalog or a computerized search is desired. Access is therefore limited to close associates of the developers or to those who use specialized data centers and know what is in their holdings.

AN ATTEMPT AT BIBLIOGRAPHIC CONTROL

Several institutions are already making attempts at bibliographic control. The Social Science Data Library (SSDL) of the Institute for Research in Social Science, University of North Carolina, Chapel Hill, by way of an example, has the goal of providing information on the existence and availability of data files to the widest possible constituency of academic users. To achieve this, it has decided to convert the bibliographic information for each data file in its extensive holdings into a format compatible with the traditional library catalog record. The records will then be automated by adopting the Library of Congress' MARC II record format. These two steps make possible the integration of information on each data file into the University's main public catalog. Beyond this, it is hoped that the same information might be: (1) incorporated into a national union catalog for machine-readable data files; (2) into a shared network system such as OCLC; and (3) into a machine-readable search and retrieval system for use by students and scholars via a computer network.

One of the most important factors influencing the University of North Carolina's decision to catalog the relevant information on data files was the American Library Association's efforts to develop standards and recommend rules for cataloging machine-readable data files. These efforts were described by John D. Byrum, Jr., Chief of the Descriptive Cataloging Division of the Library of Congress:

> In January 1970, the Executive Committee of the American Library Association's Cataloging and Classification Section instructed the chairman of the Descriptive Cataloging Committee to form a Subcommittee on Rules for Machine-Readable Data Files.
>
> This development marked the formal recognition of the need for standards by which libraries could control and access the files of data in machine-readable form which academic and other institutions had already begun to collect as an additional and increasingly important resource of educational and research value. Through the formulation of a standard bibliographic description for data files, libraries could display entries for this material in their public catalogs where records already appear for holdings in other media, such as books, pamphlets, serials, and also often for microforms, recordings, and motion pictures.
>
> Also of importance, the development of such standards could prepare the way for the emergence of a national union catalog for machine-readable data files. Already well-developed for books, serials, and book-like materials, including microform masters and manuscript collections, union lists are based on reports from a large number of participating institutions which describe holdings according to generally accepted cataloging rules. Thus a union list of machine-readable materials would enable an institution to alert a far greater constituency than that attached to it to specific files and would enable individual researchers to locate easily relevant files beyond those held by nearby institutions...
>
> It is the subcommittee's assumption that the rules for cataloging data files will be incorporated into the next edition of the Anglo-American Cataloging Rules (projected date, the fall of 1976), source according to which research libraries generally draft standard

catalog entries for their holdings. Entries for data
files, while taking into account the bibliographic and
other special characteristics of this new and unique
medium, should therefore be compatible with those
for other library materials.[5]

Based upon this Subcommittee's position papers and final report, Sue
A. Dodd of North Carolina's SSDL compiled a "Working Manual for Cataloging Machine-Readable Data Files" which was designed to assist librarians
in the task of cataloging data files.[6]

If the Dodd manual is followed, the cataloged record of a MRDF will
provide the user with the following information: principal investigator(s) or
corporate entity; title; medium designator (i.e., machine-readable data
file); place of data production, person or organization responsible for data
production, and date of data production; distributor of data, place of data
distribution, and first distribution date (if known); edition of data (e.g.,
ICPSR edition, 3rd revised edition, etc.); designation that data are part of
a series (if applicable); number of logical records and number of pages of
codebook or accompanying documentation; source of title; summary note
(which may include type of sample, universe, time coverage, other unique
characteristics, and brief statement on content of data); content notes for
sub-samples or multiple files; subject headings; etc.

The initial users of the manual prepared by Ms. Dodd are participating in an organized project to test the feasibility and adaptability of the
recommended rules for cataloging data files. This test is being conducted
under the sponsorship of the newly created International Association for
Social Science Information Science and Technology (IASSIST) and its corres-
ponding Classification Committee. It also involves many of the major data
centers in the United States, such as the Inter-University Consortium for
Political and Social Research; National Archive; National Opinion Research
Center; Data and Program Library Service, University of Wisconsin;
Social Science Library, Yale University; DUALabs, Arlington, Virginia;
Survey Research Center, University of California at Berkeley; Social
Science User Services, Princeton University; Social Science Information
Utilization Laboratory, University of Pittsburgh; and many others. Each
participating member has cataloged six data files unique to the data center
or library and has reported on the time spent per record, appropriateness
of documentation, usefulness of the manual, problems encountered, special
problems relating to special kinds of data, and recommended changes. The
final results of this cataloging experiment are being documented in a final
written report.

The manual and the IASSIST cataloging test are necessary first steps
in achieving the long-term goal of creating a widely accessible national union
catalog of machine-readable data files in the social sciences.

A second major step is a working conference to be conducted by DUALabs this spring, with the objectives of

- Identifying key technical issues requiring resolution prior to implementing a coordinated cataloging effort.

- Defining the operational components of a central clearinghouse for MRDF cataloging.

- Identifying and describing potential information services and products.

I believe we have the potential to establish a national program of information services for MRDF. Ideally, our machine-readable data resources should be integrated with our nation's other information resources. Since this is not the case, it is essential that a concerted and coordinated program be established that will provide the types of services that are required. These services will make it possible for a user to learn that needed data files exist, to learn of the content of the files so that their usefulness can be assessed prior to an investment in file access work, and to learn where and how the file content can be obtained. As a result, effective information use will be achieved.

Allen Kent closed by saying that if used appropriately, the new kind of power will become relevant both to the library clientele and to the librarian. As a library user, I want to heartily agree with Kent's prediction and to close with a plea that those attending this conference do not focus too narrowly on the potential for on-line services, seeing them only as a way of releasing you from unwanted, uninteresting and time-consuming tasks. They must be viewed in a much more creative manner, seeing them as ways to do things that were impossible before. I believe the library and the librarian are the key actors in this arena. Without them we are at the mercy of the computer technocrats, or the unrealistic demands of ultimate users. I believe the on-line retrieval solutions arrived at by either or both of these groups without the presence of librarians will be disaster.

REFERENCES

1. Hyatt, D. O. and B. K. Farris. Study of Scientific and Technical Data Activities in the United States. Washington, D. C., April 1968.

2. Bisco, Ralph L. Data Bases, Computers, and the Social Sciences. New York: John Wiley and Sons, 1970, p. 2.

3. Ibid., p. 9.

4. Ibid., p. 279.

5. Byrum, John D., Jr. "Toward a Standard Bibliographic Description for
    Machine-Readable Data Files." Paper presented at the workshop on
    Documentation of Large Machine-Readable Statistical Data Sets, National
    Bureau of Economic Research, April 1974.

6. Dodd, Sue A. Working Manual for Cataloging Machine-Readable Data
    Files. Social Science Data Library - Institute for Research in Social
    Science, University of North Carolina, Chapel Hill, North Carolina,
    1976. (Mimeo).

Chapter 5

POTENTIAL: REACTION

Joseph F. Shubert

State Librarian and Assistant Commissioner
for Libraries
State of New York
Albany, New York

Mr. Kent's paper suggests a number of issues to be addressed as we plan to exploit the potential of on-line information systems. Some of these he has made explicit and others may be suggested by further consideration of the points he makes. I have grouped these under three headings: service potential and decisions; management concerns; and planning responsibilities.

SERVICE POTENTIAL AND DECISIONS

Mr. Kent concludes his paper with a description of on-line retrieval of text as a "new kind of power," which he terms "exploitative control," permitting greater "penetration into the contents of source materials" and their further exploitation through computer analysis. He notes that appropriate use of this power is important as library users and librarians are "released from many unwanted, uninteresting and time-consuming tasks in locating information, and are able to spend more time in creatively dealing with professional decisions."

I would not quarrel with these comments on the potential of the technology for changing the work and style of the librarian, but perhaps it is appropriate to emphasize the impact upon the user. It seems to me that one of the important principles of library administration has been to organize materials, functions, and procedures in such a way as to reduce the time the reader needs to invest in locating material or information and thereby increase the time he has available for use of that material or information.

It is here, it seems to me, that the on-line technology holds its great promise. The speed of location of documents and information and the precision
with which they can be identified are already demonstrated daily: the
greater capability for working with the content of materials, and that for
analyzing and recasting information are the great potential. And it is here
that Mr. Kent's point about "rethinking current library functions with the
purpose of optimizing service objectives" may be more strongly put: the
objectives and service principles themselves must be rethought.

Mr. Kent's warning about "inappropriate use of enhanced capabilities
used indiscriminately and without skill" is well taken. Too often we have
seen a library user frustrated, overwhelmed, and irritated by having an
inexperienced or unskilled librarian kindly but thoughtlessly dump materials
on him. Readers can be unnecessarily deluged with screens of information
or stacks of printouts and copies, just as they may have been with stacks of
books and journals which only peripherally dealt with their interest.

MANAGEMENT CONCERNS

This leads me to several management concerns. That of misuse or
inefficient use of the computer should rank high among them. In some ways
misuse may be fairly easy to flag because of the precision with which the
"overt costs" are computed and made evident. Kent has forcefully pointed
out for us the need to evaluate such costs against a more realistic assessment of the "hidden costs" we have accepted because they are hidden.

A second management concern should be the balancing of the cost with
the payoff of training. Kent suggests more than once the results of lack of
training (inappropriate and costly use: excessively voluminous, irrelevant,
and perhaps misleading products; frustration; and loss of interest) and he
points out training costs can be high.

We need to quantify the extent to which skill in use of the technology
controls cost, achieves results, and meets the needs of users. Library
managers have made different decisions on the way staff are assigned and
the conditions under which they use data bases directly or through intermediaries. Perhaps the decisions are somewhat analogous to those made
20 years or so ago on the handling of reference inquiries in relation to
federal documents. Fortunately, the nature of the on-line system and its
measurement of operations and costs should enable these decisions to be
based upon greater factual rather than intuitive bases.

Mr. Kent devotes considerable space to discussion of the issues
relating to costs and fees and has developed the interesting point that "fees
for on-line services pay for services which are, in a sense, consumed

immediately." He notes that a fee must be paid even if useful results are not obtained, and that unlike the purchase of books or serials, the product is not an item--a visible codex--that will be available for other users in years to come. We perhaps are beginning to think in these terms as inter-library loan reimbursement structures include pay for unsuccessful as well as successful searches; as we assess the cost of housing and maintaining materials collections; as we use flimsier or expendable cassettes in service to blind and handicapped readers; and as we give away printed materials in some inner city program. In each of these we deal with hidden as well as overt costs and with the cost--or perhaps the price--of opportunity for service.

It seems to me that this paper might have explored in greater detail factors in comparing the cost of on-line services with the true cost of conventional materials and searches--and the implications of a shift in library practice. I expect that many library managers have computed the cost of maintaining subscriptions to printed indexes and abstracting services, and compared these with data bank cost per hour. James Fry and Richard Fisher at The State Library of Ohio a few months ago provided me with figures showing that 20 services to which we subscribed at an annual cost of $5,619 could be accessed on-line up to 6 1/2 hours per month for that same amount of money. They additionally pointed out that this figure did not cover the expense of acquisition, processing, and storage of the paper documents.

At the same time they provided me with a copy of a June 1977 article * by Donald W. King pointing out the delicate pricing balance between printed and on-line systems. King points out that the current on-line service prices are not structured to recover the substantial input costs of bibliographic data bases. To the extent input costs have been based upon production of the printed services, he says a "major shift in acquisition policies which results in increased use of on-line services at the sacrifice of subscription to printed forms will inevitably have an impact on prices of on-line systems."

If abstracting and indexing services experience a sharp decline in subscriptions, they will need to secure a larger return on the on-line services if they are to stay in operation. King suggests that "if the bibliographic search services charge a sufficiently high fee to recover the large input cost, there is a good chance that libraries in turn will begin to decrease use of on-line services and these services will not recover their costs." He

---

* King, Donald W. "A Potential Pitfall in the Economics of Information Products and Services," in Bulletin of the American Society for Information Science, Vol. 3, No. 5, pp. 40-41, June 1977.

characterizes this as a dilemma which is "the most pressing issue of our field at the present time since it has such far-reaching implications on current services as well as on development of future systems. "

PLANNING DECISIONS

Mr. Kent suggests at least two planning concerns related to the potential of on-line systems, and I shall raise another. He noted that new ways of delivering source materials are more important as users are alerted to many materials which are not held locally. He further suggests that the on-line system which provides abstracts or other "surrogates" helps to establish more precisely the relevance and usefulness of the materials identified. He also points out that the technology for transmission of images of full source materials is still not cost effective, nor are the mails a suitable mechanism for rapid delivery. He notes the use of an "electronic mailbox" and microformats as means currently utilized by vendors of services. I believe we can anticipate rapid development in the technology for rapid transmission.

Current forms of interlibrary cooperation in sharing resources are affected by on-line systems. An early indicator of the way in which on-line systems facilitate a non-hierarchical approach to document delivery was the OCLC experience which provided a means of identifying locations of materials in smaller libraries. This resulted in requests directly to these libraries, reducing the traffic and demands upon a few key resource libraries--and in Ohio this produced a substantial shift in interlibrary lending patterns over a relatively short period. Further development and cost reduction for electronic transmission of documents may swing interlibrary sharing back to heavier reliance upon a few central providers of facsimiles or electronic transmissions.

At the same time, development of added capability for retrieving local holdings information within a single community or region may solve one of the major problems facing research personnel: often it is easier to identify and obtain materials from considerable distance than it is within a single city. Witness the experience of a librarian in Columbus this summer who was working on a paper on library user needs. He began with citations from an ERIC search but then spent hours travelling from one library to another in track of a single journal article which was successively found to be missing; to be in binding; in a library unit with reduced hours; in circulation or otherwise unavailable.

Mr. Kent's point on the extent to which on-line services are integrated with conventional services bears examination as we plan library services. I suggested that management decisions on training of staff are one indicator of trend. It seems to me that these planning questions must be answered in the context of (1) facilitating access by users; (2) allocation and planned availability of staff both for alerting users to the variety and range of options open to them and for efficient assistance in the use of materials; (3) anticipated shifts in the use of systems and materials; and (4) earlier experience. Today it is still startling to visit a library which prides itself on a substantial collection in the field of management and find that cassettes by Peter Drucker or films on Herzberg's theories are not available at the same service point as are their printed works--and their availability is of no apparent concern to library staff. Many of us have a long way to go in integration of media formats and in reference organization.

Perhaps the set of planning decisions which most interests me is that which relates to extending the capability of on-line systems to small libraries. Last year when the Forest Press observed the centennial of the Dewey Decimal Classification, plaques were awarded to libraries for early adoption and continuous use of DDC. It was interesting to see the names of libraries which turned up on the eligibility lists (the reduction in size of such lists as consequence of a shift to LC notwithstanding). How and why was the decision made to adopt the DDC? What vision of the advantages of standardization as seen in the 1880's or 1890's? Of the leadership and personality of a strong librarian? Of the impact of a conference or discussion? Of the interest of a trustee or a professor?

Similarly, examination of a similar list of participants in on-line systems tells us something of the orientation of specific libraries and their administrators. The capability must be extended in one form or another (directly or indirectly) if we are to meet the NCLIS objective of ensuring that the basic minimums of library and information services adequate to meet the needs of all local communities are satisfied.

School library participation in this aspect of network development is essential and may be more within the realm of possibility than we sometimes think. I recall some 25 years ago being asked to speak to a parents' club at a Catholic high school in Nevada--they asked me to discuss informally a program for upgrading the school library. My preparation for the talk was geared to what I thought I knew about that school, its program, its students, and its constraints. Fortunately I arrived early enough to see the school and its equipment and to hear the informed and concerned discussion of the need for updating classroom electric typewriters regularly if business students were to be competitive. Given the standards these parents had set for their children's education, and their willingness to provide or pursue the resources, the school library could not be shortchanged and constraints were put in better perspective.

The sophistication of schools today and the expectations we have for them suggests we have not given sufficient attention to the ways in which they need and provide access to on-line systems. Decisions on the way in which these systems may be utilized in the school library media center and the ways in which they will impact on library service are directly related to our concept of the mission and function of libraries. A nation which spends $28 more per capita each year for recreation and tobacco than for education has an opportunity for reassessing priorities and objectives. If we recognize people as the prime resource in strengthening our economy and perceive their use of information as critical to economic and social stability, we cannot fail to address the necessity of the relationship of these services to school library media center development.

One final comment, related to service potential, management concerns, and planning: In the past few weeks I have been reading and hearing statements presented to a legislative committee looking at the problems of libraries. I sense as technology is discussed, there is a legislative concern for its widest implications--for its impact on jobs, and for what some legislators see as a depersonalizing of our libraries and schools. As we seek funds we must state for legislators our objectives for services to people, and must clearly show how these systems serve them. The "for instances" are critical if we are to have the resources we need to exploit the potential of on-line systems.

Chapter 6

POTENTIAL: COMMENTARY

Carlos A. Cuadra

President
Cuadra Associates, Inc.
Santa Monica, California
(At the time of the conference, Dr. Cuadra was General Manager,
SDC Search Service, System Development Corporation)

Allen Kent's paper has provided a clear and succinct introduction to the purpose and use of on-line retrieval systems. He identifies the kinds of information needs that modern information systems address. He shows how on-line retrieval systems satisfy (or do not satisfy) these needs. And he identifies some major points of interest and concern, particularly costs.

This paper will comment on these points and suggest some ways in which we can usefully address the matter of costs.

THE IMPACT OF ON-LINE SERVICES

Allen notes that some have described the growing use of on-line systems as an "on-line revolution," with some aspects of a bandwagon. I agree with the first part of this characterization.

At the 1975 annual meeting of the American Society for Information Science, the growth of on-line retrieval services was described as the most important innovation in the field of library and information science in the past decade. Nothing that has happened since 1975 would cause me to question that view. On the contrary, the use of on-line services continues to grow at a rapid pace, on a worldwide basis, and the increasing dependence of libraries and information centers on on-line systems is an acknowledged fact.

Does the growth represent a "bandwagon" effect? Probably not, in the sense of political or social bandwagons. The growing use of on-line services reflects almost entirely the acceptance of a cost-effective technology that helps to do a needed job.

One of the early user groups of our on-line service was the pharmaceutical-type company, which recognized the importance of maintaining highly current and highly comprehensive awareness of biomedical research findings pointing to the effects of drugs and other chemical compounds. Once it became apparent that knowledge of harmful effects could have profound financial and social consequences--one need think only of thalidomide--those pharmaceutical companies that were not yet using on-line services began to do so in increasing numbers. They realized that if they failed to take full advantage of this new information technology, they would not only be running unnecessary risks but would also be putting themselves at a serious competitive disadvantage. Within a year, most of the U.S. pharmaceutical companies were using one or more on-line services. One may choose to call this a bandwagon effect, but it should be recognized that such use was based on solid business, legal, and social considerations, rather than on matters of corporate image.

The growing use of on-line services in academic institutions may or may not have a "bandwagon" component to it. Certainly, academic institutions place considerable value on the size and diversity of their library collection as a measure of institutional excellence, and the presence of technology, in one form or another, adds some aura of prestige. Yet, I recall that among the earliest academic users of on-line services were many relatively small universities and colleges that realized that, by using on-line services, they could close part of the enormous gap that exists between their own information resources and those of the larger and most prestigious institutions.

Many large universities were rather slow to adopt on-line services, and I often had the impression, in talking with them, that there was a feeling of self-sufficiency about their collection and their literature-searching techniques that delayed recognition of the potential of on-line services. In any case, it is a fact that any bandwagon among academic users of on-line services was set in motion at least as much by the information have-nots as by the information haves.

I dwell on the bandwagon concept because I think it would be a mistake for libraries to think of on-line services as only a fad, or a necessary evil that must be endured if one is to keep one's clients in the business community.

Two years ago a colleague of mine, Judy Wanger, completed a landmark study, sponsored by the National Science Foundation, on the impact of

on-line retrieval services. The data were based on questionnaire and interview surveys of over 1200 users of ten different on-line retrieval services.
The results left no doubt that on-line services do a highly effective job and
that the job they do is perceived as being worth the costs involved. The
library that fails to recognize the fundamental basis for the acceptance of
on-line services must also be prepared to accept the loss of clients, if these
clients elect to turn to some other information services organization that is
more responsive to their needs.

RECONDITIONING THE USER OR THE SYSTEM?

Allen Kent correctly points out that some of the skills and habits
appropriate for using indexes and listings may not be ideally suited to the
use of on-line systems. He says, "The challenge is how to recondition
(emphasis mine) those who would use these systems so that they are indeed
effective supplements to their own memory." I interpret the word "recondition" in a moderate sense, to mean training the users, and I concur with
Allen Kent's premise that training will help people to make much more
effective and cost-effective use of on-line systems. But there is an alternative or perhaps complementary approach to the user-system mismatch
problem, and that is to change the system itself, rather than the user.

When interactive computer-based systems first came into being, in
the middle of the 1950's, the match between system and user left much to be
desired. For example, the U.S. Air Defense System used a large number
of complex programs that could detect a variety of possible operator errors
and, upon encountering one, trigger a flashing display at the operator's
terminal. The system thus informed the operator that he had made an error.
Unfortunately, it did not tell him what the error was. He had to figure that
out on his own.

How did one learn to diagnose such errors quickly? By providing a
great deal of rather expensive training. That was an understandable approach
in the middle 1950's, when computer technology and knowledge of man-machine
interactions were still rather limited. Today it is not an acceptable answer.
Today we believe that systems should be more helpful to the user. We believe
they should, as much as possible, adapt to the user, rather than make the
user adapt to them. Thus, if the user makes an error and the system can
determine what the user intended, it should perform the task, either with or
without a mild reproval or reminder. If it detects an error by the user but
cannot fathom the user's intent, it should at least report to the user in
English the kind of error it has detected.

These notions are fundamental and perhaps obvious. Not as obvious
is the idea that the techniques for using on-line systems should be made as

natural to the user as possible, without unduly compromising or limiting the power of the system. It was such consideration that made us design systems to speak and accept English words--PRINT, EXPLAIN, KEEP, etc. --or their abbreviations, as the medium of communication with the user.

In the near future, we can expect to see the next logical step toward accommodation with the user: the personalized system. Such a system will permit the user to establish in the system a profile, analogous to an SDI profile, except that, instead of referring to information content, it will define system behavior.

Thus a user might want the system to give all system messages in a very abbreviated form; or to give and receive all system communications (except for the data in the data base itself) in some language other than English; or to display automatically the update status of several data bases in which the user has a continuing interest; or to carry out searches in accordance with a preferred type of logic.

One can imagine a whole series of aspects in which a system can be tailored by the individual user to fit his search needs and preferences, and even his geography and culture. The user will be able to enter his profile, directly on line, and to change it any time he chooses.

When the personalized system becomes a reality, it will pose some challenges for user training, because in some respects it is more difficult to learn a flexible, multifaceted system than a simple system with a few options. I am sure that we can meet this training challenge and that, ten years from now, when we are reviewing a decade of innovation in library and information science, the advent of the personalized system, centered on the concept of user freedom, will be seen as a key event in improving our information standard of living.

THE COSTS OF ON-LINE RETRIEVAL SERVICE

It is a well-recognized fact that most on-line retrieval services cost money to use. It is less well-recognized that they also cost money to operate. In his paper, Allen mentions a range of prices for data base acquisition: from $1,000 to $10,000 per year. It is even worse than that. The license fee for using a copy of the MEDLINE data base is $50,000 for the first year and $30,000 per year thereafter, probably the highest price in the data base publishing field. SDC does not currently offer on-line service on the MEDLINE data base, so we do not have that particular cost of operation. But we do offer service on 40 other data bases, and the total cost of the license fees and royalties is very, very formidable--many hundreds of thousands of dollars per year.

The cost of storing a family of data bases on high-speed disk storage devices for immediate access runs in the hundreds of thousands of dollars per year. And even though the cost of disk storage is going down each year, bibliographic data bases grow larger, at the rate of about 15 percent a year.

But neither disk storage nor license fees and royalties are the highest items of cost for a major on-line retrieval service. Operating a modern computer facility suitable for nationwide or international on-line retrieval service can cost in the millions of dollars per year, and one must also incur substantial costs for trained people to operate the service, update data bases, and carry out user education and marketing, training, user support, billing, new data base development, and system improvements. It should be evident that a great many users must push a great many terminal keys in a great many cities for the on-line service organization to recover costs of this magnitude. I hope it is also evident that many who believe that on-line services should be "free" are either ignorant about the magnitude of the costs involved or they are simply asking for someone else--presumably all the taxpayers-- to underwrite these costs on behalf of those who currently use or might later use on-line services.

Europeans are amazed when they hear some Americans complaining about the high cost of communications. A typical user in Scandinavia pays about $48 per hour to their PTT (post, telephone and telegraph organization) for a call to Amsterdam, and an additional $22 per hour to the Dutch PTT, to be connected with an on-line retrieval service in the United States. In contrast to this cost of $70 per hour for communications, the average telecommunications cost to a North American user of a U.S. on-line service is $8 or less per hour. Allen's paper refers to the "relatively high costs." I must ask: "relative to what?" Relative to the costs that Europeans, Africans, South Americans, or Australians must pay? Relative to the costs of operating the on-line services? Relative to other ways of achieving the same quality of search in the same time?

A distinction is made in the paper between overt costs and "hidden" costs. Hidden costs are identified or illustrated as the costs of the librarian's and/or the patron's salary when time is spent in trying to locate materials in the library, by manual or any other means. I would like to suggest that we abandon the concept of hidden costs, because it impedes our understanding of true costs. All businesses, including many libraries, recognize that there are direct costs that can be associated with particular activities and there are other costs, such as for lighting, heating, space, and administrative personnel, that can more easily be considered as indirect or overhead costs. The cost of the librarian's time in conducting a reference search is either a direct cost or an indirect cost, depending on one's bookkeeping preferences. So is the cost of the patron's time. It is not constructive to consider either one of them "hidden," because it helps to perpetuate the idea that one group of people is trying to put something over on some other group of people.

I dwell on this point because the paper contains a characterization of the "eager salesperson" of on-line services, who reveals the costs to the potential client a little bit at a time, depending on whether the client flinches at the earlier revelations. The characterization is not labeled as unusual or atypical.

I cannot vouch for the selling practices of all of the organizations in the on-line retrieval services field, but I can honestly say that I have never heard any sales representative of any organization, including my most fierce competitors, ever use such unprofessional tactics. On the contrary, most of the on-line service organizations that I am aware of freely distribute standard price lists that say clearly for each data base the computer connect time cost, the telecommunications cost, the cost per off-line print, and so on. The major on-line services also have published price schedules for user materials, training, and other services.

Perhaps Allen Kent does not want to identify a particular organization or organizations that engage in the kind of marketing practice he describes, but I hope he will either name some that don't--including System Development Corporation--or else explain that his characterization was facetious and not intended to refer to a typical situation.

RECOVERY OF COSTS FOR ON-LINE SERVICES IN LIBRARIES

Whether and how to recover the costs of on-line services in libraries appears to be a subject of continuing concern in academic and public libraries, and the terms in which the issue is addressed tend to be highly emotional.

In the study by Judy Wanger that I referred to earlier, she asked the users of on-line service whether user charges are desirable and whether they impose such charges. We discovered that, more than any other user group, educational users were against user charges. We also learned that nearly 77 percent of the educational institutions had instituted user fees for on-line searches.

The reason for instituting such fees is fairly obvious. Library budgets, which are traditionally tight, were not large enough to cope with the success of on-line service, and libraries were confronted with a choice of (1) abandoning the service, (2) limiting service to a highly select group, e.g., key faculty members, or (3) instituting a charging method to recover some, most, or all of the direct costs of conducting the search. To their credit, most of the libraries chose not to abandon and not to limit the service to an academic elite.

Whether libraries wish to charge their patrons for special services, such as are represented by on-line retrieval, is up to the individual libraries involved. I do have a view on the matter, which is based on the perception that low-cost technology does not develop overnight. Automobiles, which almost everyone nowadays can afford or chooses to afford, were once the toys of the elite. As the first sales were made, the income helped the auto companies to lower the unit cost of manufacture and eventually to bring the selling price within reach of the general public. No one in his right mind would say that automobiles should not be sold to the rich until and unless they were priced at a level that permitted every non-rich person to buy one.

The same factors are apparent with the small electronic calculators that most of us here use. I bought one for one of my sons five years ago for $120. Today a calculator of equal power would cost less than $8. The keys to this kind of declining cost are (1) volume, and (2) competition. This applies to automobiles, calculators, information, and everything else that costs money to build or provide.

In the on-line services field, we are seeing both increasing volume and increasing competition. Unless the marketplace is perturbed in some way, we can assume that the cost of on-line searching, relative to the amount of information available and the quality of service, will continue to decline and come within greater reach of those who can effectively use it.

At its present stage of development, on-line service is too expensive for some. That is unfortunate for them, and it is also unfortunate for the operators of on-line services, who would like nothing better than to have them as users. We can, of course, ask the federal government to step in and, by taxing the entire public, subsidize service for those who would like to use on-line service but cannot presently afford to do so. But why just on-line information services? Why not ask the federal government to pay for all of the costs of university libraries or public libraries?

In the United States, we have traditionally tried to draw a line between those functions, such as national defense, that are so important or so indivisible, that they must be supported and operated on a unified basis, using tax funds, and those functions that can or should be operated on a local or private basis. Thus, in the United States we accept that the federal government does not typically operate newspapers, grocery stores, gasoline service stations, movie theaters, television stations, brokerage houses, or other businesses that offer services to the general public on a competitive basis. Is on-line service more like national defense or more like these local or private service activities? Should it be paid for by everyone or by those who directly benefit from it?

If on-line services are important enough to the general public that
they ought to be offered free in public libraries, shouldn't all the publications
on which they are based-- Chemical Abstracts, Biological Abstracts, Predicasts, Engineering Index, and the Derwent World Patent Index--<u>also</u> be
provided in every library ?

Since 1971, I have been a member of the National Commission on
Libraries and Information Science. Several years ago, while the Serrano-
Priest case was before the California courts, I brought before the Commis-
sion the need to make a statement of principle on equal access to information.
The discussion, which took place over several months, subsequently led to
a formal resolution expressed as the following ideal:

> To eventually provide every individual in the United
> States with equal opportunity of access to that part
> of the total information resource which will satisfy
> the individual's educational, working, cultural and
> leisure-time needs and interests, regardless of the
> individual's location, social or physical condition,
> or level of intellectual achievement.

I emphasize my contribution to this principle because I feel the need
to comment adversely on the idea, quoted in Allen Kent's paper, that buying
or selling information service constitutes prostitution. I find both the concept and the language in which it is expressed (by others, not Allen Kent) as
uninformed, confused, and unprofessional, and I am afraid that a simplistic
and rigid approach to the idea of equal access can do a disservice to the
library profession.

Information service activities are being developed all over the United
States (and in other countries) to provide the kinds of specialized services
that libraries have not been able or willing to provide. If libraries curtail
the introduction of sophisticated new services or tools until their budgets
are large enough to offer them free to everybody, I foresee a continued
erosion of the library's position in the total information environment of the
United States.

Libraries have found out two particularly important things during the
past five years. One (as witness revenue-sharing) is that they have a difficult time competing for funds. The other is that the use of on-line services
increases the use of libraries and the respect for the library as an institution
and for librarians as skilled professionals. I do not know whether libraries
can translate this increased use and increased respect into increased funding.
But I strongly believe that they cannot achieve increased funding <u>without</u>
them.

Allen sees on-line retrieval as providing libraries with a new kind of technical power. I heartily concur and I would add that on-line retrieval and other highly user-responsive services have the potential of providing libraries with new financial and social power as well. I hope that the discussion of the important issues of costs and cost-recovery can be conducted in an enlightened, comprehensive, and professional way, to ensure that this potential power is not squandered by short-sighted, uninformed, highly emotional appeals, even before it can be realized.

I recognize that a rational discussion requires solid information on on-line retrieval technology and the on-line retrieval business. Within the limits imposed by participation in a highly competitive field, I hope to contribute, during this conference, whatever relevant and useful information I can. I hope, also, that this conference can be an important starting point for consideration of on-line retrieval services, both as they really are and as they can come to be, in the years ahead.

Chapter 7

POTENTIAL: DISCUSSION

The discussion which follows has been transcribed from tape recordings, summarized and edited. Comments and questions have been attributed to speakers when their identity was provided. The editors of these proceedings take responsibility for any errors in fact or interpretation resulting from this process, since it was not feasible to provide proofs to discussants for checking.

Richard De Gennaro - University of Pennsylvania

What do we mean by "on-line systems"? Do we mean bibliographic retrieval systems (e.g., SDC, BRS, Lockheed) or any kind of on-line application in libraries (e.g., circulation, OCLC)? Unless we define the term we will be in for some confusion in the next few days.

Allen Kent

Although there were early applications of "data processing" in libraries (1930's?), these represented the automation of functions behind the scenes, not visible to the library user. One might categorize these applications as automation of the business of running a library. The first automation activity to impact the user directly was that of mechanized information retrieval. This impact was dramatized when "on-linedness" became possible. The on-line applications of circulation control, shared cataloging, serials control, and interlibrary loan then developed in parallel with information retrieval. But the power of on-line systems visible to the user is that of information retrieval. And therefore this is a major emphasis of this conference.

On the other hand, the parallel developments are becoming interrelated. So if one considers the results of on-line cataloging and on-line serials control, which lead to the opportunity for more effective interlibrary loan, these become parts of the chain of activities which results in the opportunity to deliver what on-line information retrieval locates.

So the first session addresses "retrieval, " while succeeding sessions hopefully will develop the related activities which result in aid to the user.

Mike Kobulnicky - West Virginia Northern Community College

Can commercial vendors of on-line services consider, as an alternate to fees, a cross-licensing arrangement which provides access to a locally produced data base?

Carlos Cuadra

There are a number of arrangements through which on-line suppliers acquire data bases. Some are like ERIC or Agricola and one merely mails a check to the federal government and the tapes arrive in the mail. There are other arrangements in which data base publishers (such as Predicasts) may hire an on-line service organization to operate their service. Another arrangement is a joint venture with data base suppliers offering the product at no cost to the service organization; the service organization not charging to build the retrieval system; the service organization "putting the data base on the air"; and sharing in some way that is equitable.

So different kinds of barter arrangements exist between on-line service organizations and the people that provide the data base. If a library had a data base that they thought would be of widespread interest, then payment is simply a matter of bookkeeping and arithmetic. Payment could be in dollars, or the equivalent in hours of service use.

But there are some limits to these kinds of barter arrangements. Many agreements with data base owners have restrictions which prevent access except at a certain price.

Some organizations maintain data bases for internal purposes. Some parts of these data bases might be of interest to others. To the extent that retrieval system capabilities permit, the on-line service organizations may put the data bases "on the air" and provide access to people in the organizations that own the data bases; selected portions of the data bases may then be made available to the general public (suppressing the confidential material).

Martin Robbins

One of the operations of EDUCOM, called EDUNET, provides access to data bases located at other institutions, through an on-line catalog and an ability to search from a remote location. The key problem is cataloging: how to identify the data bases, and logically build a catalog that is useable and understandable by a wide range of people.

George Thompson - International Labour Office, Geneva, Switzerland

The major advantage that we see in on-line systems is that it permits a rationalization of the processing function, thereby enabling scarce budget resources to be shifted to the servicing function. We have (1) created a data base of our own, and (2) we have contracted with SDC to make the data base available on-line. The royalties which we will get from SDC for use of our data base will enable us to search other files and to provide a service (which we have always provided) free of charge to our clientele.

The cost of communication (to access data bases) is _less_ when we go through Palo Alto or Santa Monica, California than to search the same data bases through Italy, a neighboring country to Switzerland. In Europe, the phone systems are government-owned; tremendous fees are charged; and agreement among countries is a barrier. There is panic in Europe that private enterprise will be forced out by government, and fees charged that no one will be able to afford.

Jane Hirsch - Montgomery County Public Library, Maryland

Does the government ownership of data bases, without alternative sources available, lead to the possibility of censorship?

Samuel Wolpert

I think you are on the wrong track. I think that one of the wonders of on-line systems is that it achieves the opposite effect. It is not easy to censor on-line systems--they truly open up access to information. These systems permit horizontal communication in an organization; prior to the advent of these systems, information in an organization tended to flow upward to the top, and downward from the top. These systems tend to defeat thought control and censorship.

Ted Johnson - Oberlin College, Ohio

Has there been any work done on transmission technology, e.g., by satellites as opposed to land-based systems? How might this impact at two levels: (1) communication access to data bases; and (2) document delivery?

Carlos Cuadra

We have been following developments in this area, because we see the use of satellites as a way of disseminating information at much lower cost. Regarding document delivery, the "electronic mailbox" permits the user of an on-line system to place an order for a document to some remote location. The "mailbox" is checked and the order is filled in the traditional way. This is a primitive system but better than current alternatives. Eventually, we will want the order fulfillment to be performed by machine. The document would then be transmitted quickly over great distances...

Allen Kent

...Plus the invoice...

Carlos Cuadra

Yes... I'm glad the University of Pittsburgh is concerned with such vital matters.

The costs of electronic transmission must come down. Currently it costs $200 per connect hour for someone in Australia to access our computer in California--this is, of course, much too high to access a data base that costs only $35 per connect hour within the United States.

Martin Robbins

In thinking of alternative document delivery systems, the main cost is inputting, not communication. The question is how to put the document into machine-readable form. Leaving aside the concept of facsimile, most journal materials are created in machine-readable form in order to permit computer-assisted composition. But the natural step, to transmit this information, is not too far away. That will be the true "revolution." The legal profession already has a full-text retrieval system (LEXIS), with documents searchable, and specific items printed locally in hard copy.

Tom Tennyson - Brooklyn Public Library, New York

I have heard here of advances in telecommunications and computer technologies, and competition making information available to the masses. Given these factors, will it be necessary for libraries to deliver on-line services? Will it be possible to have data delivered to my home via telephone and television?

Samuel Wolpert

I can envision some on-line retrieval at home for trivial questions. But the world is complicated, and in order to obtain understanding about a complex issue, one must use an intermediary who knows what you desire, who knows the data bases that exist, and who knows the retrieval system.

Carlos Cuadra

An interesting finding of Judith Wanger's study was the librarians' response to the question: can end-users do their own searches? Almost all replied "No." When the end-users were asked the same question, almost all replied "Yes." They are both correct, but in somewhat different ways. There are certain qualities of the information specialist that the end-users will not acquire, bacause they cannot invest enough time to do so. If end-users do not search frequently, they cannot maintain a skill-level to search efficiently. The librarian must learn to use many data bases efficiently, to keep up with periodic changes in the systems. End-users simply do not invest in that level of activity.

At the present time no data bases exist which are of intrinsic interest in the home (except the homes of scientists, businessmen, or technicians who have terminals available).

When data bases of more general interest are available, then there will be more on-line use at home.

Martin Robbins

The home computer is an obvious reality (e.g., Sears is offering one in the $600 price range). The applications promoted are for income tax preparation, checkbook balancing, and games. The development that is taking place relates to group computation (e.g., small departments) by means of "smart" terminals. The sophistication of people using such terminals will go up.

It does take an expert to search efficiently. But I expect that as sophistication goes up, expertise in searching will develop and spread.

Allen Kent

An analogy might be in order here. Historically, many computer users hired applications programmers as intermediaries to do their computer work (this continues). But many users have become expert themselves (because of interest or through frustration in not being able to communicate their problems to applications programmers). I agree with Martin Robbins, that in data base searching we will see the development both of intermediaries serving the end-users and the end-users serving themsleves. I view this parallel development as very healthy.

Dana Rooks - University of Missouri, St. Louis

Discussion of fees has centered on public service aspects of library work. Libraries all over the country are automating other functions, but there is no talk of passing these costs along to the patrons. Automated technical services are "absorbed" into the budget, and justified on the basis of cost-effectiveness. Why not charge a patron, for example, for checking out a book from an automated circulation system? Why do we think only of charging for public services?

Martin Robbins

This is a fascinating question. I've always wondered why universities charge for computing services, but not for libraries.

Anita Schiller

There has been no defense of the public interest in the matter of fees for library services. We have not opened this to public discussion. Should we not be addressing these questions?

Allen Kent

Some seven years ago, the University of Pittsburgh charged for computer services; the library services were free, as always. Then the University of Pittsburgh, like Dartmouth, offered computer services at no charge to the users (there is no way of paying). But now the library at the University is discussing institution of fees. You can't win!

Mary Eidleman - Dundaulk Community College, Baltimore, Maryland

Martin Robbins suggested that librarians should become involved in the development of a machine-readable catalog of data bases. How should they become involved?

Martin Robbins

Sue Dodd, University of North Carolina, and Judith Rowe, Princeton, are deeply involved in assuring that this development is in the hands of those who know what they are doing, rather than those who are unfamiliar with the needs.

Judith Rowe - Princeton University, New Jersey

In searching the commercial on-line services, one finds references to printed materials, but one never finds, side-by-side references to the machine-readable files which were in many cases used to create these publications. The reason is that there has never been bibliographic control of these files. Technically, they don't have titles, and are typically lacking in any standard kind of bibliographic information. Many of us have been involved in trying to bring these materials into a system of bibliographic control. The American Library Association has a subcommittee on the cataloging of machine-readable data files. The report of that subcommittee was submitted over a year ago and will form Chapter 9 of the Anglo-American cataloging rules. When published, catalogers will have a set of rules for cataloging, with the "Good Housekeeping Seal of Approval" for machine-readable files, and this will legitimize these sources of information.

Sue Dodd is preparing a manual to explain how to use these rules and to integrate entries into the public catalog. Once these files are under bibliographic control, we will then need the intervention of a data services librarian.

Jim Cogswell - University of Pennsylvania

I believe on-line services have relied on libraries as a sales medium for their own products. An example is that the training offered by the vendors was not very intensive, provided by people who know the system but not much about the files being searched. The sessions were not very convenient, offered typically only in major metropolitan areas. And the services were not offered at reduced rates for training purposes. NASIC helped to fill the void in the northeastern part of the United States. The On-Line Training Center of the University of Pittsburgh suggests that the need is still there. The need is not being met adequately by the vendors of on-line services and by the abstracting and indexing services. I would like to suggest that these services help the University of Pittsburgh and other educational institutions by at least offering free expertise or even subsidizing these training organizations. The money spent by the vendors in half-hearted training could better be spent in helping the training institutions.

Christine Borgman - Dallas Public Library, Texas

Regarding the fee controversy, we are both a public library and the municipal library for the city of Dallas. The City Manager is pushing for city departments to develop entrepreneurial ideas--charge for anything the city department can possibly charge for. We have therefore developed fee-based services (Lockheed, SDC, The Information Bank). We have developed reference services which provide the private use of a librarian for a fee. We have an on-line catalog, and are discussing special printouts at a fee. We have a COM catalog and can charge for printouts from a reader-printer. As long as we are funded in this way, we will be obliged to charge fees.

Curtis Lavery - University of Central America, Nicaragua

What are the large information services doing to provide alternative formats for small groups of users, e.g., foreign language users?

Carlos Cuadra

I mentioned earlier the personalized system, which involved being able to have an inexperienced user, or new user, "tune" the system so it behaves in a way that is appropriate for his or her level of understanding. The experienced user may want the system to "talk" and "behave" a quite different way, and that also is "tuneable." These capabilities do not currently exist, but they certainly will. We are simultaneously working on programs that will make it both more complex and more simple to address the needs of the different kinds of users.

One of the ways we plan to personalize the system is in terms of the languages the system "speaks." The users in Spain will have the system "talk" to them in Spanish; and similarly in Germany, so that users can address the system in their language. The data itself will remain in English, of course.

Regarding the comment by Mr. Cogswell, it is certainly true that in the early years (1973), none of the on-line suppliers was able to do as much as we wanted: in training; in elegant user materials; in "explain" messages on-line. All of these aspects cost money. One has to pay for them. There may be a "free" world, but we are not quite in it. Regarding training by on-line service vendors: Two weeks ago we trained simultaneously in Albuquerque, Chicago, Denver, Hackensack, New Jersey, McLean, Virginia, London, Paris and Delft. All of these were new user training sessions. We also conducted advanced training workshops in a number of those cities, and custom training at people's locations. That's an awful lot of people, doing an awful lot of training, in an awful lot of places. If someone didn't get to Pennsylvania enough, I certainly regret it. But we do not want to leave the perception that on-line vendors are unmindful of the need to get out where the user is.

Part Two

IMPACT OF ON-LINE SYSTEMS

The on-line revolution is altering library ecology. It alerts the user
to more than the individual library holds. This creates opportunities and
mechanisms for resource-sharing. The development of regional, national,
and international networks has reached the point at which we can assess the
impact on planning, policy, library functions, and especially on the user.
The economic aspects are examined: for libraries, for users, and for publishers. The relationships between the non-profit and profit-seeking sectors
are explored. Criteria and means for evaluation need current attention.

The position papers distributed in advance of the conference are
given in Chapters 8 (impact on national information policy), 10 (impact on
library functions), and 12 (impact on the clientele). Specific reactions from
panelists are presented in Chapters 9, 11, and 13; general reactions in
Chapters 15-19. Chapters 14 and 20 present the discussion at the conference.

Chapter 8

IMPACT OF ON-LINE SYSTEMS
ON NATIONAL INFORMATION POLICY
AND ON LOCAL, STATE, AND REGIONAL PLANNING*

Lee G. Burchinal

Director
Division of Science Information
National Science Foundation
Washington, D. C.

PERSPECTIVE

    Development of on-line systems is an indicator of two fundamental changes now occurring in the United States information transfer enterprise. One change involves the substitution of nonprint forms of distribution for our present paper-dominated system. The second is the shift from near total reliance on local holdings for answering users' needs to extensive use of outside services for accessing large, remote sources of information.

    Both are in early, primitive forms of development. Within a decade, however, these developments can be confidently expected to mature into integrated, network-based information services that novices will use with ease. Results of this development will include substantial changes in the structure of libraries and information services, revenue bases for operations, and competencies required of library and information professionals and users.

---

* The views expressed in the following paper are exclusively those of the author and are not necessarily the views of the National Science Foundation.

The driving forces for these changes--present and projected--lie outside the library field and its on-line suppliers. The major impetus is derived from the dynamics of the major elements comprising the U.S. information economy. Information processing requirements of business, banking, and other commercial enterprises are immense. So are those of the military and civilian sides of the federal government. All of these private and governmental organizations share two serious information processing requirements:

* The necessity to process and create ready access to an ever-increasing volume of information, with no foreseeable letup.

* To do so with the greatest feasible cost/effectiveness.

Electronic means of transmission, often coupled with micrographic storage of large files, offers the greatest hope for simultaneously achieving three objectives--lowering unit costs, managing ever-increasing volumes of information, and increasing its effective use.

Consequently, the U. S. has built up a large, innovation-oriented information processing industry. In 1973, research and development expenditures for electronics and related fields surpassed that for aerospace and missiles, our previously largest R & D field. Libraries and their information suppliers have benefited immensely from the new products and services derived from this research.

As a result, today we have low-cost terminals, large file management systems, mass storage devices, large and mini-computers, telecommunication services--all of which make networking and on-line services possible. Moreover, the cost/effectiveness of these devices and related technologies continues to improve.

In effect, our enterprise--libraries and their on-line service suppliers--is following the lead of other industries. Labor-intensive operations are being reduced, if not replaced by capital-intensive methods. These capital-intensive methods are based on successful experiences in the overall U.S. information economy, of which our enterprise is only a miniscule portion.

Two deductions follow from this perspective:

* On-line developments in the library field will not compel re-thinking or reformulation of national information policies.

* But the converse is true--decisions regarding national communication policies and practices will have profound effects on libraries and their operations.

This does not mean that there are no significant developments supporting electronic information exchange within the library field and related information services. Of course, there are, but, to repeat, the most important of these are based on applications of our advancing communication technologies and related systems. Broad directions are clear. An inevitable scenario is emerging. Disagreements are centered only on details--the timing or pace of developments or which specific technologies such as tape, discs, micrographics, holographics, video-disc or slow-scan TV will become dominant for various applications.[1]

THE INEVITABLE SCENARIO

The scenario for the future is an elaboration of our very brief computer era experience. Computers and telecommunications have and will continue to revolutionize the transfer and use of information.

Today we are in the early stages of this revolution. Let me illustrate with abstracting/indexing publications. In the early 1960's, computers were first applied to the processing of typesetting for these publications. Beginning in the mid-1960's, the first bibliographic data bases in machine-readable form were made available. In ten short years, the number of such data bases in the United States grew from an estimated two dozen or so to about 160 and the number of records available increased from approximately 880,000 to over 46 million in the same time period.[2] With the profusion of data bases, first SDC and Lockheed, and now BRS, brought on-line searching to thousands of libraries in this country and abroad. Federal agencies, notably in the National Library of Medicine, and private organizations, such as the New York Times, are providing additional services. Also, OCLC is a harbinger of specialized national and regional resource-sharing networks made possible by recent technological developments and changed views on the part of librarians. More will come, with the growth being primarily in the private sector.

A similar sequence is now being repeated in primary publishing. Beginning with automation of typesetting, computer applications have moved

---

1. For example, see: Nisenoff, N. A Forecast of Technology for Scientific and Technical Information Communities. Available from: NTIS, Springfield, Virginia; PB 253-937.

2. The 1965 data are estimated, while the 1975 data are from a recent report. See Williams, M., and T. Brandhorst. "Data About Data Bases." Bulletin of the American Society for Information Science, 3(2):20-21, December 1976. For recent data, see M. Williams, this volume, pages 149 ff.

back to on-line editing and make-up, management of subscription fulfillment, mailing, and other business and editorial functions. Computer-readable tapes are now a realistic byproduct from journal publishers. Soon we can expect to see machine-to-machine transfer of article surrogate information from journal publishers to abstracting/indexing services. In the not-too-distant future, the full text of articles will be available from remote sources through a variety of technologies--paper and micrographic facsimile, slow-scan TV, and video-disc as well as by computer networks.

Meanwhile, research is moving ahead on ways to bring electronic information transfer home for easy use by those of us who are not computer specialists. "Transparency" and "knowledge retrieval" are the related objectives of this research. Transparency means that a user needs only to input a few simple commands at a terminal and the "system" takes over to produce the requested information. The system would be structured to provide linkages among data bases of surrogate information, full text files, and numerical data files. Further, users would be able to retrieve desired information without having to learn different indexing schemes. Knowledge retrieval refers to the ability to retrieve prescribed, delimited passages from a text, tables, or numerical data from multiple, remote files, regardless of their sizes and structure. And all of this would be done from the same terminal, at one sitting, and, if users were so disposed, without the aid of an intermediary.

Transparent networks and files organized for knowledge retrieval are a long term gleam in the eyes of researchers and system designers. But all developments point in this direction.

Accessing services are fully automated today. Movement is toward developing capabilities for cross data-base searching.[3] Full text searching and reading from remote storage are sure to follow.

---

3. This is a new area of research. For example, see: Marcus, Richard S. and Reintjes, J. Francis. Electronic Systems Laboratory, Massachusetts Institute of Technology. The Networking of Interactive Bibliographic Retrieval Systems. Available from NTIS, Springfield, Virginia; PB 252-407. Williams, Martha E. and MacLaury, Keith M. "Maping of Chemical Data Bases Using a Relational Data Base Structure, " in Computers in Chemical Education and Research, E. V. Ludena, N. H. Sabelli and A. C. Wahl, eds. Plenum Press, 1977. Hillman, D., Lehigh University. Research into Knowledge Transfer Systems. NSF Grant No. SIS 75-09282. In progress. Sager, Naomi, New York University. Information Structures in the Language of Science. NSF Grant No. SIS 75-22945. In progress.

The bases for this forecast, as outlined earlier, are imbedded in the driving forces that are shaping the overall U.S. information economy. Further development of generalized automated information management capabilities will advance special purpose applications for libraries and the information services they will increasingly depend upon.

To return to the main theme of these remarks, I maintain that we need to keep our eye on the macro developments affecting the U.S. information economy. How will decisions about issues at this level affect the library-information scenario just described?

ISSUES

The brief answer to this question now is we do not know. We can, however, examine some of the policy trends that are emerging. Four sets, I suggest, are worth examining.

These are issues and related developments:

- At the federal government level--in both the legislative and executive branches.

- At the national private sector level--largely among the business and commercial organizations.

- At the local, state and regional levels.

- Across the profession as a whole.

Federal Level. The most significant development at the federal level is that both Congress and the Executive Branch of government are coming to grips with the legal demands and requirements of a post-industrial society. Widespread applications of advanced communication technology are forcing rethinking about fundamental national policies. Congress is expressing its interest in a number of ways. For example:

- The copyright revision act of 1976 represents an effort to bring this legislation in line with current technology.

- Establishment of CONTU represents a further effort to revise law in keeping with technological advances.

- The law establishing the Office of Science and Technology Policy included reference to information issues in 11 of its 45 major sections.[4] Moreover, Congress has entered the modern information age with development of its own data bases and on-line services. Today, the Congressional Research Service maintains nine data bases, and over 350 terminals are now in use in the offices of the Senate and House.

Even more basic reformulation is on the way. Congress is beginning to consider total revision of the Communications Act of 1934--the basic framework for regulation of all communications in the United States. Many experts contend that this document is outmoded and is slowing technological advancement. Revision of this Act could well have a more profound effect on the structure and functioning of the information transfer enterprise in the United States than any other single development. Obviously, organizations representing the interests of libraries and information services will want to follow and perhaps influence this development.

Numerous significant developments are also occurring within the Executive branch. The regulatory area is in ferment. The Federal Communications Commission, for example, through its decisions is opening competition with AT&T. Meanwhile, the Justice Department continues to pursue antitrust action against IBM and AT&T. The intended outcome of these regulatory and antitrust actions is to foster competition and, thereby, presumably increase benefits to the country. Issues are complex, with much of the confusion growing out of the convergence of computer and telecommunications technologies. Arguments and counter arguments come from the interested and affected industries and consumer groups. However, this is no reason why organizations representing libraries and related information suppliers should not make their views heard. But, in doing so, one should recognize the magnitude of the issues being considered and that decisions will be based on long-term national economic and social considerations.

Meanwhile, both Congress and the White House have begun to look at national information policy issues. In 1976, the Domestic Council Committee on the Right of Privacy forwarded a report entitled National Information Policy to President Ford.[5] This report, disseminated by NCLIS, has helped stir interest in broad national information issues. Since then, the Office of Technology Assessment, which answers to both houses of Congress, has begun a thorough review of national information and communications problems and issues. This is an activity that deserves careful attention.

---

4. See: Whalen, B. G., and Joyce, C., Jr. Scientific and Technical Information: Options for National Action. Available from: NTIS, Springfield, Virginia; PB 261-863.

5. Domestic Council Committee on the Right of Privacy. National Information Policy: Report to the President of the United States. Superintendent of Documents, 1976.

Even more recently, President Carter has indicated the significance of national information policy issues. Reorganization Plan Number 1 calls for establishment of an Assistant Secretary for Communications and Information in the Department of Commerce.[6] This office will inherit functions of the Office of Telecommunications Policy and will, no doubt, become a locus for analyses of national information policies.

Development of on-line services are affecting the operations of federal agencies as well. Two major interrelated issues are shaping up: (1) what are the appropriate roles of public and private agencies in the dissemination of information; and (2) within the federal sector, what actions are required to substantially improve overall cost/effectiveness? These issues are gaining prominence because of: (1) the growing number and variety of private abstracting and indexing services that are available on-line; (2) the increasing interdisciplinary nature of research, which requires information from numerous disciplines and fields; and (3) the reality of networking for searching numerous, diverse remote data bases. We can expect lively debate on these issues. In time, new policies and guidelines for federal agency operations will no doubt evolve, as a result of pressures from the private sector balanced against the objectives of agencies, as interpreted by Congress and the Office of Management and Budget.

The federal level cannot be left without consideration of the recent copyright legislation. With the new law, behavior will change. Some libraries will no doubt alter loan and reproduction practices to avoid clearance and payment requirements. Some publishers will begin testing alternative ways of packaging, marketing, and licensing their material to meet demand for separate articles. Increased use of on-line services can be expected to increase such demand. With these services, users are led to the basic unit of formal communication--the article. The journal, the traditional way of packaging articles, could give way to article availability in several forms. Today reproductions are produced in paper, as part of interlibrary loan or from commercial services. Separates are available in microfiche form as are some journals. The favorable cost-effectiveness of microfiche over paper or electronic alternatives will hold for at least a decade or so. We can expect to see a shift, therefore, in libraries toward micrographic storage of journals, with reproduction of articles on demand. Publishers are moving in this direction as well, with dual publication in microform and print. Eventually, publication will be in electronic form as well. Users and libraries then will have a choice of materials in printed or micrographic form or in electronic display, with all sorts of interchanges among these media. Cost, convenience, preference will be deciding factors.

---

6. Congressional Record. July 15, 1977. H 7231-7233.

National. By national, I refer to developments that are occurring throughout the national information economy and which are reflected in the library and information systems field. Briefly, I will mention only three major forces: (1) the hardware and software push; (2) service company development; and (3) the trend toward information management. All three are concentrated in the business world today.

Innovation in information processing hardware and software will continue. No letup is anticipated. Technologies are merging. Word processing, printing, micrographics, and computer applications are being brought together in integrated information retrieval systems. Common now in commercial and military applications, these applications will spread to other fields in the coming years.

These technological developments may be expected to accelerate the information service company movement. Examples today include services such as SDC, Lockheed, and BRS for on-line access; University Microfilms and the Institute for Scientific Information for articles on demand; micropublishers such as Congressional Information Service, Inc. and Research Publications, Inc.; and knowledge-on-demand companies, such as FIND/SVP.[7] Additional firms can be expected to generate or aggregate information products and services to meet changing market conditions. Some of these firms are now competitors with libraries. Further development of on-line services, particularly those combined with document or fact delivery, will increase the number and types of intermediaries serving users.

Another response to developments in the delivery of information, is the emergence of the corporate information manager. This development is following similar trends in other fields that began simple and became more complex. Data processing is one example; office automation and automated records management are more recent illustrations. As information choices become more complex and consequences of choices more obvious, organizations with large information-related budgets are developing information management roles. The chief contenders for these roles are managers of date processing centers, since higher level management often equates improvements in information access with computer-based systems. Directors of libraries or technical and marketing information services are in a favorable position to compete for these roles as well.

---

7. For descriptions of current information service companies, see: Information Sources: The Membership Directory of the Information Industry Association, 4720 Montgomery Lane, Suite 904, Bethesda, Maryland 20014. 1977.

With their purchasing power, these individuals could become important new forces in shaping the mix of products and services offered. For
example, information managers may wish to purchase hard copy or COM-
generated fiche of articles meeting a certain profile rather than to subscribe
to so many copies of journals and to provide copies to users on demand
through internal corporate facsimile networks. Others may want output in
electronic form. Still others will demand different services. Collectively,
however, corporate information managers will represent a way of articulating and aggregating demand for new or varied products that is lacking
today. [8]

My point here is that decisions of corporate information managers
will help structure the market for noncorporate libraries as well. In this
case, academic, public, and governmental librarians will do well to follow
corporate practices closely and seek to exploit leading developments for
their benefit.

Local-State-Regional. Changes represented by on-line services raise
several basic questions at the local, state, and regional levels. The first is
the "build" or "buy" question. By build, I mean a library maintains its own
in-house, autonomous operations. Materials are purchased, catalogued,
circulated, etc., within the resources of the library. In contrast to this
traditional role, libraries may rely on outside vendors and buy needed services, as in the case of purchase of on-line services. Complicating this
simple distinction is the development of state, regional, and national resource sharing. The many library consortia and networks are examples.
Local libraries contribute in kind services, as in the case of OCLC, and get,
in return, benefits far beyond the equivalent of their investment. This
development will spread, but will be countered, I suspect, by offerings of
information service companies. In either case, libraries will move toward
buying more of the services offered. If this forecast is correct, capital and
purchase budgets will increase, probably at the expense of personnel and
materials budgets.

A second issue swirls around the "free" versus "fee" controversy.
The trend is toward expansion of fee-based services. With increased costs,
greater automation and associated capital intensive operations, new sources
of revenue will be necessary to sustain the more costly, but far more effective, services users are becoming accustomed to having. Increased public

8. The Information Industry Association also recognizes the potential signif-
    icance of this emerging professional group. The 1977 IIA Annual Meeting
    is entitled: "The Emerging Information Manager--Bridging an Informa-
    tion Gap."

funding to meet these costs is not likely. More likely, users will be required
to pay at least part of the costs of more sophisticated services in the future.
Trends are already well established. Most libraries are charging for use of
on-line services. Federal agencies are seeking at least partial cost recovery
with some, like NTIS, committed to full cost recovery. Profit-seeking
"information-on-demand companies" have entered the field.

Here, then, is another facet of the on-line revolution in libraries--how
to combine fee-based services within the operation of "free" libraries.

Professional. On-line developments pose two additional challenges
to the professional information community. One is the development of a
comprehensive national standards program for library and related information processing systems and operations. The other is development of updated and forward-looking curricular materials and methods for information
professional and potential users.

Standards work has been carried on through the American National
Standards Institute (ANSI) Committee, Z-39. An NCLIS ad hoc committee
has recommended ways to strengthen and expand Z-39.[9] Here is an effort
that requires and deserves the help of all library and information science
professionals and organizations.

Education of professionals and users in use of on-line services and
other modern information retrieval tools has only recently begun to receive
the attention it deserves. At the university level, many library and information science schools and departments are now providing education in use
of on-line services. SDC, Lockheed, and BRS run workshops for librarians
and other users. Abstracting/indexing services, such as the National Library of Medicine, the Chemical Abstracts Service, Engineering Index, and
BIOSIS, conduct training programs as well. For several years NSF, through
its Division of Science Information, supported research on ways to introduce
science and engineering students to on-line services as part of their graduate and undergraduate instruction. Librarians and information scientists
can help by lending their skills to development of training programs for
users. At the college or university level, joint development of training
modules with professors in subject fields is particularly promising.

---

9. National Commission on Libraries and Information Science. American
   National Standards Committee Z-39: Recommended Future Direction.
   NCLIS, 1717 K Street, NW, Suite 601, Washington, D. C. 20036. 1978.

Chapter 9

ON-LINE SYSTEMS AND NATIONAL POLICY

Melvin S. Day

Deputy Director
National Library of Medicine
Bethesda, Maryland

Dr. Lee Burchinal in his "position" paper for this session (Chapter 8) has prepared a scholarly, thought-provoking treatment of the topical question. The scope and thrust of his remarks range across the technical, social, political, and economic aspects of what is really a mind-boggling subject if treated in its entirety. I admire his mature perspective and his thoughtful codification of a large number of pressing issues which must and, I am sure, will be addressed during this conference.

Because of the limitation of time and space at this session and because of the large number of items to be covered, Dr. Burchinal, of necessity, had to compress and skillfully jump from peak to peak. For my part, I plan to limit my own remarks to two major areas: (1) the impact of on-line systems on the government decision-making apparatus (federal and state); and (2) on the other side of the coin, the impact of federal policy, or lack thereof, on the "on-line revolution." I hope that a brief exploration of these two aspects will prove to be of value to you.

U.S. CONGRESS

First of all let us look briefly at the impact of on-line technology on the legislative process.

Theodore D. Sterling (Simon Fraser University, British Columbia, Canada) made a pertinent observation in 1975 when he stated that computerized management information systems increasingly determine all bureau-

85

cratic and management procedures and that they are beginning to dominate
the economic, political, and social management of society.[1]

Such changes are beginning to spread into the halls of our Congress
and these are far-reaching changes. You may recall that John Gardner in
his book "Self Renewal" says that "many Americans have a sentimental and
undiscriminating view of change." He says that "they (Americans) feel that
it (change) is without qualification, a good thing."[2]

I can assure you that the changes I am about to mention did not come
easily for the Congress and were not made for the sake of change. Congress
by design is a very conservative organization and the changes I am about to
describe came about only because they were urgently needed.

I am indebted to Robert Chartrand, the senior information science
specialist, Science Policy Research Division, Congressional Research Service for his complete documentation of the exciting progress in Congress in
automating (much of it on-line) its own information support services. I
commend to you his report entitled The Legislator as User of Information
Technology (revised October 9, 1977).[3]

He reports that for many years Congress was relatively unaware of
the potential of the new automated information devices and techniques and
was reluctant to enact legislation which included any requirement for their
use--especially Congressional use. It has only been in the last ten years
that Congress has taken action to improve its own methods of collecting,
storing, indexing, processing, and selectively retrieving information essential to its own operations and deliberations.[4] The Legislative Reorganization
Act of 1970 (Public Law 91-510) provided guidance, procedures, and emphasis
on types of information support essential to the legislative and administrative
operations of Congress.[5] More recently passage of the Congressional Budget
and Impoundment Control Act of 1974 (P. L. 93-344) has brought about the
use of advanced information technology in handling budgetary and fiscal data.[6]

Among the priority applications of ADP technology is the handling of
bill content and status information through the on-line LEGIS capability. A
remote terminal-oriented composition and editing system has been installed
for the bill drafting function and for the purpose of publishing committee
hearings. A broad array of budget analysis and monitoring projects in support of the House Committee on the Budget and Appropriations and the Congressional Budget Office have been developed. For the most part, these
systems were developed and are maintained by a number of commercial
vendors under the aegis of the House Information Systems group. By the way,
this is an example of government utilizing the expertise and capability of the
private sector. An increasing number of computer-assisted models are used

to help formulate policy alternatives, supported by such packaged programs as income modeling, statistical analysis, econometric forecasting, and income tax analysis.[7]

A "Member Information Network" (MIN) allows member offices access to various remote computerized files such as JURIS (Justice Retrieval and Information System), FAPRS (Federal Assistance Program Retrieval System), LEGIS, and the nine information files which comprise the Library of Congress SCORPIO System (Subject-Content Retrieval System). In addition, this network provides summary accounts of House Floor activities which are prepared by Chamber reporters and are directly inserted into the on-line SOPAD system (Summary of Proceedings and Debate). Terminals are also used by 18 committees to prepare their calendars of activities.

In addition Congress has come to realize that it no longer can depend solely on its own data bases for all the information support it needs, and so it is gaining access to and is making use of a number of external data bases such as the U.S. Air Force Project FLITE (Federal Legal Information Through Electronics) which allows a search of such material as the U.S. CODE and the published decisions of the Comptroller General.

My reasons for expanding on this new look for Congress are twofold. First, Congress, which in the past has been criticized by some citizens as being inefficient and not well informed, is taking giant strides to strengthen its own information support apparatus all along the line in order to increase its ability to legislate wisely in a more timely manner. The new on-line capability is bringing about major changes in the Congressional decision-making processes. Such changes are having a profound effect on the legislative process and ultimately on national policies and legislation that impact on all facets of national life.

Secondly, Congressmen as users, benefiting from the application of the new systems and technology, should be more appreciative of the value of such capability to almost every facet of American life. Hopefully, such an orientation will cause them to look much more favorably on strengthening this capability government-wide and nation-wide. If this happens then all of us should benefit from these positive and basic changes in the way Congress conducts its business.

STATE LEGISLATURES

Just a brief word about the effect of on-line technology on state legislative deliberative activities. Much of what I said about how this powerful electronic technology has provided a new dimension to the policy decision process in the U.S. Congress is also beginning to apply at the state government level. Congressional continuing interest in this area is reflected by a decision of Congressman David R. Obey, Chairman of the Commission on Administrative Review, U.S. House of Representatives, to commission a study by Congressional Research Service (CRS) of the State Legislature use of information technology. Robert Chartrand, CRS, prepared the study report which now appears in a 1977 report of the Commission on Administrative Review.[8] Two additional recent publications also carry detailed information in this important area:

1. State Use of Electronic Data Processing.[9] Contains a series of surveys prepared by James Elkins, Jr. for the Council of State Governments; and
2. Comparative Legislative Information Systems.[10] Edited by John Worthley.

(For those who may wish to refer to these publications I have included complete citations with this paper.)

In the last five years there has been a tremendous growth in the number of State Legislatures making use of automated systems. By way of illustration, in 1972 ten State Legislatures were operating statutory retrieval systems to retrieve their statutes; today there are more than 30. Several states have built automated data bases containing State regulations and case law. Several states have installed innovative on-line systems to monitor expenditures and revenues within the State, as well as providing up-to-date information on budget proposals. The trend today at the state level is not to produce more and more data, but rather to assemble it into more meaningful and more useful forms which can better serve the decision-making process.[11]

Planners are even looking forward to the interconnection via network on a selective basis, of state legislative data bases among themselves and ultimately interconnecting them with certain of the U.S. Congressional data bases.

EXECUTIVE BRANCH (FEDERAL GOVERNMENT)

I would be remiss if I left the impression that only the legislative branches of government were using on-line computerized systems to support and facilitate their decision-making process. As we all know, for the last 10-12 years executive departments and agencies have developed and installed large numbers of automated management information systems, some quite complex and many on-line to assist management at various levels of management including the policy level.

Because of the tight time constraints this morning and because I do want to leave sufficient time to touch on the information policy area, I will not expand further on this aspect of how on-line capability has influenced the making of federal policy. Suffice to say, the executive branch of our federal government has led in the application of automated systems in support of the management decision-making process.

Even in the Executive Office of the President, there is a new awareness of the need to fully utilize modern information technology in carrying out its decision-making mandate. The Office of Science and Technology Policy this past summer established an Advisory Group on White House Information Systems to identify those information system needs required to support the "decision processes" of the White House itself and of the Office of the President. An advisory group of non-governmental experts has already had two meetings, the most recent in October, at which the higher level staff members of the Executive Office of the President identified their information requirements.[12] To underscore White House interest, an on-line computer expert has been added to the limited White House staff.

Although it is highly unlikely that the President, the Secretaries of Federal Departments, or the Heads of Agencies, themselves, query and use the management on-line systems, it is equally true that with increasing frequency the data provided to them by their staffs are output products of their organizations' own on-line systems.

Decision-making at the national level has become a highly complex process because of the myriad of interrelated interacting factors; because of the wide variety and huge volumes of data, much of it changing, that must be assimilated, analyzed, and evaluated; and because of the ever present pressure for speed. Without today's computerized systems, including those for modeling and analysis, coupled to on-line capability, the process itself would be largely mired down in a morass of unintelligible facts and figures. I need not point out, of course, that the use of on-line computerized capability does not guarantee good decisions or even pretty good decisions but, if effectively used, it should make it more possible for those making decisions to better identify and evaluate their alternatives for decision-making. After that, we can keep our fingers crossed.

INFORMATION POLICY

In the time remaining this morning, I wish to address the second major problem area I identified at the beginning of my presentation, that is "the impact of national policy, or lack thereof, on the on-line revolution. "

   Dr. Burchinal in his paper spoke about the need for national information policies in a number of important areas. The promulgators of the needed
policies as he put it would represent a number of different, even diverse,
federal organizations. Here in the United States we enjoy the blessings and
benefits of a pluralistic society where the government and the private sector
have equally important roles and where successful national programs require
that the federal and private sectors join hands. Ours is a leadership role in
the broad areas covered by library and information science and technology--
a role made possible through the genius for innovation and application on the
part of all components of the private and public sectors of our country's
information community.

   Our information systems, services, and networks are the envy of the
world and yet this has been accomplished without a centrally planned structured national framework. In our field, we do not have a detailed National
Program with blueprints for implementation, nor a formalized statement of
national policies promulgated by the highest authorities in our nation, and
certainly not a National Plan proposed by these same authorities, and supported by all segments of our country's information community--public and
private.

   Overall centralized national planning in a country the size of the
United States and in our type of society is terribly complex. H. L. Mencken
has made the observation that "for every complex problem there is a solution
that is neat, plausible, and wrong." In the U.S. we do not have a neat,
plausible solution to our many complex information policy problems. Accordingly, if I subscribe to Mencken's observation, then we have not been guilty
of concocting the wrong simplified solution.

   Still national policies can, have been, and are being set but without
the help or hindrance (take your pick) of overall central coordination to tie
together all the pieces into a nice neat package.

   There are a number of attempts at national planning. For example,
this audience is certainly familiar with the hopes and efforts of the National
Commission on Libraries and Information Science. The Commission has
developed an ambitious program which is attempting to address the needs for
planning in a number of important areas. Noteworthy among them being the
Commission's plan for a National Periodicals System. My own assessment
of the impact of the Commission's efforts is that they have been positive, and
the capable and dedicated members of NCLIS and staff are to be commended.
The scope of concern of NCLIS is tremendously broad and complex.

   NCLIS as a National Commission in the Federal hierarchical structure
has many advantages by virtue of its responsibilities both to the President
and Congress. On the other hand, its organizational nature differs from that

of general executive agencies of the federal government and this coupled with its restricted manpower and fiscal resources limits to a degree the extent of its effectiveness. I understand that Al Trezza, Executive Director, NCLIS,will be a panelist at this afternoon's session, and I am sure that Mr. Trezza will have much to say about NCLIS at that time. Accordingly, to preclude duplication in the NCLIS area, I will move on to other organizations which also directly impact on the on-line revolution.

Dr. Burchinal pointed out that the Federal Communications Commission (FCC) through its regulations opened competition to AT&T by licensing other carriers. This policy decision was a national policy decision with profound implications to those of us on this continent who are users or operators of on-line systems accessible from geographically distant locations. I am, of course, referring to the FCC decision to license Tymnet and Telenet. These two networks utilizing leased AT&T lines are providing the major communications network services for the large on-line service organizations such as SDC, Lockheed, BRS, OCLC, and NLM. The network services are reliable and the rate schedules are the most reasonable in the world. The rates reflect a substantial reduction over costs for the traditional carrier system services and have contributed greatly to the reasonableness of charges for access to the major on-line systems across the country.

The FCC decision appears to be based on the long standing national policy to maintain the dynamic and entrepreneural climate in America--to foster and stimulate competition.

In almost every aspect of the on-line revolution you can feel the effect of this basic policy, the philosophical genesis of which is our free enterprise system. For example, as a matter of national policy the Federal Government by means of antitrust legislation and separately by its own purchasing regulations is fostering competition among the manufacturers of computer and peripheral equipment. Readily visible to all of us are the tremendous continuing improvements in computer equipment and at the same time continuing major reductions in processing costs. Each manufacturer attempts to leap frog the other.

Our American society encourages the efforts of the innovator and entrepreneur, with most corporate bodies attempting to become larger and more influential in their spheres of interest. Some call this progress, but this progress is not without some skirmishes and problems.

It has been pointed out that the process of marrying computers and communications has already started. For example the IBM Corporation has been authorized by the Federal Communications Commission to engage in the satellite communications business. On the other side, Western Union International has indicated its strong interest in moving into the data bank business.

How far will the giants of the communications and computer industries move into the data base business? To what extent will they be allowed to take over the marketing and possible control of data bases intended for public use? Could this lead to a situation where the knowledge nodes and communications links are under the control of the same organization? This could be a national policy issue of great importance during the next five years. What organization or organizations would be responsible for addressing this national policy issue and for developing, if necessary, the requisite policy?

Currently, national information policy is being developed on a piecemeal basis; some may even say in an Adam Smith-like process. More and more voices are demanding a change in this practice. These voices say that in order for such a change to be effective there must be an effective coalescing mechanism and framework within which a more orderly development of policies can evolve. The voices state further that if central leadership is to be forthcoming from the federal government it must start at the White House level and apply at least initially to the federal sector. The rationale being that a necessary first step is to put the federal sector in order.

During the Ford Administration the Domestic Council Committee on the Right of Privacy, chaired by Vice President Nelson Rockefeller, was commissioned by President Ford in March 1976 to prepare the Report on National Information Policy.[13] The President asked the committee to review and clearly define the information policy issues which confront federal policy makers, to determine the status of ongoing Executive Branch information policy studies, and to recommend how the federal government should organize itself to successfully deal with these information policy issues.

The committee report to the President contained a number of recommendations:

1. Recommended a unified approach to policy formulation where the many threads of policy formulation could be drawn together in one location. Dismissed the notion of Department of Communication and opted for an Office of Information Policy in the Executive Office of the President.

2. Recommended the establishment of an Interagency Council on Information Policy to serve as a forum where government-wide problems could be discussed and addressed for coordinated action.

3. Recommended the establishment of an Advisory Committee to the Office of Information Policy to assist the Office in the formulation of policy and at the same time to provide a medium of

exchange (two-way) between the Office and state and local
governments, the commercial sector, the academic community, and the professional societies.

4. Recommended close cooperation with the President's Science
Adviser and advocated that the Science Adviser maintain responsibility for scientific and technical information.

The report discussed a number of principles as a basis for the formulation of information policy--broad access for all citizens, protection of
individual privacy, efficient allocation of resources, and maintaining the
pluralism of information services. The report itself consists of 233 pages
including a twelve page bibliography of recommended readings.

The President for whom it was prepared is no longer in office, and
I know of no indication to date by the Carter Administration as to its plans
for this report. As you may know, President Carter has submitted to the
Congress his plan for Reorganization of the Executive Office of the President.
The Reorganization Plan does not appear to provide for the recommendations
of the Domestic Council Committee under President Ford. Still, it is very
early into the Carter Administration and perhaps the White House will have
an action plan of its own pertaining to the preparation and promulgation of
federal information policy or, more broadly, national information policy.

REFERENCES

1. Sterling, T. D. "Humanizing Computerized Information Systems."
Science, 190:1168-1173, 1975.

2. Gardner, John William. Self Renewal: The Individual and the Innovative
Society. New York: Harper and Row, 1964.

3. Chartrand, R. L. The Legislator as User of Information Technology.
Congressional Research Service, Library of Congress. Report 77-217
SP, 1977.

4. Chartrand, R. L. and J. P. Ernard. "Legislating Responsive Information Services." Bulletin of the American Society for Information Science,
1:18-24, 1975.

5. Chartrand, R. L. "Information Science in the Legislative Process."
Annual Review of Information Science, M. Williams, ed. Washington,
D.C., Society for Information Science, pp. 299-344, 1976.

6. U.S. Congress. House Committee on Rules. Report of the Committee on Rules on H.R. 17634, 91st Congress, Second Session. House Report 91-1215, p. 11. U.S. Government Printing Office, Washington, D.C., 1970.

7. Chartrand, R. L. The Legislator as User of Information Technology.

8. U.S. Congress. House. Commission on Administrative Review. Administration, Reorganization and Legislative Management. House Document No. 95-232, pp. 566-772. U.S. Government Printing Office, Washington, D.C., 1977.

9. Elkins, J. S., Jr. State Use of Electronic Data Processing. Council of State Governments, 1974.

10. Worthley, J. A. Comparative Legislative Information Systems, 1976.

11. U.S. Congress. Administration, Reorganization and Legislative Management.

12. American Federation of Information Processing Societies. Newsletter. Washington, D.C., October, 1977.

13. White House. Domestic Council Committee on Right of Privacy. National Information Policy. Report to the President of the United States. U.S. Government Printing Office, Washington, D.C., 233p. 1976.

Chapter 10

IMPACT OF ON-LINE SYSTEMS
ON LIBRARY FUNCTIONS

Miriam A. Drake

Assistant Director
Administrative Services
Purdue University Libraries
and Audio-Visual Center
West Lafayette, Indiana

INTRODUCTION

The theme of this conference is based on the assumption that on-line computer technology has caused or is about to cause a revolution. In this context two definitions of revolution are appropriate. The first definition of revolution is the overthrow of an established system. This type of revolution has not yet occurred in libraries because established systems of library operations have not been overthrown. While computers or terminals can be found in most large libraries and many small ones, traditional library operations have not been substantially altered. A second definition of revolution is movement in a circular path or movement about an axis. My observation of libraries and librarians is that they have been going around in circles for a long time and are likely to continue to do so unless someone says, "stop".

I believe that the "stop" signs are being posted and that traditional library systems are being gradually overthrown without violence. Although the traditionalists will blame the computer for change, the revolution will not be computer produced. The revolutionaries, who will stop the rotation of the library about its axis of the card catalog, are the people who see on-line technology not as an end in itself but as a means of providing effective and responsive information services.

The purposes of this paper are to review the relationship between on-line technology and library functions and to show how on-line services enable librarians to make significant changes in library and information services and ultimately in the work of the profession. The material is presented from managerial and planning points of view. The approach is general and is aimed at presenting a broad view rather than a detailed description. Also, there is a discussion of problems, questions and uncertainties associated with the future use of on-line systems. The term on-line services, as used here, is not confined to bibliographic services but includes all types of on-line systems. The library functions to be discussed include collections and buildings, order processing and accounting, cataloging and user services. Circulation systems will be discussed in relation to other activities.

COLLECTIONS AND BUILDINGS

There is no uniformity among libraries with regard to collection development policies and procedures. Increasingly it is being recognized that these policies are essential and that they will include some sort of co-operative purchasing or specialization. Lack of money for libraries and the likelihood of continued inflation have been the primary motivators in these decisions. The days of buying a book, film, or journal because "it's nice to have" are rapidly passing. Potential use is becoming a more important criterion in the selection process.

The use of on-line bibliographic data bases could have a significant effect on collection development. OCLC or regional data bases of mono-graphic holdings may indicate that a neighboring library holds a requested title. In this case, a library may choose to borrow rather than purchase. Searches of data bases containing information about journal articles, tech-nical reports and government documents are likely to produce citations to material which is of potential use to the researcher but is not held by the library. This material will have to be obtained elsewhere through photo-copies or borrowing. It is not economically feasible for a library to purchase and process every needed item. However, the mix of materials in the library could change if searches produce sufficient demand for a journal or technical report series. The buy or borrow decision also will be influenced, in the short run by interpretation of the copyright law, and in the long run, by court decisions on copyright.

Competitive acquisitions, based on the assumption that "bigger is better," are likely to be replaced by cooperative acquisitions, especially among the libraries which serve large and diverse constituencies. The li-brary serving a small, homogeneous population will be indirectly affected by these arrangements. The current planning activities which are being dis-

cussed among members of the Research Libraries Group and the academic
libraries in California are clear evidence that resource sharing is being
taken seriously and that the parties involved believe that it can be implemented.

Accompanying the trend to cooperative purchasing is the need for low
cost warehouse facilities or shared depositories. Lack of money again is
the basis of the need. Most library funders are unwilling to pay for multi-
million dollar warehouses to store books or other materials which are rarely
or never used. Unfortunately, many librarians cling to the notion that all
materials must be at hand at all times despite findings that only small portions of library collections are actually used during any one year.[8, 30] The
recent study of materials usage completed at the University of Pittsburgh
indicated, "...slightly less than 50% of the collection as a whole (all books)
did not circulate at all via external patron circulation during the seven year
and two month period between October 1968 and the end of the calendar year
1975."[18] Journal usage was more concentrated. The results of surveys
taken in three Pittsburgh Libraries showed that 70% of the journal usage was
accounted for by 11.4% of current titles in physics, 10.1% in life sciences
and psychology and 8.4% in engineering. In terms of journal age, the study
found, "Ninety percent of all usage can be supplied by journals published
within the last fifteen years."[18] The assumption that library usage will
decline if any material is removed to a remote location cannot be supported
by survey data on usage.

The facts of library usage, the cost of new construction, and rapidly
increasing costs of operating current facilities provide the justification for
shared storage. With construction costs rapidly approaching $100 per square
foot, large library buildings are no longer possible. As Veaner pointed out,
we will have seen the last of the great central library facilities by the end of
the decade.[34] The cost of building operation also is rising rapidly. At
Purdue University General Library the cost of building operation increased
49% between 1974 and 1976. During the same period, the cost of utilities
increased 62%, repairs and maintenance increased 17% while the cost of
insurance for the building increased 11%. In 1974 utilities represented 70%
of the cost of building operation. This portion increased to 76% in 1976.
Ellsworth Mason, in discussing the future of library buildings at a 1975 conference sponsored by the Associated Colleges of the Midwest, noted the
trend to off campus storage facilities and indicated that there would be an
increase in the construction of underground libraries so that operating costs,
especially the costs of air conditioning, could be reduced.[20]

The configuration of resource sharing in the U.S. is evolving. Currently, there are a variety of local, state and regional consortia or cooperative groups. Various schemes have been proposed to tie these groups into
larger units. Veaner sees resource sharing developing into a "distributed

library" in which all library and audio-visual materials are considered a national resource and are shared.[34] It is difficult to project precisely how such a system would work, but it is clear that library materials will travel outside the community in the future.

Resource sharing and the use of shared warehouses do not require the use of on-line systems. These activities could be carried out independently of computers; however, on-line systems will facilitate these activities and enhance their effectiveness by providing quick information regarding the location and availability of material which is housed in a depository or other library. In addition, on-line systems will enable libraries to communicate with each other directly through terminals. The order process can be expedited because availability can be determined and the request transmitted in seconds rather than days.

ORDER PROCESSING AND ACCOUNTING

Automation has been applied to order processing and accounting in many libraries. Systems range from crude batch processing with punch cards to on-line systems which perform a variety of tasks and analyses. Since purchasing involves a limited and well defined set of routine procedures, it can be automated relatively easily. Palmer points out, "When the on-order/ in-process file has a steady state of over 30,000 items, and often before the point, errors and delays that clog the system are more and more likely to occur."[25] As the error rate increases, more staff is required and control of funds deteriorates resulting in higher unit costs and poor management of money. The efficiency of materials purchasing and effective control of funds can be enhanced significantly by on-line systems. Since ordering, claiming, encumbering, and paying invoices constitute a continuous operation requiring up-to-date information, these functions and their associated records should be handled by on-line systems. Data from the on-order or in-process file can be fed to on-line catalogs so that any user can find out the status of a wanted item. The addition of these data to on-line circulation systems allows users to request materials in advance of their arrival on the shelves.

CATALOGING

In 1964 Don Swanson observed, "Most of the emphasis to date in library mechanization has been on the application of present technology to traditional practices within libraries."[29] Things haven't changed significantly, especially in bibliographic information. While OCLC has been absorbed into the library vernacular, main entry and catalog cards remain firmly entrenched. Kilgour's hopes of making resources available to more library users and putting the card catalog out of business have been only partially realized.[26]

Hopkins, in 1973, stated a conservative version of OCLC's mission, "OCLC does not conceive of its mission as merely the mechanization of library procedures of the past, but it does recognize that you have to start where you are and extrapolate toward where you would like to go, always, however, maintaining contact with the ground."[17] In terms of realizing its potential to initiate and implement new approaches to the access of bibliographic information, OCLC is still on the ground. One of the reasons for less than total fulfillment of OCLC's potential is the tendency of librarians to cling slavishly to outdated concepts. One of the excuses offered relates to the long history of bibliography which is sacred to many librarians. "Our bibliographic heritage has very long and enduring linkages to the past: historically the pace of bibliographic evolution has closely followed the pace of social and religious development and has been correspondingly slow moving."[34] I doubt that anyone can say that social change has been slow moving or that religion has stood still in the past 25 years.

New concepts of bibliographic information and access have been available for a long time. Mooers, in 1955, stated that "...machines permit new modes of information description and selection" but that librarians are not suited to design or operate machine retrieval systems because their training in traditional classification is a major hindrance to taking full advantage of machine power and flexibility.[24] Another critical element contributing to the lack of change in information description is the purpose of the library catalog. There is confusion and disagreement among librarians because there appears to be no clearly understood reason for the existence of the catalog beyond the basic purpose of providing a description of the library's current inventory. The traditional approaches to the building of card catalogs and offering access by author, title, and inconsistent and often inappropriate subject headings was sufficient when both the production and demand for information was constrained. The "monodimensional" search strategy described by Allen Kent had a higher probability of working than it does today. It is likely that traditional catalogs will be replaced by information retrieval systems which take full advantage of the power and flexibility of the computer to manipulate data and produce it in a variety of forms. The timetables for the design and implementation of new systems is uncertain; however, the need for expanded multidimensional access to all library materials is clear. Until new systems are designed and implemented the outdated and crude systems of the present will continue.

It should not be inferred that OCLC and BALLOTS have not had any impact on library operations. Libraries which have exploited OCLC, within the context of tradition, have been able to make significant improvements in cooperative purchasing, acquisitions, cataloging and inter-library loan services. OCLC and BALLOTS have facilitated the sharing of cataloging resources, an important, but often overlooked, aspect of resource sharing, while fostering the standardization of bibliographic records. Standardization, which is essential to the building of a national bibliographic data base, benefits the entire library community.

The Markuson study of OCLC users found that the major impacts of OCLC have been the elimination of local card production and faster searching for catalog information.[21] The Hewitt study of 47 OCLC charter member libraries indicated broader impact on pre-order searching, cataloging time and inter-library loan patterns.[16]

Pre-order searching is a labor intensive and expensive process. Costs vary with the extent of the search required by each library and the availability of quality searching tools. In order to search catalogs, main entry must be established. This adds to both search time and cost. OCLC, with its data base of over three million records and its easy to use search keys, offers a quality tool which has reduced search time. Hewitt found that 14 libraries using OCLC for pre-order search experienced reductions ranging from four weeks to one week.[16] The use of OCLC at Purdue has reduced pre-order search time from 57 days in April 1976 to 18 days in April 1977.

The principal uses of OCLC are for cataloging and card production. Success in using the system is contingent upon first, finding a record in the data base, and second, being able to use that record as found or with only slight changes. The mean find rate for libraries in the Hewitt study ranged from 67% to 80% with an overall average of 74%.[16] During the first five months of 1977, Purdue Libraries found records for 94% of the new titles cataloged. Original cataloging has been reduced to 6% of new titles from an estimated 15% prior to the installation of OCLC.

Finding a record in the OCLC data base does not mean instant cataloging, especially if the library uses Dewey classification. Purdue's overall find rate of 94% is somewhat misleading because 14% of the records found required the addition of a Dewey number. All records included in the 80% which contained Dewey numbers required printing or copying when the record was found so that classification numbers could be checked against the shelf list for inconsistencies. The necessity to add or check Dewey numbers reduces productivity and adds to the unit cost.

Mean cataloging time at Purdue has been only slightly reduced from an average of 122 days in April 1976 to 114 in April 1977. These data reflect the work in reducing a backlog containing materials which have been waiting for cataloging for a year or more. Median cataloging time has been reduced more significantly from 119 days to 92 days. Hewitt found that the strongest effect of OCLC "...was on the speed with which books are cataloged and ready for use." Estimates from 28 libraries showed an estimated mean reduction in catalog time of 2.8 months.[16]

While catalog cards are the primary end products of OCLC, they are limited in their usefulness. It is apparent that the card catalog, as we know it, is obsolete and about to be discarded as a working tool by large libraries. The card catalog will be replaced in the immediate future by tools which are produced by applying software to archive tapes or by modifying records on-line. The availability of machine-readable catalog data offers numerous· opportunities and possibilities to extend the distribution of catalogs, improve user services, provide useful management information and test new concepts in bibliographic information retrieval. In short, machine-readable catalog data is a valuable resource which is grossly underutilized.

Libraries are turning to alternative forms for the catalog for reasons which range from lack of space for an expanding card catalog to the desire for an information retrieval system to meet real needs.[5] Current alternative forms for the catalog include book catalogs, microfiche, and on-line catalogs. Book catalogs, even when produced by computer, are expensive and unwieldy. COM fiche catalogs are growing in popularity because they can be produced at relatively little cost, updated frequently, and reissued faster than book catalogs. Low production cost, portability, and low shipping cost make microfiche an attractive form for public libraries and academic libraries with many branches and for networks or regional cooperatives. Experience at the University of Texas at Dallas indicates that microfiche catalogs produced from OCLC archive tapes are viable alternatives to the card catalog.[22]

Although microform catalogs offer significant advantages to the library, they do not improve subject access for the user. The monodimensional search strategy, with its inherent limitations, is the same whether the catalog is on cards or film. Bates, in her study of search success using a conventional catalog, found that LC subject headings were inadequate for generalists, specialists and librarians.[27] Two experiments, the Subject Access Project at Syracuse and the BITS Project at Purdue, are utilizing standard bibliographic records enhanced by index terms to improve subject access. The Syracuse project is utilizing a sample of books in the humanities and social sciences drawn from the holdings of the University of Toronto. The MARC record for these books is being enhanced by the addition of selected words and phrases found in the book's index or table of contents. On-line searches of this data base have been conducted and are being evaluated.[28]

The BITS system (Beginning Information for Technical Search) being developed by the Purdue Schools of Engineering is designed to provide a limited amount of information about books, journals, and technical reports contained in the engineering library. OCLC archive tapes are being used to provide basic data such as author, title, publisher and date for books published after 1970. This basic record will be enlarged by entering 5-10 index terms derived from the table of contents or index in the book. Index terms also will be used to describe journal articles and technical reports. Initial

design of the system is aimed at introducing technical information to undergraduate engineering students and to train them in literature searching. The
system will contain instructional modules to aid the student in defining the
search and finding additional information.

Another productive use of OCLC archive tapes, which is just beginning
to be explored, is the provision of management information. Analyses of
acquisitions by subject, publisher, or language can be performed off-line and
fed back to librarians who can use the data for planning future purchases and
other collection development activities. The use of the tapes in on-line catalogs presents numerous opportunities to learn about user behavior in an
unobtrusive way. Information about the demand for specific authors and titles
can be partly determined by counting catalog queries. Subjects which are
queried can also be tallied. Search strategies employed by users can be
gathered and analyzed to determine the appropriateness of subject headings
or index terms.

In summary, the application of on-line systems to cataloging, thus
far, has been aimed, for the most part, at preserving traditional practice.
On-line systems for the retrieval of bibliographic information for monographs
are in their infancy but offer the hope of more effective user oriented systems
in the future.

USER SERVICES

Services offered to library users are likely to undergo significant
changes in the near future. The motivating factors come from a variety of
sources, including users, funders, the availability of on-line bibliographic
information systems, and the development of systems containing both numerical data and the software to manipulate or analyze the data.

Libraries using OCLC are finding that the service is a useful reference
tool. In my own case, I have searched the OCLC data base for a desired book
and have saved numerous trips to the card catalog. Experience at the University of Texas at Austin "...has demonstrated that OCLC improves bibliographic access to works in the local collection that are not fully accessible
through the local catalog..."[6] Improvements are possible because records
are available before catalog cards are filed, title entries are available, and
truncated search keys compensate for the effects of misspelled names or
words.[6]

Bibliographic information systems, such as those offered by Lockheed,
SDC, and BRS are having a significant impact on how users search for sources
of information. In many instances, users are paying fees for these services

and are finding that the cost is more than justified because of the time saved and the retrieval of citations which would not be found in a manual search.

The researcher who wants to search large bodies of literature can save many hours by employing the computer to do the work. My own experience is impressive. For $27 and 15 minutes of my time, I was able to retrieve 365 journal citations from a data base containing approximately 300 journal titles. A similar manual search would have required the use of at least three printed indexes and would not have been as comprehensive in terms of coverage. While the availability of data bases on-line has made a noteworthy contribution to the improvement of user services, there is need for substantial improvement in these systems. The major obstacles, other than costs, to the widespread use of these data bases is the necessity for an intermediary, terminal operator, or data base analyst/librarian. Users cannot search on-line data bases directly in an efficient manner because of unfamiliarity with the access language, the complexities and inconsistencies in the structure of the data bases, and strategies used to search them. As a result, most searches are "delegated searches." [19]

The success of the delegated search depends on a variety of factors. Among the factors cited by Lancaster are: user expectations regarding the system; user's ability to describe the need, "ability of vocabulary to describe concepts..."; and the searcher's interpretation of the user's need. [19]

Many users have difficulty in describing or articulating their information needs in precise language. The translation of concepts into words may not be exact because of the limitations of language or vocabulary. In order to ensure a successful search which meets the information need, the user must be present during the search to guide the operator in refining and modifying the terms used. The communication problem is complicated further because a single intermediary cannot be familiar with all subject disciplines or the language used by those disciplines. Rogers notes that something is lost when search requests are transmitted through an intermediary or mediator. "...the librarian may not understand fully the real dimensions of the request, or worse, the librarian may unwittingly, in difficult cases, shift the emphasis from the question put by the client to some penumbral question that the system can answer more easily." [29] The obstacles to information finding created by the imprecision of communication between librarian and information seeker have been recognized for a long time. In 1960, Mooers pointed out that customers need assistance in using machine retrieval systems because the vocabulary of retrieval systems is unfamiliar, and search prescriptions may need change as the user responds to the output. [23] Mooers stated that user assistance should be provided by the machine. Cuadra acknowledged the necessity for human intermediaries while recognizing that improvement could be achieved if the user could interact directly with the file. [11]

There is need for further research and experimentation with both human and machine interfaces. Anyone who has used an interactive computer system on a regular basis for programming, statistical analysis, or game playing has experienced a learning situation in which skills improve with experience. Individual library clients generally have infrequent needs for bibliographic data base searches and are not likely to use a system with sufficient frequency to gain the experience to use it effectively. Moderate or frequent users should have the option of learning about the system through an educational package which can be accessed through the computer. This hands-on direct approach will permit the user to become skillful in the use of the system, thereby reducing search cost and the frustration which results from poor communication.

Additional limitations are imposed by the indexing schemes used by the data base producers. Gardner and Wax point out that computers were used initially to produce the printed index. "Since these data bases were specifically developed to produce already designed printed publications, they utilize their traditional indexing schemes, and the move to computer production involved little apparent consideration of other possible uses. There was not a meaningful attempt either to design indexing schemes beyond those which were currently in use or to standardize indexing schemes among major publishers of indexing and abstracting services."[14] As Kent pointed out, the nature of search requirements have changed. Before the information explosion an alphabetic array of index terms on the printed page could be searched monodimensionally and satisfy the user's needs. The increase in the quantity of materials produced and changes in user requirements for information have made multidimensional searching a necessity. The printed index on magnetic tape and the software to manipulate the terms provide the basic tools for searching using more than one term, expanded or limited by logical operators. Since the index vocabulary on the tape has been structured for the printed page, the search strategy becomes critical to success. Clearly, the potential remains untapped and awaits further research and experimentation in order to be fully realized.

The cost of setting up and offering data base search services is of major concern to librarians. The initial cost includes the acquisition of a terminal, possibly extra telephone lines and an investment of thousands of dollars for training. The direct costs associated with the service include the charge for using the data base on-line, off-line print charges and the labor used in interviewing the client, determining search strategy, running the search and follow-up. Added to the direct costs are indirect costs of supplies, supervision, processing invoices, and overhead. Cooper and Dewath, in their study of on-line searching of Lockheed data bases in public libraries in California, found that the mean cost of searching including labor ranged from $19.58 to $35.16, with an overall mean of $28.51.[10] These costs were developed during the early phase of a two year project when searchers were

still learning how to construct search strategies and query routines. As their
skills improved, they were able to conduct searches in less time and reduce
connect time charges. Data base and off-line print charges averaged $23.46
at the National Bureau of Standards data base, and off-line print charges
averaged $22.40 from April 1975 through March 1976.[6] The costs cannot be
compared to the public library costs because they included data bases from
sources other than Lockheed. Since these studies were completed, the
charges for data base use have been reduced by the vendors.

PROBLEMS AND UNCERTAINTIES

        The previous sections presented a general review of present uses of
on-line systems. It is clear that the application of current technology to
library operations remains a latent possibility. While many day-to-day
tasks are being performed faster with computers, there is evidence that
basic concepts have not changed. The speed, manner and success with which
libraries will utilize on-line systems are uncertain and depend on solutions
to operational and philosophical problems. It is not possible to fully explore
all current and anticipated problems here. The key factors appear to be
attitudes, economics, copyright, U.S. Postal Service and user charges. At
this point in time, many questions can be raised but few answers can be
provided.

        Attitudes. Librarians' attitudes about automation, users, planning
and change are critical elements affecting the use of existing on-line systems
and the design and implementation of new systems. For many years, librarians reacted negatively to any system which altered the existing order of the
library. Computer systems were viewed as foreign elements which were
imposed or forced on unwilling librarians, who viewed computer scientists
and engineers as wanton creatures whose goal was to destroy the library.
In many instances, their views were justified. The result of these attitudes
is that librarians lost the initiative and the opportunity to specify systems
which were responsive to need. The computer scientists and engineers who
designed early systems worked in a climate of confusion, hostility and frustration brought about by the librarians' lack of participation and unwillingness
to imagine a different mode of operation for the library.

        Happily this attitude appears to be changing. The number of librar-
ians who flee to the stacks when the computer terminal arrives is diminishing. Many librarians are learning that active participation is more rewarding than stoic resistance.

        In addition to negative views of library automation, there has been a
reluctance to share negative experience. Articles about on-line systems in
specific libraries do not discuss failure or difficult problems. Auld

observed, "Instances of failure in library automation are not often discussed publicly, let alone published, for neither personal or institutional pride favors a public display of disaffection. As a result library literature does not usually mention the possibility of failure except when an author sets out to prove that library automation is not possible."[2] There is a great need for libraries to share their experiences relative to specific programs and systems. Librarians need to know about systems design and software applications that <u>don't</u> work. They need to learn about programs which have been tried unsuccessfully in other libraries so that they will not waste their time on unproductive activities that result in repetition of error. There needs to be more information on successful systems which are running and systems which are in the development stage so experiences, both good and bad, can be shared with others who are working on like systems.

Librarians' attitudes about users also are due for reexamination and reformulation. Free-lance librarians, information brokers, and for-profit information centers are presenting real competition to the traditional library in terms of information provision. Consumer awareness of information provision and alternative forms of information service are increasing. Librarians are slowly realizing that a book or journal is not information and that many library user needs cannot be satisfied with a list of citations or directions on how to use the catalog. Library users have changed their roles from guardians and supporters of libraries to consumers of information services. This change has been described as a shift from asking, "Where is the answer... ?" to "What is the answer... ?"[36] Many public and special librarians have long recognized this difference between access and substance and have tailored services accordingly.

Changing the focus of the library from record keeping to human users is a challenging task. Librarians are hampered, and often inhibited, because our understanding of human thought processes is limited. There is no catalog which accurately describes the many sets of mental steps propelling various users to the library. The areas of information seeking, assimilation, use and value are largely unexplored. Our limited knowledge of learning processes and concept attainment have, in part, acted as constraints.

Librarians have not taken advantage of the opportunity to learn more about users. Traditional reference service with its emphasis on "what," "when" and "where" has ignored the critical aspects of "how" and "why". This situation is most unfortunate because librarians are in a key position to learn about people and contribute significantly to the quest for increased understanding of complex intellectual activities.

Librarians daily are exposed to a myriad of questions ranging from fact to concept. Most librarians have little difficulty in supplying facts, such as the population of metropolitan Chicago, the year Plutarch died or the procedure for making plutonium. Answers to these types of questions usually can be supplied without knowing why the user needs to know or how the information will be used and evaluated.

Questions involving concepts, such as probability, Murphy's law or femininity cannot be answered quickly in the usual pattern. When information is supplied in response to a concept question, the librarian does not know if the answer was satisfactory unless he/she is in frequent contact with the user.

Bruner has identified processes in learning or concept attainment which involve the acquisition, transformation, retention and evaluation of information.[7] Librarians are intimately involved with the acquisition process in providing new or replacement information. The processes which follow acquisition determine the value of information to the user. Without continuing contact with the user the librarian cannot know how the information was manipulated in the users mind, whether the information was used immediately or retained for later use and whether the information supplied was adequate or appropriate to the user's purpose. In short, librarians do not know the value of information supplied or the role they have played in solving the user's information or learning problem.

Young people who have been nurtured on a diet of television, computer aided instruction, and media centers in schools will not be satisfied with traditional library fare. Their expectations of libraries and their learning modes are different from those of their parents and grandparents. The challenge of a more demanding clientele, the opportunity to contribute to knowledge and the availability of relatively inexpensive tools to implement new concepts of service provide the bases for the future enhancement of librarianship.

Implementation of these improvements is closely tied to the librarians' attitudes about planning and change. These attitudes have been obstacles in the past. The lack of planning in libraries often is blamed on the annual budget and the dependency on outside agencies for funding. The uncertainty of future funding and political pressures from the library's parent organization have inhibited thinking about any future longer than one year. In addition, librarians appear to be more comfortable resisting events than creating or shaping events. This passive stance has precluded the planning efforts which are needed to reallocate resources on a long term basis to change library operations. Planning is a way of thinking which leads to setting a future course for the library and managing the library's resources so that planned events can occur. Critical evaluation of current activities and their place in the future of the library are necessary parts of the process. Abandonment of traditional approaches is a difficult and painful process. As Drucker has pointed out, "...being budget based makes it even more difficult to abandon the wrong things, the old, the obsolete. As a result, service institutions are even more encrusted than business with the barnacles of inherently unproductive efforts. "13

    In summary, librarians need to change their fundamental assumptions about their constituents and the future. The roles of reactor and resistor must be exchanged for roles of planner and builder.

    Economics. The financial constraints which prevent librarians from thinking about new and emerging demands of the library consumer are real. The economics of library operations have changed dramatically in the last seven years. The wages of clerical staff, as indicated by the wages of secretaries, rose 35% between 1971 and 1974.[31] The salaries of chief librarians in academic institutions rose 20% and the salaries for all faculty increased 21% in the same period.[33] Salaries and wages account for increasing portions of library budgets. Indications are that continuing inflation in consumer prices will continue to push salaries and wages higher in the future. These higher costs need to be considered within a context of alternative methods for accomplishing specific tasks. While library costs have been shifting, the costs of computer systems, also, have been changing.

    Development cost now is the major expense associated with new computer-based systems. As the price of hardware has declined, the salaries of programmers and analysts have risen. The price of computer hardware as indicated by the Wholesale Price Index increased .2% between 1971 and 1976.[32] The salaries of computer programmers and analysts rose 16% in the same time period.[31]

    Mason, as recently as 1975, stated that computers are not cost effective for libraries.[20] With the decline in computer prices, and upward pressure on clerical wages, this view is open to challenge. Computer-based systems which were prohibitively expensive as recently as five years ago can now be favorably compared to manual systems in terms of productivity and cost. New developments in storage devices will mean further operating cost reductions.

    The development of commercially available "turn key" systems could have a positive effect on the cost of doing library business in the future. These systems are not suitable for all libraries but are advantageous for those libraries which can use them effectively. They provide the economic advantages of shared development costs and vendor maintenance of software, obviating the need for in-house systems analysts and programmers.

    Libraries developing their own on-line systems will make a major investment in software. When systems are being planned, librarians and programmers often do not know about software which has been developed

in other libraries, and which could be made available at reasonable cost.
As a result they reinvent the wheel at substantial cost in time and dollars.
Librarians need to share this expensive software resource and experience
so that costs can be reduced and programs improved.

In order to acquire and implement on-line bibliographic, or other
systems, many libraries will need to alter their allocation of resources.
For example, at Purdue, staff reductions were used to pay for OCLC; however, a greater volume of work is being processed by the reduced staff. In
allocating resources, library administrators will need to think beyond this
year's budget. On-line services, whether OCLC, Lockheed or other, require
investment and development costs. The return on this investment is not
usually realized in the first year, though money for terminals, training, or
development may be expended out of one year's budget. Librarians are not
accustomed to thinking about investments or return on invested capital
covering medium to long range periods. There is little understanding of
costs, benefits and the relationship between them. However, the cost/benefit
perspective is important if large investments are to be realistically evaluated.

In the past individual libraries did not give much attention to the cost
of operations, unit costs of services or benefits to customers. Major capital
costs were for buildings, for which special funding was provided, or vehicles
(trucks or bookmobiles). The line budget did not stimulate librarians to
evaluate the allocation and use of resources, especially human resources.
The desire to provide on-line services has raised cost consciousness in many
libraries.

An expanded concept of costs which goes beyond the items in a line
budget is necessary. Cohen states the economists view of library costs and
investment, "An economic accounting for fixed costs goes beyond the costs
found in a university's financial records. The latter provides data on such
operating costs as administration and maintenance but omit inputed costs--
the 'opportunity costs' of the fixed investments in the library, for example.
Such costs measure what the university could have earned had the funds been
lent out rather than being invested in the library."[9] This broader view of
investments and costs also includes the alternative uses of funds by the parent
organization. For example, an industrial firm may decide that a $50,000
market research program will yield a higher return than $50,000 investment
in journal subscriptions, or a university may decide that $30,000 worth of
computer terminals are a better investment than $30,000 worth of library
books.

The return on investment and the benefit side of the cost/benefit ratio
are elusive concepts in librarianship. There are no readily available quantitative measures which will forecast the dollar return on a dollar invested in
information systems. The standard measures such as use, document

exposure, etc., are not satisfactory measures of customer benefit. Wills and Oldman have articulated the critical questions which must be considered in library investment decisions, "What is information? How is information to be valued? For example, when it is acquired we do not necessarily know its usefulness. We may not put it to use immediately and who exactly will benefit when or if it is?"[28] These questions currently are impossible to answer and provide little guidance for the librarian who is trying to justify a major investment in on-line systems. Nevertheless, the questions raised above should provide a perspective for evaluating investment. The cost of on-line systems for public use may be difficult to justify without concrete demonstrations of reduced search time, delivery of greater quantities of information or faster location of library materials. Since manual searching and on-line searching are not likely to produce the same result, measurement of time saved is elusive, and the value of finding sources which could not be found in a manual search is not captured. Another problem is the value of the user's time. In industry, where value of people's time is measured, it is easier to guess at the dollar savings. Universities and public institutions, where cost accounting is rarely done, are not so concerned with the value of user or librarian time and may not be willing to provide tools which will enhance the value of time. The orientation of library funders is toward inputs, not the outputs of libraries. Funders are more concerned with how much money is being spent rather than value produced for library clients.

     Copyright. The most talked about unknown in library circles today is the new copyright law and its impact on library operations and record keeping. The scheme for paying royalties for uses, other than fair use, has not been decided. The government has not issued decrees on record keeping relative to inter-library loan transactions. The various options which have been discussed point to an increase in the cost of inter-library loans due to the additional costs of record keeping and royalty payments. Citations produced by on-line bibliographic searches often are for journals which the library does not own. If the user feels that this journal is essential, the librarian will try to obtain it or a copy of the needed article. It is possible that at least five articles in the last five years of a journal will be demanded by the user. The librarian cannot know if the user will want more articles from the journal in the immediate future. The decision to subscribe or to borrow may not be as simple as publishers would lead us to believe. The perceived conflicts and problems in the law undoubtedly will be decided by the courts. Given the complexity of the issues and the long periods associated with litigation, solutions to the problems cannot be expected in the foreseeable future.

     U.S. Postal Service. The need to borrow or photocopy material and the sharing of resources lead to the problem of document delivery. While postal rates are rising, the performance of the U.S. Postal Service is deteriorating and growing more unreliable. The author's experience with delivery of first class mail between West Lafayette, Indiana, and Washington, D. C̈., is normal delivery time of two to seven days. In abnormal times the delivery can be as long as two weeks. Delivery times between West Lafayette and Indianapolis, a distance of 65 miles, are similar with exceptional service of one day. The lower priority of library mail can mean additional delays in getting documents to users. When large quantities of material is needed, it may be cheaper to transport the user to the documents.

The desired delivery time for documents or library materials is contingent upon the users perception of need which can range from hours to weeks. A business or professional person who needs information in a hurry will pay hundreds of dollars for fast delivery. A university professor working on non-critical research may be willing to wait weeks for a document rather than pay for faster service. The same professor, however, will be willing to pay for fast service if a major research contract is at stake. Short documents which are needed in hours are being transmitted through telefacsimile equipment. At present this equipment is not widely available and is relatively expensive. If other than single sheets are used, photocopies must be made. New developments in this area are being pursued and are likely to result in more efficient and less expensive processes. For example, Citibank, in its effort to eliminate paper, is planning to develop the capability of transmitting reports, photographs, and charts through high speed facsimile devices and digital display techniques.[26] This form of document and data delivery will be feasible for libraries in the near future. The volume of paper to be shipped and stored will be reduced substantially. Masses of numerical data, such as the U.S. Census of Population will be stored at remote locations instead of the library. Users will gain access through terminals in the library or their offices. Text information, as well, will be accessed through terminals from remote computer-based storage facilities.

These developments will not eliminate the need for hard copy. The book as we know it is not likely to disappear, but large portions of the current paper inventory will be replaced by electronic devices and microforms.

The trade-offs between need, time, weight of material, volume of material and the fixed costs of delivery systems should be continually evaluated as new services become available. The cost of acquiring terminals and accessing large data banks may be easily justified as the cost of acquiring, processing, storing, accessing, and delivering hard paper copy increases.

In the immediate future, librarians will continue to ship large quantities of paper materials. The U.S. Postal Service and private delivery systems will continue to be the main delivery systems used. In limited geographical areas, intrastate library delivery systems, such as those which operate in Minnesota and Pennsylvania, may be feasible. The increase in postal rates and longer delivery times will cause librarians to look into this alternative for states or regions. Volume may be sufficient to meet the high fixed costs of delivery system in the short run.   As costs of vehicles, wages and gasoline increase and the volume of material shipped declines, these systems will become too expensive to maintain and will be abandoned.

User Charges. The introduction of on-line bibliographic information retrieval systems and their associated out-of-pocket cost has raised the issue of user fees philosophically and operationally. Philosophically, the issue boils down to the question of whether information ought to be a free good. If not, should the availability of information be based solely on the ability of pay? If it is free, should everyone be taxed for information which is not used by the entire population? At one extreme are the librarians who view the free library as sacrosanct. For them the library is the center of intellectual freedom and social responsibility. Eric Moon in his inaugural address to the American Library Association said, "We must loudly, insistently, affirm that free access to information for all is the very foundation, not only of our profession and services, but of individual liberty."[35]   There are many librarians who share Moon's patriotic view of the library. Berry has advocated a reaffirmation of the principle of freedom of access to information because it is "fundamental to our democracy."[4] Horn has urged, "That ALA reaffirm the concept of access to information without charge to individuals in public libraries and tax-supported libraries..."[15] These statements appear to confuse the idea of freedom to know or acquire information with provision of information at no cost. In addition, they overlook the fact that taxpayers are paying green dollars for public libraries.

The implicit assumption is that all information is a public good which is provided for the population in general rather than for individuals. "A pure public good is defined as a good or service whose total cost is completely unaffected by the number of persons served."[3] Examples include national defense, the space program, government supported research and foreign policy. All members of the population receive the same service whether they pay or not. In addition, there is no way to withhold these services from people who do not pay.

The other side of the user fee argument is voiced by people who assume that library service is not a pure public good. The reasons are: 1) libraries are used by only a portion of the population; 2) the cost is affected by the number of people served; and 3) service can be withheld from people who do not pay. The arguments in favor of charging user fees for library services involve more effective allocation of resources, the provision of output measures and the motivation to users to consider cost in relation to value received.

The people in the middle of the two extremes of the fee question have reached a compromise position in which certain basic services are fully subsidized

and offered to the public at no cost while services which are tailored to
individual needs, such as on-line information retrieval, are offered for a fee.
DeGennaro, in his version of compromise, stated, "In sum, different libraries can adopt different policies on the question of user charges for special
services depending on their own local budgets and circumstances."12

        Libraries can be viewed as having both a social mission and client
service objectives. "To the extent that the Postal Service exists to deliver
mail for those who are willing to pay for it, it is a client-oriented organiz-
ation--but the Postal Service also exists to ensure that good communication
is available to the public at large (and it therefore maintains Post Offices in
small towns that do not generate enough revenue to equal their expenses) and
to this extent it is public oriented."1

        The social necessity to have information available to the public in the
library at no direct cost is not in conflict with charging users for special
services.

        An additional argument for providing a level of taxpayer support for
libraries is the cost of collecting fees on a transaction basis. The revenue
generated by transaction fees on individual loans, in-library use and routine
reference questions may not be adequate to cover the cost of collecting fees;
therefore tax support may result in a net saving for the taxpayer. Subsidy
of routine services also ensures that information is available to people who
cannot afford to pay.

        The line between routine and special services is not easy to define.
Resolution of the user charge issue depends on the distinction between social
service to the public at large and special service to a small number of individual clients. As in the case of the Postal Service, the answer will be provided by public policy makers.

                              CONCLUSIONS

        This paper has presented a surface view of the current and likely
future impact of on-line systems on library operations as well as a review
of critical issues and uncertainties. An obvious conclusion is that on-line
systems will be integrated into more libraries and more library functions.
Used in a traditional library, on-line systems can free staff from routine
jobs, enhance the effectiveness of human resources and improve service to
users. Demonstration and research projects yielding new knowledge about
user needs and user interaction with information will provide the bases for
significant changes in the library. Forecasts of specific library designs or
operational patterns far into the future would be foolhardy because technology

and the economics of library operations are changing rapidly. The utilization of new technological devices and processes and awareness of economic change will not occur simultaneously in every library.

The decline in the price of computer hardware accompanied by improvements in software and data base access will increase availability of on-line systems to more libraries. Improvements in technology and competition will lead to lower prices in the future. While the willingness of users to pay green dollars for better service has been firmly established, public policy may dictate subsidy for tax supported libraries so that public access to information is ensured.

Finally, librarians are emerging from the catalog closet, stopping the revolution about the record keeping axis and taking charge of the revolution to come.

REFERENCES

1. Anthony, Robert N. and Herzlinger, Regina E., Management Control in Nonprofit Organizations. (Homewood, Illinois: Richard D. Irwin, 1975).

2. Auld, Lawrence, "Preventing Failure in Library Automation," Proceedings of the 1968 Clinic on Library Applications of Data Processing, Dewey E. Carroll, ed., (Urbana, Illinois: University of Illinois, 1968).

3. Baumol, William J. and Ordover, Janusz A., "Public Good Properties in Reality: The Case of Scientific Journals," address to American Society for Information Science, October, 1976.

4. Berry, John, "The Fee Dilemma," Library Journal, 102:651, March 15, 1977.

5. Bierman, Kenneth J., "Automated Alternatives to Card Catalogs: The Current State of Planning and Implementation," Journal of Library Automation, 8:277-298 (December 1975).

6. Brown, Carolyn P., "On Line Bibliographic Retrieval Systems Use," Special Libraries, 68:155-160, (April 1977).

7. Bruner, Jerome S., Beyond the Information Given: Studies in Psychology of Knowing. Jeremy M. Auglin, ed., (New York: Norton, 1973).

8. Bulick, Stephen, et. al., "Use of Library Materials in Terms of Age,"
    Journal of the American Society for Information Science, 27:175-178,
    (May-June 1976).

9. Cohen, Jacob, "Book Cost and Book Use: The Economics of a University
    Library," Library Resource Sharing: Proceedings of the 1976 Confer-
    ence on Resource Sharing in Libraries, Pittsburgh, PA. Allen Kent and
    Thomas Galvin, eds., (New York: Marcel Dekker, 1977), 197-224.

10. Cooper, Michael D. and DeWath, Nancy A., The Cost of On-Line Biblio-
    graphic Searching, Applied Communication Research, ACR-003-75-01,
    (Stanford, California: December, 1975).

11. Cuadra, Carlos A., "On Line System: Promise and Pitfalls," Journal
    of the American Society for Information Science, 21:107-114, (March-
    April 1971).

12. DeGennaro, Richard, "Pay Libraries and User Charges," Library
    Journal, 100:363-367, (February 15, 1975).

13. Drucker, Peter F., Management: Tasks, Responsibilities and Practice.
    (New York: Harper and Row, 1974).

14. Gardner, Jeffrey and Wax, David M., "On-line Bibliographic Services,"
    Library Journal, 101:1827-1832, (September 15, 1976).

15. "The Great Free Access Debate," American Libraries, 8:139, March
    1977.

16. Hewitt, Joe A., "The Impact of OCLC: The Good and the Bad, as
    Recorded by Researcher Joe A. Hewitt in Our Epic Journey to Every
    Charter Library of the On-line System," American Libraries, 7:268-
    275.

17. Hopkins, Judith, "The Ohio College Library Center," Library Resources
    and Technical Services, 17:308-319, (Summer 1973).

18. Kent, Allen, et. al., Progress Report on "A Cost-Benefit Model of
    Some Critical Library Operations in Terms of Use of Materials,"
    (Pittsburgh: University of Pittsburgh for National Science Foundation,
    April 29, 1977).

19. Lancaster, F. W., "The Evaluation of Machine Readable Data Bases
    and of Information Services Derived From These Data Bases," Evalu-
    ation and Management of Libraries and Information Centers, F. W.
    Lancaster and C. W. Cleverdon, eds.,(Leyden: Nordhoff, 1977), 73-100.

20. Mason, Ellsworth, "Balbus; or the Future of Library Buildings," Farewell to Alexandria, Daniel Gore, ed., (Westport, Conn.: Greenwood Press, 1976).

21. Markuson, Barbara E., 'The Ohio College Library Center: A Study of the Factors Affecting the Adaptation of Libraries to On-line Networks," Library Technology Reports, 12 (January 1976).

22. Meyer, Richard W. and Knapp, John F., "COM Catalog Based on OCLC Records," Journal of Library Automation, 8:312-321, (December 1975).

23. Mooers, Calvin N., "The Next Twenty Years in Information Retrieval: Some Goals and Predictions," American Documentation, 11:229-236, (July 1960).

24. Mooers, Calvin N., "Zatacoding and Developments in Information Retrieval," ASLIB Proceedings, 8:3-22, (February 1956).

25. Palmer, Richard P., Case Studies in Library Computer Systems. (New York: Bowker, 1973).

26. Plotnik, Art, "OCLC for You--and Me?!: A Humanized Anatomy for Beginners," American Libraries, 7:258-268, (May 1976).

27. Rogers, Frank B., "Computerized Bibliographic Retrieval Services," Library Trends, 23:73-88, (July 1974).

28. "Subject Access Project," Special Issue of Occasional Newsletter, Syracuse University, School of Information Studies, 3 (May 1977).

29. Swanson, Don R., "Design Requirements for a Future Library," Libraries and Automation, Barbara E. Markuson, ed., (Washington, D.C.: Library of Congress, 1964), 11-21.

30. Trueswell, Richard W., "Growing Libraries: Who Needs Them? A Statistical Basis for the No Growth Collection," Farewell to Alexandria, Daniel Gore, ed., (Westport, Conn.: Greenwood Press, 1976).

31. U.S. Bureau of Labor Statistics, Handbook of Labor Statistics, 1976, (Washington, D.C.: 1977).

32. U.S. Bureau of Labor Statistics, Wholesale Price Index, (Washington, D.C.: 1972, 1975).

33. U.S. Office of Education, Digest of Educational Statistics, (Washington, D.C.: 1975).

34. Veaner, Allen B., "Progress Toward Goals: Response," <u>Library Resource Sharing: Proceedings of the 1976 Conference on Resource Sharing in Libraries</u>, Pittsburgh, PA, Allen Kent and Thomas Galvin, eds., (New York: Marcel Dekker, 1977), 95-107.

35. "User Fees Called Peril to Libraries," <u>Detroit News</u>, June 22, 1977, 10-A.

36. Von Foerster, Heinz, "Technology: What Will It Mean to Librarians?" <u>Illinois Libraries</u>, 53:785-803, (November 1971).

37. White, Robert B., "A Prototype for the Automated Office," <u>Datamation</u>, 28:83-90, (April 1977).

38. Wills, Gordon and Oldman, Christine, "An Examination of Cost/Benefit Approaches to the Evaluation of Library and Information Services," <u>Evaluation and Scientific Management of Libraries and Information Centers</u>, F. W. Lancaster and C. W. Cleverdon, eds., (Leyden: Nordhoff, 1977), 165-184.

Chapter 11

REACTION TO "IMPACT ON LIBRARY FUNCTIONS"

John G. Lorenz

Executive Director
Association of Research Libraries
Washington, D. C.

I found it to be a stimulating paper (Chapter 10). There's some sense and some non-sense in it. I fully agree with the paper's first point that library systems and library services are continuing to go through an evolutionary process as they have since their creation and are not suddenly becoming revolutionary. My observation, however, is that the process of evolution in many of the major library systems as with many other changes we are observing in our society has speeded up within the last twenty years and that the rate of change in library services will probably continue to accelerate. As recently as 1974, only a few ARL libraries offered on-line bibliographic services. Today, almost every ARL library has such services.

That library change be evolutionary and not revolutionary, I believe, is desirable. Biologically, sociologically, politically, we are basically an evolving society. The democratic process is a process of gradual change. Biologically, it took our ancestors a long time to get out of the trees. It even took this generation of librarians a long time to get to Pittsburgh to discuss on-line services even though we can now travel by plane, train, or on our own hind legs. Nor do libraries exist in isolation. Politically, our public libraries are parts of city, county, or state governments which themselves are only changing gradually; our college and university and school libraries are parts of educational systems which change slowly; special libraries are in many cases parts of business and industry which also tend to be conservative about rapid change.

In addition, in times of fiscal restraint, many administrators and policy determining groups tend to be responsive only to priority established

needs and wants of users. Is there as yet a <u>heavy demand by users</u> for on-
line services ? Changes in library practice under these circumstances are
not likely to be sudden and revolutionary, but rather develop through study
and observation over a period of time. At one time in library history, I
seem to recall that AV services were expected to cause a revolution and these
services are still evolving; later, microforms were going to have the same
result, but we still have a long way to go to achieve full application of this
technology. I expect that use of computers and on-line services will go
through the same evolutionary process.

The paper I am commenting on states that traditional library systems
are being gradually overthrown without violence. I believe that "overthrown"
is too dramatic and not an accurate characterization of what is actually
happening and that we are still at an early stage of evolutionary change in
computer and on-line service applications--really just beginning to come out
of the trees and that for at least the next decade these services as they improve and develop and perhaps cost less will be integrated with present services.

My major criticism of the paper is its use of broad generalizations in
describing the attitudes of an entire occupational group, that of librarians,
as being a principal problem in using on-line systems and designing and
implementing new systems. For example: "For many years, librarians
reacted negatively to any system which altered the existing order of the
library"; and then the reference to "the tendency of librarians to cling slavishly to outdated concepts. " I had hoped we had reached the day when we
realized that within any broad group there are wide variations in attitudes,
perceptions, capabilities, etc. There are no objective findings to support
such general statements. They fly in the face of the many changes that have
taken place in library service, particularly within the last twenty years, which
wouldn't have been possible without the leadership and cooperation of many
librarians. I'm talking about the MARC development at LC, led by librarians;
I'm talking about OCLC and BALLOTS, led by librarians. I know that in his
Pennsylvania survey, Lowell Martin found one small town librarian who kept
the card catalog at her home because, as she said, it was easier to work on
it there. But I also know that Pennsylvania has librarians such as DeGennaro
and Doms, and many more like them, who have worked and are working hard
to accomplish constructive, effective changes in library services. I don't
think the many librarians here today are here to say: "Start the revolution
without me, "and I expect that the recent New York Metro Conference on
closing card catalogs was not oversubscribed by librarians who secretly
wanted to maintain card catalogs ad infinitum.

Here is another fallacious generalization in the paper: "Computer
scientists and engineers who designed early systems worked in a climate of
hostility and frustration brought about by the librarians' lack of participation

and unwillingness to imagine a different mode of operation for the library."
I expect many of us know many examples that deny this generalization. I
also know that occasionally there was some wisdom on the part of some
librarians in not accepting all the recommendations and promises of some
computer scientists and engineers.

But probably the unkindest and untruest cut of all is this generalization: "...librarians appear to be more comfortable resisting events than
creating or shaping events." I must rebel against such statements. Just
taking the Washington scene alone, I believe many of you have been around
long enough to have a sense of where library service came from over the
last 20 years, during which librarians have fought successfully with help
from leaders across the country to get Federal legislation and appropriations
and grants for public libraries, school libraries, college and university
libraries, library education and library research--frequently against great
opposition from administrations and Congressional leaders. In addition,
there have been many successful battles with State legislatures as well, and
all of this has shaped and changed library services significantly.

I don't want to expand this criticism further because my main point
is a general plea to all of us to get away from such generalization and negative accusations against an occupational class, not only because they aren't
accurate, but because they can be damaging in achieving the cooperation and
good will needed between librarians and information scientists and accom-
plishing more rapid and effective change, cooperation and progress. Let's
really bury the old cliches about all librarians and, if anyone is tempted to
generalize about librarians, tell him or her to go to an ALA conference and
observe how much alike they all are.

I believe that maximum time and energy in papers and at conferences
should be spent in developing constructive ideas and steps to the solution of
problems. This paper does accurately point up the problem of economics
in library services and library change, and I would underscore this key
problem in relation to speeding up the introduction of new technology and
services in libraries.

I believe if we really want to hasten evolutionary change in library
services, that nothing will accomplish this as effectively as the introduction
of new money, new capital, and the most intelligent regional, state, and
national planning for the use of those funds. My observation is that most of
the beneficial change in library organization, technology and services that
has occurred over the last 20 years has been the result of new and additional
federal, foundation, and, in some cases, state funding.

For example, the entire MARC development at LC was begun in 1965
with an initial $50,000 grant from the Council on Library Resources and

continued with added foundation and then Federal funding. The entire National Program for Acquisitions and Cataloging began with a small Federal appropriation in 1965 to the Office of Education for transfer to Library of Congress to accomplish this major evolutionary change. And, as you know, the early development of on-line bibliographic services received considerable initial support from the National Science Foundation, NASA, and Federal appropriations to the National Library of Medicine and the Library of Congress.

What the virtue of new and added funding provides is that it greatly increases the opportunity for creative and fruitful planning within library systems and between library systems. Particularly in a period of rapidly rising costs, it is not realistic to expect that existing financial resources of sufficient size can be successfully harnessed for significant change. This possibility should always be rigorously examined but neither should it be considered the only alternative if significant change is to be accomplished within a reasonable time.

New capital also will continue to be needed for new research, but I believe the large proportion of new capital is now needed for purposes of development and application, development and application of those changes which we already know will result in more cost-effective library services. I often think of the farmer who was asked by the county agricultural agent if he needed more agricultural research pamphlets. He said, "No, but I could sure use some money to help me farm as well as I know now."

Specifically, I believe there is one piece of new Federal legislation, Title II C of the revised Higher Education Act for "Strengthening Research Library Resources," that has great potential for helping to move us toward the development of a national library system by providing new funds which could include expenditures for the application of computer and communication technology. The dual objectives of the Title are to strengthen research resources across the country in the major research libraries and improve access to these resources. The initial appropriation for fiscal 1978 is only $5 million, but the authorization for fiscal 1979 is $20 million which, I believe, could make a considerable difference in speeding up national library system development. In addition, the Library Services and Construction Act has recently been extended for five years with a strengthened Title III for Interlibrary Cooperation, also with an authorization of $20 million per year for fiscal 1979-82. To get these amounts appropriated by the Congress will take good planning, organization, and communication at state and national levels and lots of superb education of Congressmen and government officials. But I think it is worth out best effort because it may be our best chance to improve the economic status of libraries and get the new money to speed up the rate of progress toward improved library service for all.

I also agree with the paper that continuing support by all funding bodies of new library and information services, including on-line services, will require good data on cost-effectiveness. Again, this is no easy job, but it is clearly worth the investment in money and time and the assignment of responsibility, planning and implementation to achieve. Who will step forward to provide the leadership and coordination to get the data on cost effectiveness that is needed?

The paper has a brief section on the subject of copyright. I may be able to add some later information. For copying beyond the provisions of fair use in Section 107 and the provisions of Section 108 of the new copyright law, and particularly for the payment of fees for multiple copies needed by libraries and educational institutions beyond Section 107 and 108, I expect that the new Copyright Clearance Center, Inc., will be the major vehicle for receiving royalty payments. The initial overhead charge of each copy made is expected to be 25¢ which will be taken out of the per copy cost which will begin to be noted on some periodical articles in January 1978. It seems clear that the costs to libraries of multiple copying beyond Section 107 and 108 will increase in calendar 1978 but to what degree each library system will have to estimate and then determine by experience.

On document delivery, I have no difficulty in agreeing with the paper that the U.S. Postal Service is a problem. (This is probably the understatement of the conference.) I also expect that high speed, hopefully less expensive, facsimile transmission and display is the best alternative being developed and will assist in time in substantially reducing this problem.

On user charges for on-line services, I would agree that there is probably no one solution to the problem for all libraries and that individual libraries at least for the time being will adopt different policies based on their type of library, their objectives, their budgets and other circumstances.

Here are some further random reactions on this question. Since many libraries, I expect, are in development, testing, or experimental phases with on-line services, I can understand having interim policies on payment for such a period with more permanent payment policies to be based on results found.

Perhaps a fundamental question for our society, which extends beyond libraries and on-line services, is can we as a nation provide both high quality service and equality of access. One educational leader recently said that the two achievements which keep our nation strong on the world scene are: the production of food and the production of new knowledge. He questioned whether we as a nation could afford to sacrifice quality in research in favor of equal access.

Jimmy Carter, in defending his position on no federal funds for abortion, recently concluded that "Life is not fair." Also speaking from a Washington point of view, I know that to get from here to there often requires compromise. The new copyright law is certainly an example of compromise and so is much of our library legislation, but overall I believe they both represent progress. On-line services in libraries will probably go through the same evolutionary trauma as we proceed from fees for on-line services toward subsidized services when in the national interest.

The paper concludes, as will I, with one more "librarian" generalization--used this time in what I expect is supposed to be a backhanded compliment: "Librarians are emerging from the cataloging closet...and taking charge of the revolution to come." All I can do is to try and top that with this generalization which I believe has just as little validity or sense: "You've come a long way out of the closet, baby. Comes the revolution, don't use the frozen card catalogs for barricades. They're shot full of holes already."

Chapter 12

IMPACT OF ON-LINE SYSTEMS
ON THE CLIENTELE

Paul Evan Peters

and

Manager
Social Science Information
Utilization Laboratory

Ellen Gay Detlefsen

Assistant Professor
Graduate School of Library
and Information Sciences

University of Pittsburgh
Pittsburgh, Pennsylvania

INTRODUCTION

The promise of on-line retrieval systems for libraries and their clienteles is one of access to computer-based information handling systems at manageable and predictable cost levels. This is not to say that on-line systems do not offer advantages when compared with batch, off-line systems and traditional manual techniques. Rather, on-line systems are not, on the whole, replacing existing search services; they provide the means by which such services are being established. They enable libraries of all sizes to consider instituting individualized, personalized search services which generally have been cost-prohibitive. Not only libraries are involved; any organization or individual desiring a richer information environment may now reasonably consider the necessary improvements--a person, a computer terminal, and a budget for telecommunications and access charges expanding and contracting according to actual use. The on-line revolution represents a new phase in the on-going development and use of computer-based information systems in that we now have a service-oriented marketplace with capability and price competition where none existed before. After twenty-five years of discussion and demonstration, we are on the verge of computer-based search services as a rule of library operations rather than an exception. Libraries and their clienteles cannot fail to benefit.

These articles of faith should not be allowed to obscure pressing and unanswered questions, many of which cluster around the impact of these on-line systems on library clienteles. Three matters are of concern: 1) a framework by which client impact questions can be addressed not only by researchers but in the daily professional lives of information workers as well; 2) results of recent research and commentary devoted to this issue; and 3) suggestions on useful directions for future research and development. Our discussion begins with the definitions of "clientele," "on-line system," and "impact," and continues by surveying the existing corpus of pertinent literature. Finally, the adoption of an admittedly user-sympathetic perspective allows us to assess the steps that remain to be taken to consolidate, institutionalize and personalize both the on-line revolution and the new "information world" which this on-line revolution is bringing into being.

CONTEXT

Our deliberations should be placed in context because on-line systems are not found solely in libraries, and those which are found there are not used exclusively for the purposes with which we are concerned.

The development of on-line systems is a computer industry-wide phenomenon. Three types of technological innovation are most responsible for this: 1) the maturation of computer language design to a point at which sophisticated understanding of machine characteristics and processes is less and less required of users; 2) the emergence of data transmission networks which enable coast-to-coast and, soon, intercontinental telecommunication at cost levels much lower than those of telephone communication; and 3) the development of typewriter-like computer terminals which enable a user to contact a computer through a familiar piece of office equipment.

On-line systems have improved computer service in some very straightforward ways. Although computers have always had the ability to process data rapidly, the preparation of input and the scheduling of access to a computer have not been similarly rapid. The introduction of on-line systems results in dramatic improvements in these areas, as these systems allow data to be prepared using the computer itself and the time required to detect and correct errors is reduced. The results of a computer analysis of data, moreover, become available much sooner in an "on-line" environment, so it is not an overstatement to say the on-line systems can make computers access in time frames more similar to those in which human problem-solving proceeds.

On-line systems, then, have begun to be widely incorporated throughout society. Businesses use them for inventory control and for tracing shipments and deliveries. Retail stores, banks, and other agencies use them for financial accounting and credit authorization. Brokerage firms use them to stay in touch with quickly changing market conditions. Police departments use them to exchange statistics and information on crime and criminals. Educational institutions use them for computer-aided instruction and course and grade registration. In general, it seems that there is a place for on-line, computer-based systems wherever large amounts of frequently changing data must be made available to numbers of users.

This activity seems apt for many types of library operations. On-line systems have been introduced to assist acquisitions processing, cataloguing, and circulation and collection control, to name three prominent applications. The application of concern to us in the following, however, is that of reference librarianship; we shall devote our attention to the use of on-line systems in the reference function. We shall focus primarily on academic/research and special libraries. It should be understood that this limitation arises from the simple fact that work to date has concentrated in these areas. The use of computer-aided reference techniques in public libraries, for example, is very attractive in principle. It is, however, a possibility which has yet to materialize in a form comparable to the experience of academic/research and special reference librarians. Insofar as some clienteles of public and school libraries are very different, it is important to be cautious in regarding on-line systems as suggestive rather than decisive in their implications for reference librarianship in general.

DEFINITIONS

Our concern is with "on-line information services"--those types of computer-based information services characterized by the manner in which the computer and its user, the searcher, cooperate. Two distinctive features are key: the searcher is able to issue instructions to and to receive responses from the computer in a step-by-step, interactive fashion which approximates the conversational give-and-take of human communication; and, on-line systems usually process search requests immediately upon receipt. The major computer-based alternative to this is the "traditional" or batch approach, offering economies of scale but doing so at the cost of making users wait. Although all on-line systems offer "immediacy" of response, not all do so exclusively. Some allow their users to specify whether immediate or delayed processing is desired and price the two options differently. A concept of "file aging" is usually present, with the effect that "new" information can be searched immediately or in the delayed manner, whereas "old" information is available only through batching. On-line systems also distinguish between processing of searches and printing of results, making it possible for these systems to search and report how many items were retrieved immediately and yet to delay printing of items until the user is "off-line." With the on-line system there is an immediacy of contact between users and on-line systems not found in other types of computer-based systems. This immediacy is a distinctive feature, making the on-line experience the one machine-based process most similar to the traditional reference service offered by many libraries.

The "client" of an on-line service is the person who makes use of it; the "clientele" is a group of clients. The person who actually uses an on-line system--the person who sits at the computer terminal, operates its keyboard, and reads its display--is certainly the most basic type of client. This is, however, but one of at least four types which can be described-- "searchers," "end-users," "service managers," and "decision makers." All four can be embodied in a single person, but it is common to find each as a separate individual within a given organization.

The "searcher" is typically a trained librarian or someone who works in a library or information center. A reference or information science specialty is also common. Searchers know system procedures and the contents and organization of system files; they receive statements of interests and produce reports which cite pertinent information. Searchers are an important, if not the important, element in an information service, and their relationship to an on-line system can be conceived in craftsperson/tool terms. In the same way that almost anyone can learn how to use a hammer, almost anyone can learn how to use one of the new on-line systems. Carpenters, though, use hammers with more skill than do less experienced individuals; a similar expertise can be found in searchers. On the other hand, it is sometimes difficult to explain what is needed in terms a craftsperson can appreciate and it is also often difficult to find a competent worker. For this reason, do-it-yourself approaches to both home improvement and information searching have become popular. These are useful not only as the means for circumventing unwanted or expensive intermediaries but also as educative experiences to prepare for dealing effectively with experts when a project requires it.

An "end-user" is someone for whom a search is conducted and to whom its results are routed. Many end-users have no interest in the techniques of information storage and retrieval, traditional or modern. They are interested only in the products these techniques can generate. The typical end-user is someone who has a question or topic in mind, wants to bring information to bear on it, but does not want to face an information problem in addition to the problem which motivates the inquiry. This person enjoys being able to delegate an information problem to a searcher. For reasons of personal preference, or because of the traditional reluctance to trust, however, some end-users want to be their own searchers. On-line systems are particularly well-adapted to these persons but most end-users have yet to exercise this option.

Two other clients are notable even though their roles are not the same as those of the searcher and end-user. Searchers use systems and end-users use information; "service managers" use searchers and "decision makers" use all parties involved. Both view on-line systems in an administrative light, service managers viewing them through searchers, while decision makers look at all three types, including service managers. Questions of cost, benefits, and productivity are on the minds of both. Service managers are concerned with the quality of service their searchers provide. They are the first to become and remain interested in the impacts of on-line systems because it is their responsibility to make changes, to determine and evaluate cost, equipment and space requirements, to recruit and train personnel, and so forth. Decision makers, on the other hand, are ultimately responsible for performance of both information services and the people who are served by them. Service managers examine alternatives for allocating resources among competing collections of information and the techniques for handling them, while decision makers investigate alternatives at other levels of organizational functioning and can conclude that improved information services are less important than increased research and development staff, carrying a larger inventory, recapitalizing a production line, or acquiring new library materials.

These four types of clients, depending upon the characteristics of the organization under scrutiny, can be found as four or fewer people. Some organizations may have an even more diversified clientele group. The vendor or developer of an on-line system is a class of client on whom and for whom the system has an immediate and very direct impact. So likewise might be the file suppliers.

Each client brings a varied perspective toward and response to information services and on-line systems because each has a unique organizational role in the establishment, operation, use, and evaluation of a system. Where more than one role belongs to a single individual, attention must be paid to the very real possibility of conflict and a resulting inconsistency and confustion in attitudes and behavior. No investigation of clientele impact can be conducted without first carefully considering the "clientele." First-order clients, those who use the system or who use the information from it, are not themselves a sufficient class for analysis. Attention must be given equally to the second-order clients--those who manage first-order clients. Clientele impact can thus be addressed in a manner compatible with the structures and dynamics of organizational functioning.

An "impact" implies the determination of the effect one thing has upon another--on-line information services on one hand and library clienteles on another. Effects on clients can take two basic forms depending upon whether the focus is on attitudes or behaviors. Care must also be taken to distinguish between effects for which the service is a contributing cause and those for which it can be said to be the sole cause. The separation of impact questions with a simple descriptive intent (e.g., "what difference does this system make?") from those with a comparative tone (e.g., "what system should I use to achieve a certain impact?") must be made as well.

To know the differences between attitudes and behavior is a caveat for research involving human subjects. A troublesome and familiar feature of such research is that people can express a belief in one thing, behave in a way suggestive of a contradictory belief, and be genuinely surprised, even irritated, when the discrepancy is made obvious. Administrators of academic libraries, for instance, face this difficulty when they try to reconcile faculty demand for "all important materials" with steadily rising financial pressures. One effective response is to attempt to make an exact statement of areas of inconsistency so that they can be examined on the basis of reliable information. The methodological key here is to ask the same question more than once, in different ways, and to link attitudinal data acquired through questionnaires and interviews with behavioral data obtained through observation. Consistency is then measured in both internal and external ways.

The distinction between a sole and a contributing cause is necessary if proper generalizations are to be made on the basis of an impact study. If an assessment of the impact of a system is made by calling attention to a state-of-affairs afterward, then the possibility exists that something else, in addition to the arrival of the new system, may also have altered or have played a role in bringing about the noticeable change. Things which vary over time in complex, open environments are subject to these mutual effects. The core of the issue is, then, one of "appropriate attribution" of impact, with the clear understanding that the attribution of causality is always a risky endeavor.

The conceptualization of "impact" must also be responsive to the difference between descriptive and comparative investigations. The initial impact study attempted within an organization should be a descriptive effort, to describe attitudes and behaviors at regular intervals using very similar methods and materials. A creditable baseline from which change can be measured must be established and simple descriptive techniques have this as an objective. The identification of those attitudes and behaviors which must be studied intensively to explain their changes is critical, but these data are seldom available as the normal routine. Organizations which commit resources to a continuing analysis of themselves and the people they serve are better prepared to determine impact than those which do not. Over time, however, descriptive methods yield to the more informative comparative techniques. With a recognition that no analysis of a system can be entirely separated from an analysis of competing alternative systems comes the understanding that systems and states of affairs are more often modified than simply accepted or rejected. When questioning "what is the impact of this system?" one of the first thoughts should be "compared with what?"

The impact issue can thus be reduced to four allied questions: 1) what can be done now which couldn't be done before (added benefit); 2) what can be done now which could be done before (maintained benefit); 3) what can't be done now that could be done before (lost benefit); and 4) what can't be done now which couldn't be done before (unrealized benefit). The introduction of cost consciousness into this structure produces the familiar cost/benefit or price/performance formula, a reliable and widely accepted manner by which to assess impact. Nevertheless, it represents an advanced stage of research, whose first step is to produce descriptive data.

LITERATURE SURVEY

An early attempt to develop a comprehensive perspective toward the users of on-line information systems was made by the participants in a 1971 workshop held in Palo Alto, California. The information scientists in attendance gave serious consideration to the "user/computer interface." In the workshop's proceedings,[1] statements of opinion and philosophy, discussions of design features of and experiences with some well-known systems (NASA/RECON, SUNY/BCN, SDC/DIALOG, SPIRES and BALLOTS, AIM-TWX and ELHILL, BASIS-70, and PROJECT INTREX) were given, as well as the record of the workshop deliberations. The primary emphasis was on the presentation of systems designers' views. Thus, the proceedings are not necessarily the best source of user reaction or impact data. Their "user," moreover, seems to be a combination of our "searcher" and "end-user."

John L. Bennett's "challenge paper" was the starting point. He identified eight issues which are critical when examining the user dimensions of on-line system design, development, and operation:

1) Characteristics of the Searchers Served by the Facility--the environment of system use, the expectations and preparation of searchers, and the attitudes and behaviors of searchers which pertain to information and computers.

2) The Conceptual Framework Presented to the Searcher--the structuring of the searching process required by the system and the appropriate locus of control, e.g., whether the system should guide the user or the user command the system.

3) The Role of Feedback to the Searcher During the Search--the timing and volume of system responses and the provision of user evaluation and control mechanisms.

4) Operational Characteristics of the Facility--the command language, display formats, response time, etc.

5) The Constraints of the Terminal and Techniques to Ameliorate Them--the device by which we state our requests to and receive responses from interactive systems, the provision of compensatory procedures on the part of the system, and the design of new and more appropriate devices.

6) The Effect of the Bibliographic Data Base on the User Interface for Search--the various collections of information to search and their contents, organizations, formats, and size.

7) Introducing the Search Facility to the User--the orientation and training program and the manner in which it is conducted (manuals, seminars, computer-assisted instruction, and so forth).

8) The Role of Evaluation and Feedback in the Redesign Cycle--the user/designer interface, behavioral science methods, and data collection and analysis roles that systems provide.[2]

In a response to this position paper, Thomas H. Martin and Edwin B. Parker suggested guidelines for system designers who seek to insure user acceptance:

1) Study the information needs and information-seeking habits of a sample of the target population to insure that the design goals are plausible.

2) Create a series of user profiles to illustrate the frequency, volume, and variance of different types of system interactions.

3) Plan from the beginning for multiple design iterations by requiring that features be broken into modules. It should be possible to add, replace, or modify modules without revising the entire system.

4) The detailed design and test implementation of the user interface should take precedence over other parts of the system so that adequate data can be gathered.

5) The interface design should include an elaborate facility for gathering information from users (both by unobtrusive monitoring and by question asking).

6) Alternative test versions of the system should be implemented and tested experimentally.

7) System evaluation is necessary if the system is to stay viable and if lessons learned from the development process are to be useful for later versions of this or other systems.[3]

These guidelines are complemented nicely by Siegfried Treu's notes on the human characteristics which are important to the searcher-system interface. Treu wrote that:

Designers of interactive search systems, in purposely planning for an effective searcher-system interface, must deliberately take into account that the human searcher has a sense of (or need for):

1. Spatial reference (or perspective)
2. Order (or file arrangement)
3. Completeness (or comprehensiveness)
4. Association (or connectedness)
5. Simplicity (or clarity)
6. Accessibility (or convenient access)
7. Responsiveness (or prompt action)
8. Control (or manageability)
9. Versatility (or variety in means and modes of access)
10. Compatability (or harmony among means and modes of access)
11. Reliability (or confidence)
12. Support (or advice and assistance-on-demand)[4]

While these reflections are directed primarily at designers, they are instructive for users of all types. This knowledge equips users with an understanding of how they themselves might become more actively involved as co-designers or critics of established systems.

Most of the remainder of the published proceedings of the 1971 workshop was a set of seven papers devoted to specific on-line systems. These papers outlined the features of the systems as seen by users and presented comments about users' reactions to them. Some of these designer observations provided a provocative reinforcement for the earlier ideas. Roger Summit, for example, concluded a discussion of DIALOG with:

The design criterion most often ignored, perhaps because of historical inability to include it, is that of flexibility. It is no longer necessary to find the "one best way" to design a retrieval system; it is now possible to design a system that is responsive to individual differences in user needs as well as individual differences in the approach to problems.[5]

Janet Egeland also offered some interesting remarks from her experience with the SUNY Biomedical Communication Network. She warned that it is more likely that users will overstate rather than understate the coverage and capabilities of an on-line information service, and cautioned that it "is most important at the outset that all users be made aware of the exact scope of the searching system so that they will have an objective base on which to judge the value and quality of the service they receive." She has also found that many users of information do not necessarily want to operate the search system itself:

> After the initial novelty of the system had worn off, however, even the users who had at first expressed willingness to sit down at the terminal and to do their own searches became less and less interested in spending the time that was involved...

> For the initial three months of system operation, there was no trained supervision available to terminal users. It became evident...that this arrangement was unsatisfactory from many points of view. It was much more practical to have assistance on hand for users who wanted to perform their own searches, to retrieve additional citations...for users who had done an initial query...and to actually process searches for the users who did not want to use the terminals themselves or who did not have time to wait if the terminals were busy. Most importantly, the trained professional was necessary because of all the problems that users were experiencing in trying to find the right vocabulary words and the proper search structure.6

Robert V. Katter and Davis B. McCarn presented a very well-structured report on user dimensions in the development of the AIM-TWX and ELHILL systems, and were particularly concerned with the changes in user reaction and impact over time. They observed that achieving system goals takes place in phases, with two pertinent aspects:

> ...First, each phase can be thought of as a collection of obstacles, each of which, unless the user is able to surmount it, may operate to inhibit or prevent his developing the kind of relationship with the system that allows him to extract its full potential so far as he is concerned. The second pertinent aspect of "phases" is that explanatory materials and user-system interface arrangements that are appropriate before the user reaches a certain transition point are often less appropriate after he passes that point, and vice versa. This raises the dual problems of finding out what the appropriate arrangements and materials are for various phases, and of finding ways to determine when the user has reached or passed a given transition point...7

Katter and McCarn proposed three roughly sequential phases. The first, termed the "confidence" phase, accounts for a user's initial hesitancies, fears, and eventual assumption of a relaxed attitude. Problems include a system's "response press" by which a quick response from a computer-based system can result in an impression that users must respond rapidly as well, or "conspicuous consumption," by which users may feel that their needs are not sufficiently important to justify the employment of an expensive system, and "error tension," the familiar fear that an error may have disastrous consequences for the system as a whole. The confidence phase is followed by an "insight" phase, during which users begin to comprehend a system's potential and underlying structure. The onset of the insight phase can be recognized by a user's perception of consistencies in a system's operations, a comprehension and appreciation of system flexibility, and an ability to make shortcuts in system procedures. A system offering "graduated memory support" for prompting and assistance at varying levels of detail and extensive "feedback channels" for making comments and observations as well as receiving news concerning the system and its data bases is essential. The third and final phase is "incorporation," when a system becomes an absolutely necessary feature of the user's professional life.

Pauline Atherton, in a paper that would specifically "...ask more questions than it answers, prod more than it guides, and offer few solutions for the myriad of problems which lie ahead,"[8] was concerned with a larger problem: given the emergence of attractive, effective information delivery mechanisms in the form of on-line systems, is the re-evaluation of the contents of such systems, the data bases themselves, a necessary corollary? She cited four outstanding problem areas relating to user interface:

1. The principle of least action--a user must encounter little resistance when entering a system, when understanding how to use it, and when transferring from data base to data base in cases of multi-file searching.

2. The problem of compatibility--much must be done by groups or individuals to insure that various on-line systems operate by similar principles, structures, and languages or that data are produced in similar formats.

3. The problem of flexibility--the bibliographic conventions being followed in the production of computer-based resources are derived from those originally developed for a radically different information world than that being created by on-line systems.

4. The problem of auxiliary aids in bibliographic retrieval systems--on-line systems in their current form are not

making use of the powerful assistance offered by auxiliary
aids such as thesauri or dictionaries.[9]

Atherton saw these as barriers to the development of a truly "integrated"
bibliographic system. Without attention to these issues, on-line systems
might only offer users data processing advantages (in that large volumes of
materials can be processed in short amounts of time) without significant information processing advantages. This observation is as salient today as it
was in 1971.

The deliberations of this workshop are placed in perspective by a
study done at the System Development Corporation during 1974 and 1975, and
published last year.[10] The principal investigators, Judith Wanger, Carlos
A. Cuadra, and Mary Fishburn, stated their primary purpose:

> ...to describe and assess the impact of the introduction and use
> of on-line bibliographic information retrieval systems, focusing
> primarily on three major areas: 1) the impact of on-line re-
> trieval usage on the on-line searcher; 2) the impact of on-line
> literature-searching services on the using organizations; and
> 3) the impact, as perceived by the information intermediary
> organization, of on-line literature-searching services on the
> information-seeking and -use habits of the information con-
> sumer.[11]

The results of their efforts should be mandatory reading for anyone
with a serious interest in on-line systems in libraries. They presented data
drawn from 1,273 respondents, divided into two classes: 472 managers and
801 searchers. These were users from some 546 organizational units found
in 469 different parent organizations--either commercial, educational,
governmental, or other, agencies. Each respondent had experience with one
or more of the following ten on-line service suppliers: Battelle Memorial
Institute (BASIS), European Space Agency (RECON), Lockheed Missiles and
Space Corporation (DIALOG), Canadian Institute for Scientific and Technical
Information (CAN/OLE), State University of New York (STAIRS), System
Development Corporation (ORBIT), United States Energy Research and
Development Agency (ERDA/RECON), United States Defense Documentation
Center (RD&TE On-Line System), United States National Aeronautics and
Space Administration (NASA/RECON), and the United States National Library
of Medicine (ELHILL III). Each supplier made a service available to external users--individual or organizational, concentrated on bibliographic data
bases, and was willing to cooperate in the study. The motive for involving
the various suppliers was not evaluative or comparative in the strictest
sense; no particular service supplier was identified by name. Each supplier
either furnished the SDC study team with a subscriber list, or mailed the
materials itself.

This research covered a number of important areas: the introduction of on-line services, the selection and training of staff; the levels of on-line use; the selection, access, and use of on-line sytems; the selection and use of on-line data bases; the costs of using on-line services; the problems in using on-line services; the special challenges, the major areas of impact; and a final discussion. An appendix provided the two survey instruments. Four of these areas are particularly useful in our present discussion of on-line systems--the respondent backgrounds, the problems in using on-line services, the special challenges, and the major areas of impact.

Only 32.2% of the managers and 30.8% of the searchers worked for commercial organizations, 30.7% of managers and 33% of searchers worked in educational institutions, 21.3% of managers and 24% of searchers worked for governmental agencies, and "other" organizations accounted for 15.7% of managers and 12.2% of searchers. Over eighty percent of all respondents worked in libraries and traditional information service units. Nearly 55% of the managers had a year's or more experience with their first on-line system, while only 27% had as much experience with a second system and only around 18% had equivalent experience with a third and fourth system. Overall only 11% of the respondents indicated using as many as four systems; 51% indicated the use of two systems, and 25% indicated use of three. A conclusion that use of more than one on-line system was just beginning was obvious.

Six familiar system-related problems were documented: supplier's computer, disconnection from the host computer, apparent loss of control of the program, loss of data, intermittent transmission of "garbage" characters, and totally unintelligible transmissions. Four-fifths of the searchers indicated that they were "generally bothered" by variations in system response time arising from numerous hardware, software, and environmental factors. Nearly half, however, said that they simply put up with this, 80% said that they rarely or never terminated their sessions in favor of completing the search another way, and 57% said that they sometimes terminated their current sessions to try again later. Almost half of the searchers indicated that all these problems in the aggregate did not interfere very seriously with their work but a third said that these problems were "somewhat serious".

An examination of problems associated with data base use was also made. Less than 10% of searchers reported difficulty most of the time in formulating search strategies, 47% said they had difficulty some of the time, and the remainder are troubled rarely or not at all. Only 2% had frequent difficulty in selecting appropriate data bases and 17% had occasional problems, but the majority of searchers surveyed did not have trouble in the selection of data bases. Finally, the assessment of relevance was never, or rarely, a problem for 55% of those surveyed while 36% encountered occasional difficulty and 10% were troubled by this most of the time.

The issue of on-line system supplier/user communication was investigated. While two-thirds of the respondents thought telephone assistance from the supplier to be essential, only one-fourth saw terminal-to-terminal consultation as equally useful. Almost 75% of the searchers reported that they found supplier-distributed newsletters and bulletins very useful.

One "special challenge" considered was that of the "end-user interface," and an extremely significant finding was expressed by the SDC team:

> Our study clearly shows that most on-line bibliographic searches are performed by information intermediaries. In the early days of on-line systems, there was a strong belief among many designers and planners that these systems should be designed for, and used by, end-users. This belief is still held by some but it has not been translated into practice. However, on-line systems permit--and, some would say, demand--a new relationship between the end-user and the information intermediary, and the challenge today is to define the kinds of interfaces that take full advantage of the potential of the on-line, interactive technology.[12]

The SDC research indicated that in 45% of the cases, the end-users were actually present while an intermediary conducted a search (the "side-car" interface) and in 8% of the cases the two were in telephone contact (the "information operator" interface). Where end-users are doing their own searching, they have been trained to do so by library staff. In fact, 60% of the respondents believed end-users could assume responsibility for their own searching, although some felt that, as a result, some end-users would then never go beyond the on-line system, to the detriment of their general information needs. Managers believed that in 63% of the cases, end-users were changing as a result of the on-line system; the major change was a preference for on-line searches over those done manually. Fewer than a third of the managers, however, saw no changes at all in end-user behavior and believed that none would be found.

An investigation of challenges introduced by the use of more than one system and more than one data base was also undertaken. Obviously as a searcher moves from system to system or from data base to data base, confusion arises as to procedures, contents, structures, etc. Searchers did not, however, report the expected kinds of problems. In a third of the cases searchers indicated that multiple system use had not been a source of confusion; about a half reported occasional confusion while only 3.8% said that the confusion was a major problem with serious effects on efficiency. In a consideration of multiple data base use, a similar pattern emerged; 51.5% reported no confusion, 39.0% reported occasional confusion and a mere 1.7% reported serious confusion. These major findings of the SDC study bear upon the on-going "standardization debate," indicating that the projected benefits to accrue from standardization may not be worth the costs.

The study of "major areas of impact" began with an examination of managers' expectations of the benefits resulting from the institution of an on-line service: 72% anticipated faster turnaround time, 67.5% anticipated access to additional sources of information, 56.9% anticipated reduction in staff time, 47.2% anticipated greater precision in retrieval, 44.4% anticipated serving more end-users, and 43% anticipated introducing their first literature-searching service. Obviously, then, 43% of the respondents did not offer any literature-searching service prior to their introduction of on-line systems. Organizationally, these "nothing-before/something-now" agencies were broken down: 38.6% of governmental users, 34.9% of commercial users, 60% of educational users, and 32.4% of other users. In almost all cases the managers said that nearly all expected benefits had been realized; only 4% dissented. The managers' one complaint concerned the accuracy and currency of information, an issue that can be traced through the on-line supplier to the data base vendor and developer.

Searchers and managers were also asked about the cost-effectiveness of on-line searching vis-a-vis both manual and batch computer-based techniques; three-fourths found interactive on-line searching more cost-effective than manual searching and half saw it as more cost-effective than batch searching.

The impact of on-line systems on modes of operation and service images was also investigated. Although 91.8% of the organizations surveyed have continued manual searches and 34.6% have continued computer-based batch searches, their heavy reliance on on-line techniques was striking; 54.6% of the responding organizations do one-half or more of their searches on-line, 16.3% do one-half or more partially on-line, while 13.0% do one-half or more without using an on-line system. Over half of the managers surveyed found more end-users are being served now than ever before. Over half of the searchers thought the quality of their work improved when using an on-line system. The managers, moreover, felt strongly that on-line systems had increased staff productivity, but split evenly on the issue of improved staff attitudes and morale (48.7% saw a significant change while 42.3% did not). Searchers, on the other hand, were very positive in their personal feelings about the use of on-line systems.

These two monographic items are nicely supplemented by a few articles from the journal literature. The vast majority of materials retrieved in our literature search on users and on-line systems were either dated examples of the type of literature commonly christened "how-I-run-my-library (read "on-line service")-good," or they were technical reports from R&D teams and systems specialists apparently operating in a user-free arena.

Three articles and a single ERIC report stand out as examples of current literature with a strong sense for users (all classes of users) and a

positive attitude about the present impact and future promise of on-line
systems in user-sensitive services. The articles, in chronological order,
are Martha Williams' essay from Special Libraries in December 1975,
Jeffrey Gardner and David Wax on the general state of the art in the Library
Journal for 15 September 1976, and J. S. Kidd on faculty use from College
and Research Libraries in March 1977. These are non-technical, blessedly
free of jargon, and well-suited to the needs of reference librarians, library
administrators, educators, and potential users; in short, they are intro-
ductions to the world of on-line systems for differing clienteles.

    Martha Williams, in her article entitled "Criteria for Evaluation and
Selection of Data Bases and Data Base Services,"[13] does not specifically
address the issue of evaluating on-line systems and services, but her per-
ceptive examination of the factors to be considered in, first, choosing to
offer data base services, and, second, choosing the appropriate data base
from among the many now available, are easily applicable to on-line services.
Her advice reflects an understanding of the categories of users, particularly
the end-user and the searcher, and her ability to ask straightforward and useful questions is laudable.

    Gardner and Wax, on the other hand, write more generally and histor-
ically. Their overview and description of the three basic models for developing and delivering computer-based searching services are useful, particularly
for the individual or institution beginning planning, or working with an uninitiated audience. Two important points about users and the impact of such
services on them were made: "Users have become uninvolved bystanders,"
and "the librarian-intermediary is a regrettable and expensive necessity."
The authors' hopeful notion that "on-line searching will begin to reach its
potential when the individual scholar sits at a terminal and interacts directly
with the data base"[14] is, it is devoutly to be hoped, not a fantasy. The eight
items cited in the bibliography of the article also serve as a mini-reading
list for those wishing to pursue the ideas in greater depth in the literature
of both librarianship and management.

    Kidd's "Toward Cost-Effective Procedures in On-line Bibliographic
Searches,"[15] is, despite its blunt title, an example of some of the innovative
uses to which on-line search services can be put. Kidd described an experiment in which pre-packaged results were distributed to faculty members,
and their responses to each of two formats were recorded. The dichotomy
between the expectations of the searchers ("advocates of on-line bibliographic
systems") and the faculty who received their output prompted Kidd to observe
that "it seems increasingly unlikely that it is either feasible or desirable to
deliver 'packages' of actual documents on an unsolicited basis to an unpre-
pared client," but that "the response was generally positive, not to say,
enthusiastic, to the bibliographic list as opposed to the document package."
Alas, it is the innovative notion of providing the highly selected (and one

hopes) highly relevant documents instead of the moderately selective biblio-graphic list that should or ought to characterize the full-blown use of these systems. Kidd seemed to point to the perhaps Herculean task of re-educating the end-user as the major challenge for those who promote the use and serv-ice of data base tools.

A fourth document worth perusal is a modest ERIC report from Jeffrey C. Griffith, of the University of Southern California School of Library Science, entitled "On-line Bibliographic Retrieval: An Instructional Resource for Classes."[16] As Kidd did, Griffith described another new use for the skills and services emanating from libraries possessing data base reference services and systems. He demonstrated formats for the inclusion of on-line information in library instruction for the large class, for group work with students in smaller classes, and individualized research methods for students in advanced seminars. Despite its "how -I-run-my-library-good" approach, it contains much of interest to the library or individual planning new uses for on-line services within the fiscal constraints of an academic setting.

Finally, an article which appeared in a recent issue of the Archives of General Psychiatry deserves mention, particularly because it may not have seen wide use among those in librarianship and information science. Entitled "The Lithium Librarian: An International Index,"[17] it described an on-line information retrieval system developed by a group of physicians and researchers (in three countries) dissatisfied with the results obtained from searches initiated on their more familiar data bases (MEDLINE, Psycholog-ical Abstracts, BIOSIS, etc.). It is the first example of a purely user-based on-line system, and is remarkable for its efficiency and simplicity in pro-viding access to the voluminous literature on lithium as a pharmacologic agent in a variety of disorders. As its authors concluded,

> While some library scientists may regard this approach as
> trivial or unsophisticated in terms of library science theory,
> it is a system designed by clinicians and medical researchers
> to meet clinical and research needs and it does this very well.
> A similar 'sophistication' argument is often advanced by com-
> puter scientists who deplore the 'antiquated' computers and
> programming language that physician users advocate. Com-
> puter scientists are simply not challenged or reinforced by
> stable and reliable computer systems that provide no oppor-
> tunity for them to use their skills and knowledge. In contrast,
> physicians working in clinical settings place a high priority on
> stability and reliability and are not concerned whether a partic-
> ular computer process is completed in 300 or 700 milliseconds.
> The Lithium Librarian, with its emphasis on a specialized, com-
> prehensive and up-to-date registry of all lithium references,

rapid search capability, widespread and constant availability, and ease of use, provides a model for problem solving library resources needed by clinicians and researchers.[17]

Systems developers, vendors, librarians, and information scientists need look no further for a concise description of user needs, interests, and impact. That no information professionals were apparently involved in the creation of the "Lithium Librarian" is an embarrassing admission.

DISCUSSION

This examination of the impact of on-line information services on their clienteles suggests ways to improve the operation of these systems in the interests of users and suggests ways that research on these concerns could be sharpened. The on-line revolution is still very much in process, and the issue of the potential of these techniques is very much alive.

The most curious feature of this study of users is the general lack of involvement of end-users. Since the late 1940's when Vannevar Bush articulated his notion of MEMEX, there has been a widespread assumption that information technology would reach the point at which end-users could assume complete responsibility for their literature searching activities. This development is not yet obvious.

Possibly, on-line systems are too new to justify a sweeping conclusion based upon this absence of "hands-on" end-user involvement to date. Possibly, despite the good intentions of librarians and information scientists, they are not seeking end-user involvement in an active way--one which would lead to the futuristic information environments which we visualized before we had access to the technologies these concepts required. These two possibilities may very well be related. Because of the novelty and expense of these systems, searchers and service managers may be unwilling to turn searching over to the end-users until they are absolutely certain that the results will be positive. Is this a reasonable caution on the part of those who have the most to lose--the searchers and service managers who have broad responsibilities and who regard on-line systems as but one tool among many that they use to serve the information needs of these clienteles? Or, is it a simple distrust of those who lack library and information science training?

A further possibility is also obvious. End-users may never want to assume total responsibility for their searching. At the very least there will always be those end-users who want personal involvement in literature searching, those who shun such involvement, and those who sometimes do and sometimes do not. It is appropriate then for systems designers to aim at the goal of universal end-user involvement because the attainment of this goal makes end-user involvement possible whenever desired. It is not clear, however, that the current lack of end-user involvement necessarily implies that on-line systems and the services delivered by their use are radically deficient. To learn that end-users vary in their needs, wants, and willingness to do certain things is to rediscover something known for years but to find it in a new context.

An analogy may serve to clarify these thoughts. The American telephone system allows a user to determine the telephone number of someone by either looking it up in a directory annually prepared for and distributed to subscribers at great corporate expense, or by dialing 411 and requesting directory assistance from an operator, a service provided at greater expense. The telephone company is trying to reserve the directory assistance service for those situations for which it is required: new listings, changed listings, long distance calls, handicapped persons, etc. The "regular" inquiry should be a matter handled by the subscriber using the printed directory supplied to each user. Users and developers of on-line systems may someday discover a similar division of labor. Searchers may become "directory assistants" with access to basically the same resources and tools as end-users and they may use on-line systems to accomplish tasks which are beyond the skills developed by end-users through occasional use. End-users, on the other hand, could become self-sufficient in a number of ways in which they are not at present.

There is not now a reliable resolution to this question of the lack of end-user involvement. If descriptive studies can produce results which lead to more intensive and carefully comparative controlled studies, then the elucidation of the end-user involvement issue is the one which must be singled out for an in-depth examination. Efforts must be directed at characterizing the forms and extents of end-user involvement, identifying the features distinguishing organizations exhibiting a high degree of involvement and those with a low degree, profiling the traits of those end-users who seek high involvement versus those who do not, and developing recommendations for the profession on fostering the involvement of end-users in the total process. Research of this variety will transform the discussion of end-user involvement from a matter of opinion to a subject for empirical exchange.

Two types of research methods not widely used at present bear upon these concerns: extensive instrumentation of the systems themselves and longitudinal studies of clientele groups. "Instrumentation" implies unobtrusive collection of data performed by the systems as they are being used--a heretofore unexploited potential of the on-line, and perhaps of all, computer-based systems. The discussion of differences between searches performed by end-users and those performed by professional searchers or information intermediaries is often phrased in terms of user satisfaction with results and the general quality of products. These important attitudinal aspects of

on-line system use deserve continuing study. There are other behavioral
aspects, however, which can be effectively approached by implementing on-
line data collection features. Each time an on-line searching session is held,
the system involved could add a summary record to a growing "transaction
file"--a record containing data on such interesting usage characteristics as
numbers of terms selected, numbers and types of combinations performed,
numbers of items examined on-line and printed off-line, length of session
measured by both computer-time and connect-time, etc. These data can be
collected with a record being generated for each file used during a session
as well as an aggregate profile for the session as a whole. A modest capability of this sort already exists in every commercial on-line system that is
automatically invoicing for services rendered. This capability could be extended to produce data which will greatly improve our understanding of how
on-line systems are used.

If the data could be arranged by user and organization type as well as
by extent of experience and other similar concepts, useful and enlightening
comparisons can be made. This second possibility, however, may be difficult to realize, not only for reasons of confidentiality, but also for reasons
arising from the methods for capturing the data. The imposition of a questionnaire as an overhead item which could inhibit on-line system use and
thus compromise the quality of any data gathered must be avoided. To respond to background questions might distract users from their prime purpose
in using a system; if the system made the answering of questions an optional
feature, the data from those who elected to participate would inform us only
about "cooperative" users rather than users in general.

A possible solution to this dilemma would seem to be available by
presenting the background questionnaire only once, when a given user first
subscribed, and by entering those responses into a system's "accounting
files"--for retrieval or incorporation into "transaction records" on a session
by session basis. Although the identification of individual users by their system access codes is presumably unique, this is not always true in practice
and is impossible to police at any rate. As a result there is not an absolute
assurance that any single person is the only one using the system and identifying herself or himself with a specific access code.

These thoughts lead us in a familiar direction. On-line data gathering
of a descriptive nature can be implemented in a straightforward fashion and
will yield useful information. To accomplish more than this objective, however, requires something beyond "routine" operation. This highly focused
research calls for the provision of incentives for user cooperation which will
make the results less conditional upon the "good will" of system users.

The longitudinal study of a clientele group can be a periodic examination of the same group of people over an extended period of time. Ideally

an investigation of this type would begin prior to the introduction of an on-
line system, not only to identify reactions to the system per se but also to
detect changes occurring in people's attitudes toward and habits concerning
information acquisition and use. Longitudinal studies are particularly well-
suited to noticing and tracking trends as they unfold. Although usually expensive and very demanding in terms of time and effort, they yield types of
data difficult to obtain otherwise. The most basic form of a longitudinal
study has a distinctly descriptive tone. Anecdotal treatments of this type
are useful and the literature is full of them. However, they involve looking
backward from a single vantage point at the end of a succession of activities.
They provide a record of what happened as someone remembers it. It is
difficult to discount investigator bias and to account for the natural influence
of point-of-view. Such reports do serve, however, to point out either common or provocatively dissimilar reflections which may need further investigation. In their most advanced form, logitudinal studies involve observers
from outside the organization or clientele group in which the changes are
taking place and are generally improved if the data analysts and data collec-
tors are separate groups.

CONCLUSION

        A final observation which isolates some of the concerns mentioned by
Pauline Atherton can be made. It is a mistake, at least in principle, to
regard the impacts of on-line systems as occurring solely at the end of the
cycle by which information is produced, acquired, organized, stored,
searched, retrieved, disseminated, and used. The exposure of end-users
to the information made possible by on-line systems is very much greater
than anything we have known previously. This can eventually result in the
formation of new and more discriminating opinions about the entire set of
processes now labelled as librarianship and information science. It is difficult to say exactly what role on-line systems can and should play in order to
bring about this possibility, but it is certain that this matter deserves more
attention than it has been receiving. A second, allied thought is that on-line
systems in their current forms have to be regarded as the first step down a
trail of technological development --the end of which is not yet in sight. For
example, most of the available on-line systems do not make use of existing
library and information science tools; the general omission of computer-
readable thesauri or posting dictionaries for use while preparing search
strategies is an important omission. We will either have to come to view
these techniques as unnecessary, thereby saving money and time when ready-
ing materials for incorporation into computer-based files, or their useful
place will have to be acknowledged with obvious effects in the structure and
operation of on-line systems. On-line systems someday may have to provide
users with processing options designed to analyze the results of a search and
retrieval operation. Again, what form these operations may take is difficult

to perceive, although preparing a word-frequency report, a concordance, or a keyword-in-context index from a set of retrieved documents seem to be useful information processing capabilities of on-line systems. The point of such open-ended thoughts is to encourage the recognition of the stunning advances made by system developers to date and then to point toward those mechanical processes which deliver better services.

That there is and can be an impact of on-line systems on our user groups is undeniable. A single look at the job descriptions for searchers, at the budgets proposed by service managers for review by decision makers, or at the program plans laid by end-users assembled for scholarly meetings, is evidence enough of the increasing interest in on-line machine-based information. The reference process in traditional libraries is changing; the number of disciplines whose knowledge has been until now unrepresented in data base files is daily diminishing. The availability of information in new or different formats calls for the establishment of new sources and new centers for such services, whether institutional or extra-institutional.

User resistance on every level is shrinking slowly, either because access to on-line files is now a fait accompli in many academic or special libraries or because a machine-based file is the only way to find certain kinds or bits of information. The once fantastic vision of on-line access in every office is now less surreal, and more likely. There may not be universal, physical, and interactive, on-line access in every office, but the vision of daily personal access to an information specialist or data services librarian is genuine.

This on-line revolution is here to stay. To paraphrase a revolutionary from another age, those users who are not part of the solution are part of the problem. If users--whether end-users, intermediaries, or managers --do not respond to the inevitable impact of these systems, they risk having crucial decisions made for them by systems developers, vendors, and others less interested, and less educated, in their welfare and their needs. The second revolution (third? fourth?) must be that of the user, rising up to participate critically and positively in the planning and production of new services and in evaluation of existing ones.

A prominent library leader said it well in a recent speech to librarians assembled:

> ...We must speak up. And more than that--we must think, and having thought, move on--to action. And not to action prompted by short-term expediency, but motivated by principle. For if we do not, there is nothing more certain than that others, and particularly those who see the material potential in information as a commodity, will move before us to grab off this energy

source as they have oil and gas and coal, and who will use it
and develop it with perhaps no more social concern than the
record from the Industrial Revolution on down should lead us
to expect. [18]

On-line information systems can affect, and benefit, us all enormously so
long as we are all involved in their use, evaluation, and development. The
phenomenon of the mechanical manipulation of information has led to the on-
line revolution. Where now are the users?

ACKNOWLEDGEMENTS

Our thanks to Thomas G. McFadden, an MLS student in the Graduate
School of Library and Information Sciences at the University of Pittsburgh,
who sought out the literature both mechanically and manually, and who participated in the hours of conversation that preceded our writing, and our
special thanks to JoAnn Hartz for her patient typing and retyping of the document.

REFERENCES

1. Interactive Bibliographic Search: The User/Computer Interface. Pro-
    ceedings of a Workshop..., Donald E. Walker, ed. Montvale, N.J.:
    AFIPS Press, 1971.

2. John L. Bennett, "Interactive Bibliographic Search as a Challenge to
    Interface Design," in Ibid., p. 1-16.

3. Thomas H. Martin and Edwin B. Parker, "Designing for User Acceptance
    of an Interactive Bibliographic Search Facility," in Interactive Biblio-
    graphic Search..., op. cit., pp. 45-52.

4. Siegfried Treu, "A Conceptual Framework for the Searcher-System
    Interface," in Ibid., pp. 53-66.

5. Roger K. Summit, "DIALOG and the User: An Evaluation of the User
    Interface with a Major On-line Retrieval System," in Interactive Biblio-
    graphic Search..., op. cit., pp. 83-94.

6. Janet Egeland, "User-Interaction in the State University of New York
    (SUNY) Biomedical Communication Network," in Ibid., pp. 105-120.

7. Robert V. Katter and Davis B. McCarn, "AIM-TWX--An Experimental
    On-line Bibliographic Retrieval System," in Interactive Bibliographic
    Search..., op. cit., pp. 121-141.

8. Pauline Atherton, "Bibliographic Data Bases--Their Effect on User Interface Design in Interactive Retrieval Systems," in Ibid., pp. 215-223.

9. Ibid., p. 216, 217, 218, 219.

10. Judith Wanger, Carlos A. Cuadra, and Mary Fishburn, Impact of On-line Retrieval Services: A Survey of Users, 1974-1975. Santa Monica: SDC, 1976.

11. Ibid., p. 1.

12. Judith Wanger, et. al., op. cit., p. 193.

13. Martha E. Williams, "Criteria for Evaluation and Selection of Data Base and Services," Special Libraries, 66:561-569 (December 1975).

14. Jeffrey J. Gardner and David M. Wax, "On-line Bibliographic Searches," Library Journal, 101:1827-1832 (15 September 1976).

15. J. S. Kidd, "Toward Cost-Effective Procedures in On-line Bibliographic Searches," College and Research Libraries, 38:153-159 (March 1977).

16. Jeffrey C. Griffith, "On-line Bibliographic Retrieval: An Instructional Resource for Classes," Los Angeles: University of Southern California, School of Library Science, 1976. (ED 121 242).

17. John H. Greist, James W. Jefferson, Ann M. Combs, Mogens Schou, Ann Thomas, "The Lithium Librarian: An International Index," Archives of General Psychiatry, 34:456-459.

18. Eric Moon, "Data Base is Two Four-Letter Words," unpublished typescript of his ALA Presidential Inaugural Address, Detroit, Michigan, June 21, 1977, p. 5.

Chapter 13

THE IMPACT AND FUTURE OF ON-LINE RETRIEVAL
AS THEY RELATE TO THE CLIENTELE

Martha E. Williams

Director
Information Retrieval Research Laboratory
University of Illinois
Urbana, Illinois

INTRODUCTION

This paper will provide background information about data bases and on-line retrieval, define the clientele for on-line systems, that is, indicate who the users are, discuss problems associated with on-line searching, propose requirements for solving those problems, and indicate the future trends. This paper is a reaction to the Peters/Detlefsen paper;[1] however, I find little to disagree with and will concentrate on further elucidation and expansion, rather than providing counter arguments. With respect to clienteles as users, there are problems that can be alleviated by fruitful research --research about users and research that will help users in their on-line searching and search-related activities. Research about users would help us understand the nature of users as users, their actions, reactions, the motivations and reasons behind them, and the impact they have on the users' work. The Peters/Detlefsen paper discussed research about users; I will discuss the need for research that would be directed toward helping the user, by making systems more user-oriented.

BACKGROUND

Volume of Activity On-line. First of all, I think there really is a revolution in the field of information retrieval. This is evidenced by a number of factors. It is evidenced by the fact that the majority of the world's A&I

literature is now in machine-readable form. There are some seventy million[2] computer-readable records of the abstracting and indexing type (A&I). These are contained in about four hundred bibliographic data bases. There are also dozens of on-line software packages such as ELHILL, DIALOG, ORBIT, STAIRS, and the New York Times system, and there are also at least a dozen major on-line systems including those operated by the National Library of Medicine (NLM), Lockheed Information Service (LIS), System Development Corporation (SDC), Bibliographic Retrieval Service (BRS), and the Times Information Bank (TIB).

Although there are seventy million records in machine-readable form, not all of them are on-line yet. Approximately 75% of them are on-line[2] on one or more of the systems throughout the world. There are many different services being provided by the on-line vendors, and the number of searches being conducted in the U. S., Europe and Canada is growing rapidly. Based on data I have collected for searches of systems in the U. S. and Canada (European systems not included), the search volume has grown from 700,000 on-line searches in 1974[3] to more than two million in 1977.[2] These search figures are restricted to bibliographic and bibliographic-related data bases-- those that do not contain bibliographic references but pointers to bibliographic references or indexes, such as the CASIA file of Chemical Abstracts Service. There are also factual/numeric and representational data bases, but they are not included in the figures presented above. Representational data bases contain pictorial or graphic information. Currently, the majority of the action in libraries is with bibliographic data bases, but I anticipate a great increase in the use of numeric data bases.

Data Base Production. The file that we search on-line is a computer-readable data base. These data bases are, or have been historically, created in several ways.[4] Initially, they were by-products of A&I publication, then they became direct products, that is, A&I publishers produced data bases together with hard copy products, taking into account the search requirements of the data base, as well as the hard copy product. Both products were produced for distribution. Somewhat later we saw the direct production of data bases with no hard copy counterpart, i. e., distributable tapes but no printed publication. Finally, there are systems that produce data bases for on-line searching with no print product and no distributable tape. In the future, we are going to see more of this kind of activity. The A&I sources will be less and less used in hard copy form, and there will be more electronic distribution of and access to information.

Reasons for On-line Searching. There are many reasons for using on-line services.[5] The systems are used because users are satisfied, and they are satisfied for a number of reasons. They find they get very fast turnaround and access to very extensive files. They can access many different sources without having to move from one location. It is easy to ask a

search question. Hard copy output is provided as well as CRT displays.
The output is formatted in a standard manner. It is easy to demonstrate on-
line systems; it is easy to show a client what he is likely to get. The re-
quester has control over his on-line search, and, in fact, the requesters
usually are present during an on-line search session so that they can change
the direction of the search when they want to. It is easy for the searcher to
switch from one file to another file without moving from the terminal; alternatively, a manual search in a library might require that the searcher change
location several times to access several A&I sources. It is possible to store
questions for reuse at a later time against the same data base. The same
question can be stored and used against a different data base, thus saving
input or typing time. Overall, on-line searching makes it possible to provide more searches for more clients with fewer staff members. Probably
the most significant feature and the reason for client satisfaction is that there
are economic benefits. The availability of data bases on-line decreases the
need, on the part of individual organizations, for purchasing or leasing data
bases, computers, and associated equipment for developing, maintaining,
and operating computer search software systems, and for providing the operating, management, and marketing staff for the system. These expenses run
to hundreds of thousands or millions of dollars. A large number of searches
can be provided for tens of thousands of dollars, even when accounting for
the staff time used in searching and search-related activities.

On-line Services. On-line services are of many types. We are
principally concerned with on-line retrospective and on-line current awareness (SDI) searches. However, there are other on-line services now available, and even more in development. These include:[6] numeric data retrieval;
library activities in addition to reference services (selection, acquisition,
cataloging, and interlibrary loan); location of library resources; document
ordering through vendors of data base searches (e.g., the SDC Electronic
Mailbox Service); referral to data base resources and services; referral to
people, places and conferences; news announcements; electronic mail service;
teleconferencing; data base transferring within networks (i.e., transferring
a file or portion of a file from one location to another location); data base
augmentation (i.e., transferring a desired portion of a file or a data item
from one file to another to augment data in the other file); personal data base
maintenance, which is being done now by several of the on-line vendors via
special contract arrangements; Teletext or home television search services
--two such experimental services are operated in England; and, finally, in
the future I hope we will see widespread fact retrieval and, eventually, even
computer-assisted knowledge retrieval on-line.

CLIENTELES

Clienteles can be defined in terms of the data base use chain,[7] which
involves: the data base producer; the first-party user, or the on-line vendor,

who acquires the data base through a licensing arrangement and processes
it; the second-party user, or broker, who searches a data base on-line and
sells the results to a third-party user; the third-party user, who may be an
information specialist in some other organization; and the fourth-party user,
or end-user. Either the information specialist or end-user could be a second-
party user, if he/she does his/her own on-line searching.

The data base use chain can be looked at in more detail, bringing in
others who are involved, but are less directly involved with the specific bibliographic references than the 1st, 2nd, 3rd, and 4th party users. An expanded data base use chain involves producers, processors, search service
managers (may be either a brokerage organization or an organization that
requires search services for its own internal purposes), searchers or intermediaries, end-users, and managers of end-users.

Each of these has a different kind of responsibility and a different
motivation for providing data base services. The data base producer is
interested in obtaining sales or use of his data base. He also wants to ensure
that the files are used properly. The data base processors are interested in
sales/use of their systems--not specifically the data base, but the data base
on their system. They are concerned that the files be properly used and the
system be properly used, because improper use leads to dissatisfied users,
or dissatisfied customers. The managers of search services are interested
in the use of the system, but they are also interested in increased productivity
of their staff and improvement or expansion of services. The searchers, or
intermediaries, are also interested in sales or use of the system, because
they have to promote it or be sure that it is used, or they themselves will not
function effectively. Searchers are also interested in the proper use of files
and systems, or they cannot provide an effective service to their users.
Both end-users and the end-user's management are interested in results.
They are concerned with the impact that on-line searching (just as any other
service) has on the research or development that is carried out in the organization. They are interested in the increased productivity of their researchers; they are interested in anything that saves dollars or time. They do not
want to spend a lot of time in doing manual library searching, but could use
an on-line searching service to save time in acquiring information. The
motivations differ for the different clienteles or members of the data base
use chain.

One can also look at these classes of data base users in the reverse
direction. That is, the impact is not only on the users, but the users can
have an impact on the providers. The users at every level may communicate
their needs and views in order to change or improve the resources or the
services that are provided to them by those above them in the chain. In terms
of providing near future response or having an impact that will be fairly close
at hand, the end-user may communicate his problems or needs to the search

services, to the on-line vendor, and, eventually, back to the data base producer. And, at each level, the number of contacts required decreases.
Impacts can be made not only for near future results. Long term results
can be effected, too. Data base producers and on-line vendors are more
likely to be interested in short term changes than in changes that may require ten years to produce. They have immediate economic concerns; they
must be at least self-supporting, hopefully make money, and provide a useful
and good service. They may not be interested in doing the kind of research
and testing that is necessary to produce very long term changes. Needs that
require long term research should be communicated by users to researchers
or research sponsors who then can see that research is done. The results
of those research projects, when completed and publicized, can be used by
data base producers and/or on-line vendors for the subsequent benefit of
search service organizations, searchers, and end-users.

PROBLEMS

        The fact that on-line systems are good, useful, and economically
viable is evidenced by the fact that we have gone from 700,000 searches per
year to two million searches per year in only four years time. There is,
however, room for improvement. Some improvements can be made quite
readily, some require short term research, and some require long term
research. There are still more users or potential users who could benefit
from on-line services. Many of these people are not now using on-line services for a number of reasons. Systems are not easy enough to use for many
of them, i.e., they are not willing to invest a few days time to learn a system. Reasons for the complication of systems are related to the variety and
variability found in the resources and services. Variety and variability exist
with respect to the data base sources themselves. They differ with respect
to content, type, data elements included, format, years covered, vocabularies and codes, etc. Systems differ with respect to command languages,
protocols, features, system responses, data element labels, and data base
loading. The existence of all this variety and variability is included among
the reasons why we have intermediaries and professional searchers. They
are the people who can use systems effectively if they keep up with all the
variety and keep up-to-date as change takes place, as new data bases, new
vocabulary structures, new vocabulary terms, new commands, and new features are introduced. They must keep up with these changes so that they can
provide a good service to the end-user. The end-user does not want to contend with all this variability. It is a fact that data bases are increasing in
number and size, new systems are being introduced, and the straightforward
problem of knowing what is available on-line and where, is becoming increasingly more difficult.

SOLUTIONS

This leaves us with a bit of a dilemma, because if the number and variety of data bases and systems increases, the need for intermediaries increases. The end-user himself is less able to cope. The end-user has more confusion. His confusion increases as all these other factors increase. What can be done to simplify the situation and to make people aware of what resources are available and how to use them? There are several possibilities. Traditionally, people became informed about the use of systems and sources through training sessions, such as workshops and seminars; through educational programs, such as university courses or continuing education sources; through the use of tools, such as instruction manuals and user aids; and through the use of CAI programs and on-line training systems. There is, however, another alternative, and that is the development of more user-oriented systems for retrieving desired information.

There are several steps involved in retrieving information.[6] The user who wants information (or his representative who is a searcher) will need to 1) identify and select A&I sources, 2) locate the A&I sources, 3) search the sources to identify the documents he wants to see, 4) locate the primary document, 5) order or access that primary document, 6) search the text of that document, 7) locate the facts in the document that are needed, and 8) assimilate that information for his own research. The lapse time required to go through the steps is not trivial. Parallel to that, you can look at goals for retrieval. Retrieval goals include:[6] a) retrieval of information sources, or a directory type of activity, b) retrieval of information or data itself, c) fact retrieval, and d) knowledge retrieval. The user ultimately wants to eliminate the uncertainty that he has. At present, most of the systems are type "a" systems. They are involved in retrieval of information sources. In fact, retrieval steps 1 through 5 are really associated with locating information sources rather than the actual information. Very few systems are type "b" systems. Some systems retrieve explicit facts but none provide true fact or knowledge retrieval. These are much more sophisticated activities and much more elusive. Considerable research will be needed to achieve fact and knowledge retrieval. We need to do research aiming in that direction in order to improve the user-orientedness of systems. We should work toward reducing the obviousness of the eight distinct steps. The user should not have to be aware of the distinct steps of selecting a secondary source or locating the source or questioning the source, etc. He should be able to enter a question and get back as much information as he needs to answer the question. It is quite conceivable that steps 1 through 4 could be interconnected and appear as one step. Once the full text of primary documents is available on-line, steps 5 and 6 could be integrated into the search procedure. Steps 7 and 8 are certainly going to be more difficult to achieve and will require considerable research.

There are some research projects being conducted right now that aim toward making systems more user-oriented. Some such projects include: the automatic logon work being done at MIT; the design of an automatic data base selector at the University of Illinois; network modelling at EDUCOM; development of user-cordial interfaces at NLM; data base mapping for switching from one data base to another within a distributive network, at the University of Illinois; analysis of architecture for distributive networks at Lehigh University; data tagging being done at Chemical Abstracts Service and Engineering Index; automatic conversion of access protocols at the National Bureau of Standards; vocabulary switching at Battelle; design of a common command language at MIT; subset clustering research results at IITRI; and text understanding work at New York University. Some of these projects are quite elementary and will require considerably more effort to reach the stage where their results can be used by on-line services. They are, however, working in the right direction.

TRENDS

Finally, I would like to mention some of the trends that will affect the future of on-line retrieval.[7]   There are two types of trends--quantitative and qualitative. From the quantitative point of view, we can definitely see that there will be more data bases, they will increase in size, there will be more systems, more terminals in use, more networks, more inclusive networks, more minicomputers and intelligent terminals for local processing, more storage permitting larger files to be maintained on-line, more access to systems and data bases, more on-line data bases, more searches per year of the bibliographic data bases, more searches per year per user (as users find other reasons for using the on-line services), more users of numeric data bases, more textual data bases, and more searches of textual data bases.

We can also anticipate some qualitative changes. The quantitative changes are pretty much related to current and near future technology, and they will happen as soon as the economics are favorable. From the qualitative point of view, though, we are going to see some other changes. There will be data bases covering different subject matter. There will be different types of data bases, thus more use of pictorial or graphic data bases, etc. We will see the development of distributive data bases where files or portions of files reside in different locations with logical interconnections. There will be ties between different types of data bases, whether they are numeric, bibliographic, pictorial, graphic, or any other type. There will be more local processing of subsets or retrieval sets through mimicomputers or intelligent terminals, and, hopefully, we will eventually reach the stage of fact retrieval and knowledge retrieval.

REFERENCES

(This paper synthesizes ideas presented by the author in several
other papers. These papers are cited here.)

1. Peters, Paul and Detlefsen, Ellen. "Impact of On-line Systems on the
   Clientele," Chapter 12 in this volume.

2. Williams, M. E. "Data Base and On-line Statistics--1977," Bulletin
   of the American Society of Information Science, Vol. 4, No. 2,
   December 1977, pp. 21-23.

3. Williams, M. E. "Data About Data Bases," Bulletin of the American
   Society of Information Science, Vol. 3, No. 2, December 1976, pp. 20-
   21.

4. Williams, M. E. "The Impact of Machine-Readable Data Bases on
   Library and Information Services," Information Processing and Management, Vol. 13, 1977, pp. 95-107.

5. Williams, M. E. "Networks for On-line Data Base Access," Journal
   of the American Society for Information Science, Vol. 28, No. 5,
   September 1977, pp. 247-253.

6. Williams, M. E. "On-line Retrieval--Today and Tomorrow," In:
   Proceedings of the First International On-line Meeting, London, England,
   published by Learned Information Ltd., 1977, pp. 1-15.

7. Williams, M. E. "Education and Training for Data Base Use," (Key-
   note address) In: Proceedings of the EUSIDIC Conference on User
   Education, Graz, Austria, December 1976. Aslib Press, London,
   England, 1977, and in Journal of Library Automation, Vol. 10, No. 4,
   December 1977, pp. 320-334.

Chapter 14

IMPACT: DISCUSSION

The discussion which follows has been transcribed from tape recordings, summarized, and edited. Comments and questions have been attributed
to speakers when their identity was provided. The editors of these proceedings take responsibility for any errors in fact or interpretation resulting
from this process, since it was not feasible to provide proofs to discussants
for checking.

Leon Montgomery - University of Pittsburgh

My question is directed to Dr. Burchinal: The recent report of the
task force which reviewed the NSF Division of Science Information recommended a number of substantive changes. These changes included more
emphasis on information science. With this background, I have two questions.
(1) Can you provide us with some insight as to what these changes might
mean? (2) In this new environment, are general guidelines available with
regard to appropriate proposed research areas? For example, is on-line
systems research within the area of the new domain of research?

Lee Burchinal

I believe there is confusion and anxiety in the field today. NSF did
have a task force looking at the area of "science information" activities,
which is technically the name of our program and of our "budget line" for
the research work that is carried out in information science. The task force
did make a report. The director chose not to act on the report as it was
received. Instead it was sent to 50-60 chosen people around the country.
Another 20-30 volunteered comments. So a large number of comments have
been received in the Foundation. These comments raised, in my opinion,
sharper sets of issues than were delivered by the task force report itself.
Consequently, the management of the Foundation is still reviewing the task
force report as well as the comments received. However, we have made

157

one decision: to make, in effect, "de jure" what has really been "de facto".
By this I mean that, although our program has been called "science information" activities (also in the budget line), about 80-85% of the awards are
really for "information science" research. So there should be available
within a few weeks a new program announcement from NSF, calling for research in information science. We have identified three areas, as suggestive
areas (although there are no real limitations on what may be submitted, as
long as it qualifies as information science research): (1) stimulation of
fundamental, basic research in information science--toward the theoretical,
conceptual end--to try to strengthen the bases of this emerging discipline;
(2) applied research--at any point of the information transfer cycle, starting
with the recording of authors' output and continuing through information
capture, distribution, transfer, storage, and retrieval, including on-line
services as well as other technologies, management questions, economics,
etc.; (3) continued work on collection and analysis of data on the structure,
functioning, and changes in the scientific and technical communications system, maintaining the kind of work supported with NCLIS in the photocopying
study, or Don King's work on the size of the STI enterprise, etc. For those
who are research oriented, and want to obtain a copy of this announcement
(NSF-77-77), call my office (202/632-5824) or write to the Publications
Office, NSF. Proposals may be submitted at any time.

We are in business; there is an active program; there is $4.8 million
of research money available this fiscal year for information science research.
Because of some degree of uncertainty in the field, the normal flow of proposals is a little below the level that we would customarily have at this time.
So you have a good "shot" at some research opportunities: take it!

I should note, finally, that most, if not all, of the research studies
cited at this conference were supported by NSF.

Gaya Agrawal - Robert Morris College, Pittsburgh

Question to Martha Williams: I recall an announcement that you
received a grant to prepare a data base of data bases. Is there a report
available?

Martha Williams

The grant was not for the purpose you mention, but it was done any-
way. The grant was to do a feasibility study on mapping of data bases to
show the relation between various data bases. The final report should be
ready January 1978. The data base of data bases exists "in-house" and is
used for generating directories of data bases, etc.

There is a data base directory which was published in 1976 by the American Society for Information Science.

Sidney Winn - Gulf Science and Technology Company, Pittsburgh

Question to Martha Williams: You indicated that you were doing research on switching from one data base to another. Our experience has been that most of our searches are carried out in multiple data bases; we always have the problem of handling the duplicate references. Is there any work being done on elimination of this duplication, with a combined printout as the result of a search of several files?

Martha Williams

We recently submitted a report to the Illinois State Library on identifying duplicate records in multiple files (relating to monographs). The results are quite satisfactory even when dealing with different formats. This method could be applied to journal references as well. The report will be sent to ERIC and NTIS for distribution.

Sue Martin - University of California, Berkeley

Regarding the mention by John Lorenz of the Copyright Clearance Center: This center is not required by law; and libraries are not required to join. A library would be well-advised to examine its own photocopying experience before making a judgment as to the usefulness of the center.

John Lorenz

I agree. Libraries should take advantage of all rights and privileges under "fair use" before going to any commercial service.

Sue Martin

Regarding Martha Williams' discussion of variety and variability in data bases: In Lancaster's book on "The Measurement and Effectiveness of Library Service," he cited a study which compared data base retrieval and retrieval from published "hard copy" services with retrieval from personal searching of library catalogs and other sources. He found that there was a significant proportion of references that could not be located because of the original indexing. This is another factor that should be considered.

Martha Williams

With such techniques as subset clustering, it may be possible to locate references even when the exact search terms desired are not available.

Mary Jo Lynch - American Library Association

Regarding the Copyright Clearance Center: The latest issue of the Washington Newsletter deals with the things librarians should consider. This is the first thorough analysis from the librarians' point of view.

Barbara Robinson - Council of Governments, Washington, D. C.

Regarding Martha Williams' discussion of research problems on protocols and loading problems: How much can we expect from the systems such as SDC and Lockheed in cooperation, and reconciliation of the design problems, to reach the goal of one point of entry? We understand that the content of data bases must be different, but what about the "container"?

Martha Williams

Standardization of data bases would effect some positive changes; however, the data base producers have huge investments, and it is unlikely that they would standardize with regard to vocabulary, for example. They may standardize on a few of the data elements; there is a study underway by NFAIS, ASIDIC, USIDIC, and ICSU/AB to develop a minimal set of required data elements for all data bases. So far, the data base producers involved have been quite responsive, and probably will implement.

There are many ways of achieving "transparency" for the user of on-line services. Translation programs can be developed; alternatively, one standard command language can be used to translate into the language of a specific system. Or Lockheed might develop another entry into their system for users who want to use the command language or ORBIT (SDC) or NLM. Other systems could do the same thing if they have the motivation to do so.

Some things cannot be accomplished technically. There are some features that exist in one system and not in another, obviously preventing translation.

Douglas Price - National Commission on Libraries and Information Science

Returning to the Copyright Clearance Center, the 25¢ charge per transaction is paid by the publisher for processing the payment for them. This amount is substracted from the royalty fees established by the publisher. This charge is for post-1977 material that is coded (fee printed on the item). For uncoded, pre-1978 material, the charge is 50¢.

Some publishers will not require royalty payments. Other than these, it should be expected that the fee will be substantially higher than 25¢ or 50¢ (some publishers expect to charge several dollars).

Use of the center is not mandatory, but may prove very useful to those libraries whose circumstances warrant its use, e.g., need for rapid turnaround.

John Lorenz

The center will not provide copies, but only collect royalty payments. The copies will have to come from elsewhere.

Christine Borgman - Dallas Public Library

Regarding impact on clientele, are libraries using on-line systems to serve essentially the same clientele and to provide the same information in alternate form, or are we really redefining our clientele? This would force new marketing and user studies and a new definition of hiring requirements and job descriptions.

Paul Peters

A little bit of both. I feel it is primarily new clienteles. In certain libraries it is old clienteles served in new ways, as in special libraries. User surveys that have been conducted in special libraries are applicable. In academic and public libraries, I'm not so sure. I think that the statistics show that in academic libraries, generally, these systems are being used to introduce a new service. Consequently, I think they are designed to serve a new clientele. In the sense of need, the clientele may always have been there, but the response of the library to the need is new.

Chapter 15

IMPACT OF ON-LINE SYSTEMS

Alphonse F. Trezza

Executive Director
National Commission on Libraries
and Information Science
Washington, D. C.

The National Commission in its enabling legislation does have a
mandate. Public Law 91-345 declares a national policy for information.
I'll read the very brief statement in the law, Section 2, that: "Congress
hereby affirms that library and information services, adequate to meet the
needs of the people of the United States, are essential to achieve national
goals and to utilize most effectively the nation's educational resources, and
that the Federal Government will cooperate with state and local governments
and public and private agencies in assuring optimum provision of such services. " Now that, in my opinion, is a strong national policy statement. Our
problem is that we forget it's in the law. And we forget to remind the
decision-makers that it is in the law, and that either they ought to support
implementation of it or they ought to delete or change it.

During the time the National Commission was developing its national
program document, and as Carlos Cuadra read to you, they did adopt a basic
overall goal. It is important enough to repeat "to eventually provide every
individual in the United States with equal opportunity of access to that part
of the total information resource which will satisfy the individual's educational, working, cultural and leisure time needs and interests, regardless of
the individual's location, social condition or level of achievement. " And in
the preface of our program document, Dr. Burkhardt, our Chairman, states:
"Users of information, the American citizens, have been paramount in all the
Commission's deliberations. The proposed program aims to increase each
person's access to the nation's rich knowledge resources. "

So clearly then, the National Commission is user-oriented. We exist to assure service for the residents of the United States. And not to serve the specialized needs of any group, be they librarians, information specialists, government agencies, or the private sector. It is a difficult role. It imposes a real dilemma for the Commission, because it is awfully easy, too easy I'm afraid, to enunciate goals and high sounding ideals. The big problem is how do you translate goals into action and produce results. Of what value are all these large and comprehensive data bases if they never really serve the needs of users.

For the last day and a half we've been discussing just who is the user. Is it the university faculty and students who require the sophisticated science and technical information? Or is it the user who walks in off the street to go to the local public library? Or students who use their school libraries? Or businessmen who use the special libraries? Of course the answer is simple. It is all of them, isn't it? We really are not trying to say it is one or the other. We're saying it's all, but that immediately imposes the dilemma I mentioned. When we adopted our broad goals, the dilemma presented was can we economically afford it?

Someone referred to that this morning and said that the conclusion was that you can probably not have excellence in service and also equal opportunity of access. Well, I must say that I personally, and I'm sure the Commission, is not prepared to accept that conclusion. Absolutely not. It is possible and it can and will be done. You know, we keep hearing about tight money policy. I can't remember in my professional career, which started way back in 1949, when we did not have a tight-money year. I get a little tired hearing that federal and state money is tight, institutional budgets are tight, etc. They have always cut budgets, especially library budgets. I was at the University of Pennsylvania in the early 1950's and we lived through six years of nothing but tight budgets. I'm sure Dick De Gennaro is living through tight budgets again, and we will continue to do so in the 1980's and 1990's.

The dilemma is this. You and I, as library and information specialists, have failed to convince our immediate decision-makers, our bosses, local and state legislators and our Federal Government that information really is so important that library and information services deserve a higher priority and, therefore, a greater share of the money that is available. We're probably spending more money today than ever in the history of the United States. But, yet, we keep saying there is not enough money around. The money is there. We're just not getting our fair share. It's a matter of priority, isn't it? Think about that for a moment and relate it to the problem we've been discussing of fee or free service. I think that the words fee or free are a misnomer. What we're really saying is when can services be paid for indirectly through taxation and when can services be paid for directly

--out of the user's pocket? That's really what we're saying. At what point does the institution say, I cannot get it from my budget and, therefore, it comes from a direct user charge.

Public libraries are supported by local property taxes and some state funds. A large proportion of the academic libraries are supported by state funds with some federal help and all the school libraries, at least the public schools, are supported by local and state funds. So, obviously, all of us are already paying once for all of this service. We traditionally have called library service in that context free. And that's a legitimate description. Let's not play games, as Anita Schedler said, with the quotes. We know what we mean when we say free service. That's what we mean. We mean we pay for service by our taxes. Now, should we offer all of our services with no direct payment by the user? It's a delicate question. It's a complicated question. The profession does not have an answer yet. The profession has only started to seriously discuss it in the last year or so. The National Commission, for example, at one or two of its meetings, has briefly and gingerly discussed the subject. We have not arrived at a firm policy that we would like to recommend for consideration.

We have some ideas, the general feeling is that the decision as to whether there is to be a direct fee paid really should rest with the institution and not with the Federal or State Goverment. We should not, that is the Commission, recommend a policy which says there ought to be direct fee services, or there ought to be only free services. We want to encourage more debate and hopefully to better understand the ramifications of the problem. We are saying to the institution--local public, academic, school and special library, you make the decision at your local level, just as you do when you decide how to hire staff, how to buy books, when to build a new building, when to buy new equipment, etc. It's a budgetary decision based on priorities. You decide the priority.

Think back a little. After World War II, the book budgets at universities increased dramatically, but look at them today, and you will notice the tremendous shift in the amount of the book budget that is spent for journals compared to the amount that was spent years ago. You will discover that what the decision-makers decided was, as a matter of priority, to put more of the acquisitions money into journals and that meant less for books. Okay, then by following the same reasoning a library might well decide that data base services are so basic, are so important, that they deserve a priority in the budget and, therefore, will be charged to the book budget and something else has to suffer for it--less monographs or journals, for example, or perhaps less staff.

The point I'm making, strongly I hope, is that the best place to make the fee or free decision is at the local level, the local institutional level, and not have it handed down from above, be it from the government or the private sector. The private sector doesn't care where they get their money as long as they get it. And, as long as their service is good and is effective and supplies the need, we'll pay for it. It's that simple.

Let me toss in a couple more ideas before I run out of time. Someone asked me what the Commission's views have been in the whole area of the provision of resources. As you know, the whole idea of a national network is based on a philosophy of what we call a full service network. We're not primarily interested in an automated network. We're not primarily interested in a manual network. We're interested in a full service network. That means total library services. Now, we obviously want to use the latest and the best in technology, give the best possible services in the most cost-effective way. Thus, we strongly advocate the effective use of technology.

A Commission study undertaken about three years ago recommended the sharing of library resources at the regional and national level. The conclusion was that it must be done in an organized fashion. We obviously could not attack the whole problem or all of the elements at one time. We decided we would begin with periodicals. Our plan was to then look at monographs and at non-print media. The periodical report, as you have all read in the literature recently, has been completed by an NCLIS task force after about eighteen months of work. The report on The Effective Access to Periodical Literature has been released. It recommends a national system of three levels. We recognized the fact that at the state and regional level you are already supplying 80% of need. MINITEX, for example, supplies an even higher level of demand. We recognize that that last 5% is very elusive and should be provided for by those very large academic institutions such as Harvard and Yale, the University of Pennsylvania, Illinois, etc. And it is that middle gap that presents a problem and our report recommends that there should be a dedicated national periodical center and that the Library of Congress ought to assume the responsibility for its administration and operation.

The recommendations of the task force were adopted by the Commission. They were shared, both in their development and final articulation with the library profession, through the Association of Research Libraries, the American Library Association, and a number of other groups representing the public and private sector. The first phase of implementation, the design phase of the National Periodical Center, the dedicated center, will be starting January 1, thanks to a grant from a consortium of foundations to the Library of Congress through the Council of Library Resources. The design phase is expected to take nine months. If all goes well, come 1979, we would hope to be able to start actually providing services from the National Center.

We are now going to start deliberations on how to share monographic
resources. John Lorenz mentioned Title II C of the Higher Education Act
(HEA) which obviously is going to give us some concrete help in resolving
this problem. The NCLIS task force is going to study the problems of
how to designate which collections represent a national resource. How many
regional collections do you need? Are the full collections or only portions
of the collection truly a national resource? These problems will be considered
and it is expected that a report with recommendations, which reflect what the
people in a field feel will satisfy the needs of users, will be issued. The third
area of library materials, AV, is currently receiving attention through our
project called Project Media Base. What we've discovered is that that's the
one area where there is, at present, no real bibliographic control. That
study is considering how we can develop an effective system of bibliographic
control of non-print media. You heard the discussion about the bibliographic
control of data bases. It is the same area.

I am sure you've heard enough about the problem of copyright. All I
want to say is that the Commission's study on the patterns of library photocopying which was jointly funded by the Commission, the National Science
Foundation and the National Commission on New Technological Users (CONTU)
is now at GPO and will be available for distribution by the end of the calendar
year. It's a very good report. It has a lot of information which I think will
be very helpful to you in trying to form a base line as we work with the new
law which becomes effective January 1, 1978. I can only echo what John
Lorenz and some of the others have said and that is, don't forget you have
your basic rights of library photocopying delineated in Sections 107 and 108 of
the law. Make sure you understand it. And only when you've exceeded those
provisions do you have to then be a law-abiding librarian and pay your just
royalty fees. The publishers have a right to expect us to be honest in the way
we handle the copyright responsibility and we have a right to expect publishers
not to unduly pressure us to try to get us nervous and force us to pay for photo-
copies which meet the fair use test.

The National Bureau of Standards in cooperation with the Commission
is just completing its study on protocols for computer to computer interface.
I understand from my staff that that study is going to be ready for presentation to the Commission meeting in December, and shortly thereafter will be
released. You heard mention of a publication on the National Information
Policy that was developed by the Committee on the Right of Privacy under the
Ford Administration. The National Commission assumed the responsibility
of publishing and distributing that report. We are also assuming the responsibility of trying to move on implementing those parts of it which effect the
library and information community. If you haven't seen the report, you
should. Later this year or early next year we hope to appoint a task force
which will work on implementation of the recommendations in the national
information policy report that are of basic importance to the library and

information community. The task force will cooperate not only with the various library and information services groups but also with the private sector.

Let me close by talking about the White House Conference on Library
and Information Services for a moment. As you know, the Congress passed
and the President signed the bill for a White House Conference on Library
and Information Services. This is the only time in the history of our country
that we've been presented with this opportunity. The national conference
will be held in Washington, D. C., in 1979--October 28 to November 2.
There are going to be fifty state, six territorial, D. C., and a conference
for American Indians living on or near reservations involved in the preparation of the national conference. Georgia and Pennsylvania have already held
their conferences. There will not be another state conference until this
spring. And sometime between this spring and April 30 of 1979 the remaining
56 conferences will be held. The purpose of the conference is clear. The
administration and the Congress, as recorded in the Congressional Record
and in statements President Carter has made since he has been in office,
have stated that they are looking toward the White House Conference to set
the legislative goals for the eighties.

You think about that for a moment. The impact of that on all of us
is great. We've got to make sure that grassroots involvement in the decision-
making process, both at the state conference and the national conference, is
truly effective. All of the elements of library and information professions
must be involved. You can come up with a few--not fifty, but a handful of
major issues with recommended policies and programs derived from those
issues which will then be considered and discussed at a national conference.
The areas of data bases, fee or free service, the area of categorical aid
versus block aid versus general revenue sharing are all issues that are
essential, if the White House Conference is going to produce results that are
going to effect our problems and your careers for the next ten to fifteen
years. The challenge is yours. All the Commissioners can do is to offer
leadership and instruction and to coordinate efforts. We are a small agency.
We have no operating responsibility whatsoever. We are a coordinating body,
an initiator, an irritant. We're sort of a pin that pricks people into action.
That's our role--we'll try to do the best we can.

Chapter 16

IMPACT OF ON-LINE SYSTEMS: RESPONSE

Roger K. Summit

Manager
Lockheed Information Systems
Palo Alto Research Laboratory
Palo Alto, California

VIEWPOINT

Several observations can be made regarding the three papers which discussed the impact of on-line systems. The overall viewpoint of the presentations is interesting. No longer is the feasibility of on-line retrieval being discussed; rather problems and prospects of on-line are discussed. Such discussions reflect the maturity of the process and problems resulting from its rather rapid development and acceptance. One such problem concerns how to fund these new services. A second problem involves the appropriate roles of the government and commercial sector in the provision of information services. A third problem which seems to thread its way through the papers concerns the overall effect of this new technology on existing institutions and on institutional practices such as those found in libraries and information centers. Another primary topic found in each of the papers relates to the future of on-line systems. As seems to be frequently true in assessing future trends, the scripture often appears to be written according to the patron saint of extrapolation rather than analysis. In particular the reasoning goes that although for the most part on-line searching is being conducted today by librarians with specialized training, if the retrieval languages were made to be simpler and the data bases were constructed more consistently (as they surely must be in the future), then novices will be able to effectively employ these systems with ease.

I would like to present a conceptual framework for on-line systems and relate this framework to the major points and issues presented in the three papers. Consider if you will the following premises:

A. Hardware technology provides the opportunity for innovation in information systems.
B. On-line retrieval has developed because it has made the process of identifying relevant information easier, faster, and cheaper.
C. As a result there will be a trend away from exhaustive collection in favor of selective acquisition on demand.

HARDWARE TECHNOLOGY

Current on-line information systems were made possible by the introduction of the third generation computer technology in 1963. The necessary hardware adjuncts for today's on-line services were:

- Mass random access store - to provide a means for non-sequential access and processing of data

- Terminal control processing - to allow the introduction of a human being in the data processing cycle

- Timesharing - which allows the high costs of large scale data processing to be shared by multiple users

- Telecommunications - which allows demand from widely dispersed geographical points to be concentrated at a single facility

If we wish to anticipate developments in on-line systems, we must look to today's state of the art hardware technology, for it provides the opportunities for future development. The hardware areas of most consequence for on-line systems involve large scale integration (LSI) in electronics, and the development of relatively inexpensive, lightweight ground stations for satellite communications.

LSI means smaller, faster, cheaper and more flexible computers and storage equipment. This, in turn, will allow a greater distribution of processing tasks throughout networks. You will be able to select, store and re-process the results of searches.

Low cost ground stations will most likely be located in every city of any size, and perhaps on the roofs of many organizations. They will provide direct satellite links to any other point on the globe without high cost, terrestrial communication linkages. The development of such ground stations can pave the way for highspeed, low cost facsimile, for example, and can make access to the world's literature feasible from lessor developed countries.

What is not so clear is the basis for assuming that systems will become easier and easier to use. I can recall a required two-week course at Stanford entitled "Sources of Business Information". Even with this two weeks of training, none of us could match the skill and acuity of the librarian in identifying needed information. It now takes us about one day to train a person in the use of the DIALOG commands for searching data bases. While efforts to standardize data bases and simplify the retrieval languages are to be applauded, we should keep in mind that the basic difficulty lies with the very roots of communication itself. The process of describing an information need to the computer is certainly no more simple than describing that need to another knowledgeable human being. Thus, we should not expect that standardized data bases and simple retrieval languages will overcome the fact that most users do not have the "search sophistication, " i.e., the insight as to how to tackle a retrieval problem, that the trained reference librarian acquires with training and experience. Although research work has been carried out over the past decade in trying to program the computer to carry out the inductive and deductive processes required, little progress has been made to date, and the forthcoming dramatic changes in hardware will not change this situation. Furthermore, if a process requires extensive training, it becomes uneconomic to train the occasional user.

We can, however, anticipate the areas of on-line direct end-user use by identifying analogous familiar functions they now perform that can simply be transferred to a computer. Two such functions occur to me: index lookup as in a telephone book, and subject category lookup such as in catalogs or yellow pages. Note that in the first case there is a one-to-one (index) relationship, and in the second case a one-to-many relationship (yellow pages). These functions would suggest the possibility of automation of the card catalog, for example, with direct use by end-users (which indeed has occurred). On-line retrieval, however, involves a many-to-many relationship (i.e., many terms ANDed and ORed which define multiple documents). This is a much more difficult operation than simple index lookup, and there are no analogous intuitive processes occurring in everyday life.

PROBLEMS AND CHALLENGES

Now let us examine some of the problems and challenges addressed in the three papers (Chapters 8, 10 and 12). The first is appropriate roles for the public and private sectors in on-line systems. The government currently plays an all-pervasive role in information. This role extends from the development of mission-oriented data bases by NASA, ERDA, NAL, NIE, NTIS, NOAA, Defense Documentation Center, National Library of Medicine

and others, through the sponsoring and training of librarians in the use of
on-line systems via National Science Foundation and other agencies, to the
direct offering of on-line services both on an intra-agency basis as well as
subsidized offerings to contractors and even the general public. Professional
as well as commercial organizations are also developing data bases which
are offered by commercial and government information retrieval services.
The two sectors complement each other insofar as the following:

- Training and education of users

- Providing awareness of and promoting the use of on-line services

- Sponsoring of research and development of information systems
  and data bases

The government further supports on-line activities through the offering of
direct subsidies to potential users for trial and evaluation of the services.

Conflicts between the two sectors occur as a result of:

- The pricing of government services at preemptive or non-com-
  petitive rates which discourage commercial services in similar
  areas

- Differences in accounting methods which tend to make costs non-
  comparable between the two sectors

- The withholding of government data bases developed with public
  funds from commercial services or the pricing of these data
  bases at rates which discourage commercial acquisition

Aside from these issues one must consider the First Amendment and
competitive implications inherent in a total reliance on government-based
information systems. It is the case that government services tend to drive
out commercial services in similar areas. Throughout history we have
vigorously defended the independence of the primary information providers
and limited the right of the government to control published information; we
should give the same consideration to secondary information. This point
was alluded to yesterday by Jane Hersch of Montgomery County Library when
she suggested the difficulty of finding non-supportive Viet Nam War literature.
As to competition, the existence of more than a dozen on-line information
services around the world would seem to offer a high degree of protection to
the on-line system user. Competition is the user's insurance policy to assure
the provision of a wide variety of data bases at a high level of service quality
at competitive prices--and, incidentally, competition is increasing in every
respect. It would not seem to be in our national interest to encourage total
reliance upon government provision of these services.

A second point which received considerable attention in the papers (particularly in that of Miriam Drake) is the question of the funding of on-line services in the library. First of all, we must realize that costs are costs; that the fundamental economics of systems operation do not differ across the three segments of our pluristic society other than as a result of the efficiency of operation and the economies of scale reached by the particular organization in the offering of services. The bills must be paid. And what are these bills? I can recall the installation of DIALOG at the European Space Research Organization in 1969. At that time the entire European space program was supported by an IBM 360/65 computer. It was on this computer that we installed the DIALOG programs providing access to the NASA data base to some half dozen terminals. In addition to DIALOG, this same computer processed telemetry from satellites, controlled launches of the European satellites, and did the myriad of additional processing necessary to support a space research program.

Currently, just to support the DIALOG service, we are operating two dedicated IBM 360/65 computers and have perhaps twenty times the amount of disk storage which was available for that initial application. Add to this the costs of the computer programmers, the operations and maintenance people, the customer support personnel, and the substantial royalties paid back to the data base suppliers and you have a multi-million dollar annual budget simply for the provision of on-line retrieval services. It takes a large number of $10.00 searches to pay the bills for this order of resources. So the question really becomes one of who pays, the public at large or the using patron? Again, Miriam Drake offered practically all the arguments which are fit to print. One point of view, however, is frequently overlooked in these discussions--that of the patron receiving the search. Also overlooked is the question of the cost of not getting information--as illustrated by Allen Kent in looking for a saccharin substitute.

Our recently completed experiment sponsored by the Division of Science Information of the National Science Foundation which investigated provision of on-line retrieval services via public libraries shed some further light on the question of user fees. To recap the experiment, four public libraries in the San Francisco Bay area were involved. The experiment ran for three years to determine the feasibility of public libraries providing data base access to the general public. Because of already over-burdened budgets, it was felt that for on-line searching to be viable in a public library environment, fees would have to be charged. Consequently, during the first year searching was free to the user; during the second year charges were levied at 50% of commercial rates; and during the third year full rates were charged. Although fee-for-service was probably the most emotionally charged and difficult issue that we dealt with during the experiment, it turned out in actual experience to be a non-issue. Anticipating patron dissatisfaction, collection difficulties, and other difficulties commonly associated with commercial services, we established an elaborate refund mechanism within the experiment. To

my knowledge not one refund has been requested, nor has there been significant displeasure registered by users of this service. A second concern is
that fees discriminate. Again we found that the service was not used by those
who could not afford to pay (with the exception of local students) even though
it was widely publicized and free of charge during the first year. What we
did find, however, was that the retrieval service was used quite differently
during the free period than it was during the fee period. For example:

- During the free period, teachers at San Jose State gave classroom assignments wherein each student was to have a search
  performed. This resulted in a substantial overload on the
  facilities at San Jose Public Library.

- Time per search on the terminal was much longer when
  searching was free than when a fee was charged.

- The library was less able to accommodate to the overall demand
  for service during the free period.

- The amount of the fee, as long as there was some charge,
  seemed to make relatively little difference in the level of
  demand, whereas when the cost went from free to fifty percent
  charge, demand dropped by eighty to ninety percent.

One last argument on funding: whereas the economic sense of libraries comes from a one-time investment in resources (namely books and periodicals) with multiple or unlimited usage, the on-line search is a custom
product--the cost of which cannot be shared across several users of that
product. The question thus becomes one of fairness: whether the taxpayer
should bear the cost of that search or whether the individual for whom the
search was conducted should bear the cost. This is not to argue that subsidies should not be made available to those who are unable to afford the cost
of searching. Such a procedure would seem far less costly than spreading
the total costs across society.

AWARENESS

Probably the biggest problem and challenge we all face is that of providing awareness to the profession and to the public at large. Over the years,
the interest in using on-line retrieval has moved from a starting point in
1966-1968 in a couple of federal agency libraries, through special libraries
in large companies in 1969 and the early seventies, and to the university
libraries three years ago. In the last one to two years, interest from public
libraries has begun to emerge (like waves and incoming tide). On-line retrieval has not yet caught the interest of the popular writer nor is it used by

people other than those in well-established professions. This is not because of the cost of searching, the inconvenience of using a terminal, or lack of coverage in the systems; it is rather simply a matter of lack of awareness among the population of the powerful tool that exists for everyone, but is used by relatively few. Dr. Burchinal indicates that these tools have only recently begun to receive the attention they deserve.

THE FUTURE

Just as five years ago none of us would have likely predicted the level and scale of on-line services available today, five years from now we are likely to be equally surprised. What we observe is not a shift in information usage from traditional sources to on-line sources, but rather a new influx of information users who were previously put off by or unable to utilize the traditional tools effectively. We can anticipate that the librarian will continue to play a critically important role in the provision of these services.

In evaluating the status of the on-line revolution, it is more useful to look at direction and trend than to try to assess position. The current position of on-line is analogous to the immediate post-Gutenberg period: then relatively large numbers of books were capable of production but such production faced a largely illiterate usership. We now need to educate the public into information literacy.

Chapter 17

IMPACT OF ON-LINE SERVICES
ON THE ACADEMIC LIBRARY

Richard De Gennaro

Director of Libraries
University of Pennsylvania
Philadelphia, Pennsylvania

In 1973, I wrote a paper to try to counter the view that was widely
held at that time that academic research libraries were going to have to begin
subscribing to the growing number of tapes of bibliographic data bases in
machine-readable form and to provide current awareness and other services
from them for their local users. (The paper was published in the December
1973 issue of the Journal of Library Automation with the title "Providing
bibliographic search services from machine-readable data bases; the
library's role.") In the paper I said that high costs and the nature of the
demand would make it unfeasible for libraries to subscribe to tape services
and to establish local processing centers, and that it looked as though the
newly available on-line commercial services would become the dominant
means of gaining access to these data bases and that librarians would become
brokers for on-line services. The critical question then (and now) was: will
the user be charged for the services he/she uses or will the costs be absorbed
by the library? The answer to that question would determine how and to what
extent the on-line services would be used in the future. If they were free,
the use would be high. If the user had to pay, then use would be more moderate. I predicted that a combination of institutional subsidy for indirect costs
and individual charges for direct costs would evolve as the dominant method
of paying for computerized bibliographic services.

My purpose then was to try to put these powerful emerging capabilities
into perspective for library decision makers--and that is my purpose today.
Like all the other speakers, I, too, believe that on-line search services are

going to revolutionize libraries, but there are other revolutions competing
for our attention. Now I don't want to appear old and wise or cynical, but I
have been experiencing revolutions in libraries ever since I got my first job
at NYPL in 1956. At that time, the current revolutionary technology was
microphotography. We were told it would solve our space problems and
transform our way of servicing readers. The use of microfilm has become
routine since then, but we can hardly call it a revolution. Ultrafiche was
going to revolutionize libraries in the late 1960's but that didn't pan out either.

Actually, the closest thing we had to a revolution in libraries in the
1960's was the Xerox machine, but no one called that one in advance; it just
happened quietly and was taken for granted. But no other technology has had
as much impact on libraries and the way they are used as the copying machine.

There were other revolutions. In the 1960's, the second generation
batch processing computers were going to revolutionize libraries and many
technologists were predicting that the contents of the Library of Congress
would soon be converted to computer tapes via optical scanning and would be
made instantly accessible to anyone anywhere. The conventional library
with books and journals would go the way of the dodo. Then came the MARC
tapes revolution, the OCLC on-line revolution, the network revolution, the
participatory management revolution, the media revolution, the minicomputer
revolution, the resource sharing revolution. No one would deny that we are
living in a period characterized by rapidly accelerating technological change
in libraries (by now it is a cliché), but we have to learn to take these changes
in stride. We live in a real world where we have to make day by day and
week by week decisions in a political environment where the people are real
and demanding and where funds and choices are limited.

The situation we are in today with on-line search services reminds
me of the mid 1960's when we were facing the "computer revolution" in
libraries. Engineers, information scientists, and even some librarians
were predicting the end of libraries. No thinking person can deny that fundamental change (call it revolution if you like) was coming in the next decade
or two in libraries from new technology such as computers, telecommunications, and microtechnology. That is obvious but not very helpful to those of
us who have responsibility for managing libraries. The important questions
are: when and how are these developments going to be implemented in the
working library environment? Timing is everything.

Theoreticians can and should take the long view. They can look ahead
and try to tell us what is coming five or ten years hence, and if they are off
by a few years in their predictions--no harm is done and no one can fault
them for it.

In the case of library technology, the rate of development proved to be slower than was predicted by many in the 60's. The job of automating the library proved to be more difficult than was anticipated, and in fact is happening in ways that were totally unforeseen 15 years ago. OCLC started the on-line revolution in 1971 and over 1,200 libraries are on-line today. Nevertheless, those libraries that tried to go on-line in 1968 failed because the technology and state of the art were not yet ready. A two or three year error in forecasting for a theoretician or anyone without responsibility for acting on his predictions is not serious. However, for those of us who have to act and commit ourselves and our limited resources to a new technology, a mistake in timing of one or two years can be a minor catastrophe. (Larry Buckland of Inforonics used to say that it was the fate of pioneers to get arrows shot in their rears by the Indians.)

Anyone who has pioneered the development or implementation of a new computer-based system knows how serious the consequences can be of a poor choice of equipment or a mistaken conceptual design. Those who planned and built libraries in the early 1960's without expansion space because they believed that microfilm was the storage medium of the future know the consequences of bad timing. Those who built libraries in the 1960's with large rooms in the basement to house the massive computer that would be required for the library in the 1970's also know the consequences of bad timing. One library uses the space to store a collection of little used books. Prudent managers know that it is better to be a year late in adopting a new technology than a year too early.

Fortunately, there are virtually no risks for a library that wishes to get a terminal and offer search services. The investment is small and the systems work. The only mistake you can make is to exaggerate the importance of the service and lose perspective on your other needs.

The first commercial search services came on-line only four years ago in 1973, and now we are told that they are going to revolutionize libraries. We believe it; but when is it coming? How long will it take, five years, ten, or twenty? And what are the various impacts that it will have on journals, A&I services, on libraries, on research? When and in what ways will they be impacted? Nobody really knows for sure. That is the subject of this conference and this panel. My role is to try to forecast the impact that on-line search services will have on research libraries. It is a risky assignment, and I will limit myself to a time frame of three to five years.

At Penn, we were one of the first academic research libraries to begin offering on-line search services with SDC, Lockheed, and the New York Times Information Bank. We started in September 1973. Our policy is to subsidize the indirect costs and change for direct. The impact to date has been slight when viewed in the perspective of the University Library as a whole. We increased our reference staff by one and trained the entire reference staff to use the technique. They loved it. It increased their skills, broadened their horizons, and increased their already heavy workloads. Less than a hundred searches a month are provided for a small but satisfied and ever-increasing number of library users. Despite our best efforts at advertising and selling, the majority of our faculty and researchers have not yet tried the new service and most of them know only vaguely that we are offering it or what it could do for them. In the next few years, the services will continue to expand but the overall impact will continue to be modest.

Perhaps by 1980 the cumulative effects will begin to be felt at an accelerated rate--not just or even primarily at the various reference desks but in the acquisitions department, in the science libraries, and in the budget. On-line services could become one of the important driving forces in a larger context of change. Why?

Rising prices, declining budgets, and increased resource sharing will help bring about the demise of many journals. Libraries may soon begin to rely on on-line searches to turn up a demand for particular articles in lieu of having increasingly expensive subscriptions. This could lead to basic changes in the allocation of library acquisitions funds away from large numbers of subscriptions to little used journals and more reliance on on-demand acquisitions of specific articles and reports through NTIS and ISI's OATS service.

Many libraries can be expected to cancel some hard copy subscriptions to expensive A&I services in favor of relying on on-line searches. This could cause A&I services to raise their prices both of the hard copy editions as well as the tape versions they provide to the vendors. The vendors may have to raise the prices of their services, and this could cause a serious decline in the use of such services by libraries. A price increase could also exacerbate the already bitter debates about whether libraries should give these services free to all their users or only provide them to those who can pay for them. Those libraries which are fully or partially subsidizing these services now may be hard put to continue the subsidies if the prices go up.

A sharp increase in the cost of on-line searching is not merely idle speculation on my part. Donald W. King, President of King Research, Inc., has expressed the dilemma as follows:

> My major concern is that increased use of the on-line services at the sacrifice of subscriptions to printed forms will not yield enough return to A&I services. The reason is that current on-line service prices are simply not structured to recover the very large input costs of bibliographic data bases. If A&I

services get caught with a sharp decrease in their traditional subscriptions and without appropriate return on the on-line services, they could be in serious difficulty. Just as NTIS increased microform prices, the price of on-line services must also increase as users switch from printed form to on-line services. However, if the bibliographic search services charge a sufficiently high price to recover the large input cost, there is a good chance that libraries in turn will begin to decrease use of on-line services and these services will not recover their costs. This is a dilemma which I consider to be the most pressing issue in our field at the current time since it has such far-reaching implications on current services as well as on development of future systems... (BASIS, June 1977, p. 40).

We have to guard against the very human tendency we have to see the future as a continuation of present trends. Because we have seen a 20% annual increase in on-line searches in the last few years, we assume that it is bound to continue and increase indefinitely. Anyone who has experience in the stock market knows that this is a dangerous fallacy. Who could have predicted the depression in higher education that began in 1970 or the energy crisis in 1974?

It is not at all certain at this time that libraries will be the primary searchers of on-line data bases in the future. This is an area where commercial information brokers who have no qualms about charging could take over a substantial part of the market. They could perhaps do the searches more efficiently by having skilled subject specialists working on a high volume basis.

Perhaps libraries, as a result of political and philosophical considerations, will not be able to charge their users enough to cover the high cost of these searches or they simply may not have the money to subsidize them.

There are indications that suggest that over the course of the next decade academic research libraries will undergo substantial changes. Their acquisitions policies may be greatly restricted and their growth rates may diminish. This will be partially caused by and will cause in turn a substantial diminution in the size of library staffs. Increasing staff salaries and benefits will cause some operations and services to be priced out of the market and on-line search services could be among them in many poor libraries.

Chapter 18

IMPACT ON PUBLIC LIBRARIES

Keith Doms

Director
The Free Library of Philadelphia
Philadelphia, Pennsylvania

I represent a very large group of potential consumers of so called "on-line services." We belong to the people of this country for whom, by their mandate, we provide free service. According to the American Library Directory, there are 8,504 public libraries in this country, plus 5,477 branch libraries of city, county, and regional systems--and most of us are not yet in any way on line, although participation is increasing.

However, times have changed and old "show me" attitudes are being displaced rapidly as practitioners have begun to savor some of the benefits of on-line services in both technical and public service areas. As Allen Kent noted in his paper (Chapter 1), the bandwagon is moving and there are riders who are eager to get on board.

Now imagine this little scenario. A large crowd of people is waiting in line to enter a relatively small restaurant that has been receiving rave notices from the critics. As we draw closer to the scene, it is clear that this group is orderly and dressed impeccably. Also, they bear the appearance of indoor, sedentary workers; ah, could they be...yes, they are librarians and information specialists. You can tell because some of them are wearing lapel buttons that read ASIS, ISAD, and "I'm a Knowbody." And as to the restaurant itself--a small discreet sign identifies it as the Alexander Graham Dewey Electronics Commissary, Fred Kilgour, Chef. And what an inviting menu. Not gourmet to be sure, but very nutritious. Among the entrees listed are computer-based circulation control systems. Further down, we see featured as the Chef's special, an OCLC cataloging and location

183

service. It is available either medium or well-done, or can be prepared to
meet special dietary requirements. The next offering is a palate-tickling
COM catalog. I can't think of anything more delectable! And as we proceed
we've just begun to get into ORBIT. Think of it, an assortment of no fewer
than 160 computer-based data banks to choose from! What could be more
"Times-ly"? By the way, an intermediary has just advised me that this
menu is merely a reasonable facsimile.

I assure you that the public library community is eager to feast at
this groaning board. Perhaps this group of consumers is comparable with
the tens of thousands of rural households who eagerly awaited the advent of
a rural electrification program which, when it came "on line, " opened entire
new worlds to countless Americans.

Since I seem to be serving up an uncommon stew today, I would like
to present a notion that has simmered on many a back burner for the last
twenty years or so. The assumption is that if information really is the
national resource we believe it to be, why not view networking and the provision of selected on-line services as a national utility?

Can we accomplish for our clientele what REA achieved in large parts
of our nation? Can we illuminate the nation with information? Are we not in
the same spot as the potential customer for a new car who wants it ever so
badly, but has not been able to arrange the financing?

Public library managers must deal with the question, "How do we
move into the Computer Age?" Will it be in an orderly, planned way, or
willy-nilly? Are we willing to accept the fact that planning based on growth
may be an obsolete concept. Public libraries, generally, large and small,
with few exceptions simply lack the funds needed to take full advantage of
available on-line services. Fiscal constraints are severe and cutbacks and
retrenchments are reported regularly in both the library and commercial
press. What's more, there is virtually no money for research and development, except from a limited number of federal and private sources. And as
inflation continues, there appear to be fewer and fewer trade-off possibilities
left in the typical public library budget. That is to say, reduction of staff in
exchange for purchase of services, or reductions in the materials budget,
with the savings to be used to buy on-line services is surrealistic if not down-
right unreal.

Again, with certain notable exceptions, a large number of public
libraries are stacked in hold patterns with many losing altitude rapidly. On
November 6, the New York Times likened many of our larger, older cities
to federal dependencies. The same newspaper, one day later, noted that
desirable cities such as Seattle and Tucson are currently beginning to be
caught up in the same demographic shifts that proved so ruinous to so many

East Coast cities. It is a grim fact that many of our city libraries would
literally have their backs against the wall if it were not for large numbers
of federally funded positions available under programs such as CETA.

In my opinion, fiscal constraints are the greatest barrier to adequate
and appropriate public library participation in the entire area of electronic
communications. Therefore, I believe that there will be no large scale involvement for the next nine or ten years unless higher levels of government
share their wealth with local public libraries, which currently receive most
of their funding from local government. As I noted earlier, I don't believe
that "show me" attitudes are a barrier any longer. The technology no longer
frightens us. Nor are so many of us terribly concerned about the possible
threatened loss of certain prized clienteles, such as the business community.

Quite frankly, I believe that there are numerous other constituencies
whose needs for information may be even more pressing and deserve priority
consideration. And even if you don't agree with that, the public library constituency is so broad and diverse that it might be an advantage to be able to
narrow our mission and reduce the number of target populations to be served.
Current, authoritative career and vocational information delivered on-line
and provided by a public library for motivated kids trying to break out of the
poverty cycle is an example of just one type of service that may be more
meaningful than our attempts to provide advanced research data to a clientele
who already has access to an abundance of information available from other
sources. One of the chronic problems of the public library is that we have
always felt that we must be all things to all people.

I suspect that some of my statements have already gotten me into hot
water, so I might as well continue to expound views that may not be popular.
Quite frankly, I would like to see a National Information Policy which in part
would provide for the subsidization of local and regional electronic networks
and on-line services, as well as at higher levels. More specifically, for
public libraries to plan for the computer age intelligently and in order to
implement their participation as quickly as possible, local governments and
their local libraries will need outside funds to capitalize such investments
in the future. To reorganize or expand into a computer-related library--
beginning at the beginning with acquisitions right on through to information
retrieval stations for staff and public use--new capital and operating funds,
too, will be essential. I can't begin to estimate what these initial costs would
run on a library by library basis, but it is quite possible that if all LSCA
Funds, I repeat ALL, could be allocated for two consecutive years for these
purposes, the nation's public libraries, small and large, would soon be on
line and fully prepared for network participation. In other words, I believe
in the long run that it could be to the nation's advantage to declare a mora-
torium on federal funds for (1) bricks and mortar, (2) for one-shot demonstrations and (3) for a host of other projects that by themselves lack significance and/or visibility. It is high time that we tool up for the future.

Chapter 19

THE ON-LINE REVOLUTION:
SOME EMBARRASSING QUESTIONS

Ellen Gay Detlefsen

Assistant Professor
Graduate School of Library
and Information Sciences
University of Pittsburgh
Pittsburgh, Pennsylvania

I have been reading and re-reading the position papers and listening and re-listening to the presentations and reactions thus far, waiting to hear some discussion of a couple of ideas of great concern to me, ideas with real impact. What I have heard are several common themes. These common, if unfortunate, themes, in no particular order, include (1) cost-recovery from users is inevitable, but how we do it in the least painful manner, or in what we perceive as the least painful manner, is the real question; (2) hardware costs will be lowered, and thus charges for the services may be lowered (the familiar digital watch or pocket calculator syndrome), but how long must many of us realistically wait for this to happen?; (3) librarians are on the whole still perceived as timid traditionalists, and here I agree with Miriam Drake and not with John Lorenz, but must we be dragged kicking and screaming into the machine-dominated future depicted for us by the information industry, by researchers or by fiscally-conscious corporate-style managers? Can we not and should we not choose our own directions?; (4) academic and special libraries, particularly those in science and technology, are (by some divine right) predominant in the areas of information science and information services, and all other libraries must play catch-up ball as quickly as they can; (5) the only suitable end-users for these on-line systems are sophisticated, literate adults--whether the system allows access to data files, bibliographical materials, or cataloging information; (6) files are, and will continue to be, produced and supplied by organizations external to the library and to librarians--how can we expect them to listen to us or even to negotiate with us?; and (7) the present corporate model for on-line services with information as a commodity or utility is somehow perfectly acceptable for libraries.

I'd like to focus on this model for a moment, on a model that has tremendous impact on us all--librarians, information specialists, managers, library educators, suppliers, users. We are looking at a model drawn from the military-industrial or competitively-oriented corporate structures of mid-twentieth century America--a model where users are frequently referred to as "customers" (to use Samuel Wolpert's description) or "clients" (a Madison Avenue phrase in vogue with many librarians), or the old familiar term "patrons," based on a highly selective group of users (those persons or organizations with the bucks to buy into a commercially-available system, with the bucks to hire the exquisitely-well-trained "information intermediary," "information counselor," "data services specialist," or (dare I say it?) "reference librarian," and with the necessarily demanding group of special users. This model is an elitist one; we may protest vigorously that these services are, and of right ought to be, freely available to all, but a plain old fact haunts us: with rare exceptions (Pitt's Social Science Information Utilization Laboratory, for example) we are now serving only those who can afford to pay the going rate.

Our model can be illustrated with the highly successful on-line searching services available to those in the health sciences--first with MEDLARS and MEDLINE, and later with CHEMLINE, TOXLINE, SDILINE, CANCERLINE, CATLINE, and AVLINE, etc. The users have borne the costs of these services from the beginning, but these are users who are, or who are perceived, as wealthy (either by reason of high personal income, or because of large research grant funding), as active in life-and-death situations (the soap opera scenario of the surgeon at the table pausing to look at the most recent article from the Annals of Neurosurgery before plunging on into the procedure), and thus as somehow more deserving of our services. To the extent that those of the medical world can afford to beat down a library's doors with $20 bills in order to have on-line services, they are unique. Patterning a model for on-line information services after this example will have disastrous impact on and for users perceived in less dramatic terms, and on and for users with far fewer financial resources.

Is this corporate or medical model then, necessarily, the only or the most effective one? Are we forcing not-for-profit social service organizations into an inappropriate profit-style model? Are we falling into a trap described by Allen Kent when he perceived the "business community" as the "prize client" of libraries? Can we avoid what Burchinal describes as the "driving force" behind the on-line revolution as this corporate/industrial model? Must we necessarily adopt the corporate or medical or industrial model in the age we so frequently describe with Daniel Bell's overworked

buzzword phrase as a "post-industrial society"? Can we create successful
user-based, service-based on-line systems for modern libraries?

In a counter-response to these common themes, I should like to suggest some additional ideas for the discussion on the impact of on-line systems.
We can be, and are, directly affected by those things we have done, and by
those things we have left undone. Among the things we have left undone thus
far is the issue of quality control. Martha Williams alluded to this--I would
like to make her allusions more concrete.

What good, for instance, is a fancy on-line system that organizes and
makes available information that can at best be described as garbage, in its
familiar construct of GIGO ("Garbage in, garbage out"). Why pay money for
such garbage? Any library that attempts to "sell" its users on the value of
on-line information systems solely on the strength of the ERIC data files (the
cheapest, and therefore frequently the one chosen for a trial service) risks
alienating its users from the service because of the poor quality of the material retrieved. Joe Shubert's notion that speed in access, and thus greater
time for the analysis of information, is fine, so long as the information thus
located is valuable.

Catalogers have long had to deal for instance with the problem of poor
quality data in the OCLC files; cataloging identified as the input from a mid-
western academic library is immediately suspect to many technical services
people. Selectivity in information files is another quality control problem.
Beware for example when approaching the New York Times Information Bank;
you are accessing what a colleague of mine neatly calls "all the news that's
fit to automate." If you think you are getting early and quick access to information from the Times and from seventy other news media, you are not.
You are getting only what the folks at the Information Bank choose to include
from the Times and the seventy other papers and journals. Do we score
another point for quality control?

A data base--such as ISI's Social Sci Search--that goes no further
back in time than the 1970's or does not include the small but reputable state
historical journals, is next to useless for an American historian. Obviously,
then, in considering the acquisition of a data file or the provision of access
to one, we must look at the material being indexed or made accessible. Is
it worth our time and our money? How will it affect its potential ˙ sers?
How the data file, and its access structure, is organized is another important area for quality control. Are the indexing terms relevant to current
practice in the field? Or are they chosen from the words used in titles--not
a very careful way to construct an indexing language in many disciplines
(locating an article entitled "Reflections on Miltonic Prolegomena: Second
Thoughts" with a permuted term index or a KWIC index is only partially satisfactory). How do the subject skills of the indexers or file preparers affect

the user? Is a posting dictionary citing how many times a term is used (and thus indicating which terms are favored by individual incumbent indexers) not also a necessary tool for the successful use of an on-line system? Is such a tool available from suppliers on a routine basis? No.

We must also be very wary about the hasty choice for a glamorous on-line service if a significant portion of our users are coming from those disciplines underrepresented in the long lists of available data files--particularly users in the humanities or the softer social sciences, disciplines where currency of information may not be the most important factor, or where the monograph is still as honorable and viable a source of information as the journal article. Different kinds of files with different kinds of access may be necessary for those practicing these disciplines, but data base and on-line service suppliers have not always perceived this. If they have, they have probably also perceived that these folks do not have the bucks more readily available to social and medical and pure scientists. After all, as Anita Schiller pointed out (and here I merely rephrase), for the information industry, a sensitivity to user satisfaction is a vehicle for the attainment of a corporate goal (profit), but for the library, user satisfaction and the sensitivity to user needs is a goal in itself.

Another area that we have neglected in our discussion of the on-line revolution is that of the missing end-users, the missing conference participants, and the missing data files. We have all been guilty of defining users --real and potential--in terms of those who have already expressed an interest in these systems. We overlook a vast number of people out there with genuine information needs that can be well served by the new technology and the inventive interactions afforded by on-line information systems. We are not just serving "executives and researchers" (in Samuel Wolpert's phrase), or just physicians and health care specialists, faculty scholars and graduate students, or legislators and government decision-makers (as Mel Day suggests), although a glance through any directory of on-line services might suggest that that is the case.

Where are the children, the school age youth, the functionally-literate or low-literate adults, the undergraduates, the people in trade and vocational programs, the continuing education students in community college, the adult or lifelong learners sitting for the GED and CLEP exams? Where are the data bases and on-line services that can have an impact on these large groups of users? How many of these people--these potential users--know what a Wiswesser line number is, or a permuted term index, or a stock option model? How many of them care? Do we run the risk of creating a dodo-like on-line information service that does not and cannot respond to social need or urgent user demands? Where are the on-line community information and retrieval services, providing instant access to life-and-death information in the storefront or bookmobile library setting? Where are the bilingual data

files for the millions of Spanish-speaking Americans or French-speaking
Canadians? These are among our missing users, and we cannot afford to
ignore them.

Just as there are missing users, there are also missing data files.
When will we have on-line, interactive access to information about social
service agencies nationwide, or to health, nutritional and consumer information for the lay public, or to career information for the job-seeker (the
machine-based Job Information Service of the Federal government is one
small step in the right direction)? When will we have on-line, interactive
access to evaluative data files of audio-visual materials for children and
schools (in the vein of AVLINE, but aimed at a different audience), or information about materials and services for special students, whether gifted,
handicapped, or retarded? The creation and availability of this kind of on-
line information service may have a far more real impact on the public,
whether or not they are now library users, than any sort of service now available to us. We must think of the consumer, the institutionalized person, the
child, the un- or underemployed adult, the newly emerging ethnic minorities
or women; we must see them as potential users of information, and thus of
on-line information systems, and we must construct files and systems that
are responsive to their special needs. There are more of them than there
are scholars, executives, researchers, physicians, or librarians and information specialists.

Finally, there are the missing conference participants. An advance
look at the persons registered for this conference and a glance through the
hands raised for Roger Summit's survey reveals a heavy attendance by academic and special librarians, especially library managers and reference
or retrieval specialists, plus a few catalogers and technical services types.
There is a significant proportion of attendees from the information industry
itself, and a goodly number of library school students, no doubt here to see
how the heavies and the hot shots perform and to scout possible job opportunities in the tight job market. There are some public librarians, but many
are from the large and therefore possibly more sophisticated of our country's
public libraries. There are a few library educators, checking up on Pitt's
faculty and programs and gathering a few notes for next week's or next se-
mester's classes. But--where are the children's specialists, for example?
They've probably all gone to the Allerton Park Institute on Children's Services in Public Libraries, meeting in Illinois at this very hour. (Undoubtedly
the two sets of conference planners felt that those who would attend an on-
line conference and those who would attend a children's services conference
were mutually exclusive groups. Wrong--the children's specialists are today hearing a paper that calls for increased activity in resource sharing and
on-line information systems for children's materials.) Where are the school
librarians, the media specialists, the learning resource center staffs?
They're not into on-line systems, you say? Then, why is the forthcoming

issue of <u>School Media Quarterly</u> entirely devoted to networking and on-line systems? Where are the institutional librarians, those of our professions serving users in prisons, mental hospitals, nursing homes, and other long-term facilities? Where are the librarians serving the blind, the physically handicapped, the deaf? Their users have perhaps a greater need for on-line, and quickly efficient access to, files of information about the materials and services available to them. And where are the information brokers and the free-lance librarians? The information vendors do not require an institutional or organizational affiliation before allowing a customer to purchase access to their files and services, and an entrepreneurial soul might be well-supported by a consulting or free-lance service for libraries unable to justify access through the more "traditional" models described at this conference.

These are a few comments on the themes that have pervaded this conference thus far, on the corporate model that is described for us in most contemporary literature and discussion, on quality control issues, and on the missing users, the missing data files and services, and the missing conference participants, upon whom and by which an impact could certainly be felt, and may yet be felt.

I'd like to close with two final thoughts: does Allen Kent's perception that the on-line revolution will free librarians for more "creative dealing with professional decisions" necessarily mean, or even imply, that these professional decisions will equal good public service and a strong sensitivity for users, current and potential? And finally, at the risk of making another horrible pun, the real on-line revolution may not be the introduction of these sophisticated new services within libraries, information centers, and data archives. The revolution may be, rather, that of the persons who stand <u>on line</u> in welfare offices, mass transit queues, picket lines, student registration areas, and public health clinics, people not so patiently waiting for basic and vital information with which to make day-by-day decisions. Are we yet ready to supply these people on their lines with on-line information?

Chapter 20

IMPACT: DISCUSSION

The discussion which follows has been transcribed from tape recordings, summarized, and edited. Comments and questions have been attributed to speakers when their identity was provided. The editors of these proceedings take responsibility for any errors in fact or interpretation resulting from this process, since it was not feasible to provide proofs to discussants for checking.

Jane Kelly - Pueblo Regional Library District, Colorado

Question to Keith Doms: Isn't what you are discussing really cost-benefit analysis, where you weigh not just the investment in computerized services, but the benefits (not only to the library) to the library user. What has bothered me in the past two days has been hearing about cost-effectiveness. I think this is a confusion of goals; I don't think cost-effectiveness is possible when considering computerized services. If one looks at benefit, then public libraries might better be able to justify participation.

Keith Doms

We have to relate cost to institutional goals and objectives. We must then examine these in terms of short, intermediate, and long-range planning. As a manager of a public library, I must look at two areas in connection with on-line services: (1) technical services, and (2) public services. Based on our experience, when we have been able to integrate an on-line service with some of our traditional services, we have improved the quality of service. We do not have enough depth of experience to know whether it is cost-effective, but we hope to evaluate our public library services and our objectives and goals, and to determine where we are and might go in light of current constraints. There are numerous constraints, not only financial, but those imposed by demographic trends. All I can say for now is that I believe we are meeting, more efficiently, some needs that have been met only partially in the past.

Ellen Detlefsen

In looking at benefit rather than cost-effectiveness, it implies that
we know who our users are and what their needs are. I am not certain that
we know, and it would therefore be difficult to measure benefit.

Norma Burns - Canada Institute for Scientific and Technical Information,
    Ottawa

We hear a great deal about benefits in staff reduction through more
use of computers in libraries. I don't believe this is considered a benefit
by everybody, particularly those who lose their jobs. Has anyone in government given any thought to the social unrest which may result from more
unemployment in libraries due to increasing use of computers? I think that
students in library schools will have more trouble finding jobs if this trend
continues.

Alphonse Trezza

Technological unemployment is a reality not only in libraries, but in
all of industry, manufacturing, and business. Librarians as well as others
all have to face up to it. Our problem is not that we have an overabundance
of librarians, but rather an underabundance of jobs. We are not anywhere
near meeting the library standards. If we came close to meeting the standards, we would not have enough students coming out of library schools to
fill the jobs. Thus we should not use this as an excuse to hold back technological advancement. We should fight that battle on its own ground: better
library service and sufficient staff to meet the standards we believe are so
essential. We must sell our budget people on the principles that we are
important, that we deserve support, but not stand in the way of progress--
it won't work.

Mary Eidleman - Dundaulk Community College, Baltimore

I wish to address the question of the image of the librarian as conservative and obstructive. We are the only profession I know which spends such
an incredible amount of energy on such compulsive self-criticism with so little
basis in fact. I suspect that it is a myth continued to support the self-worth
and self-righteousness of its disseminators. Eleven years ago I was working
on my master's at Columbia University and I heard the same thing. I want
to know what the graduate schools have been doing for the past eleven years
if they feel that the same situation exists--I personally do not. I have had
considerable experience and I have benefited from it richly--I have worked

in public libraries, in school libraries, and in special libraries. Of the librarians with whom I have worked, only 20% (at most) could be called "conservative and obstructive. " I would feel incredibly more comfortable if I could feel the same way about the medical and legal professions.

I have been in my current position for four weeks--I have been assisting public librarians in the development of information and referral services to the public libraries in Maryland. Eighteen of the 24 counties deliver such services through their public libraries. I've worked with urban, suburban and rural librarians, none of whom have exhibited these conservative or obstructive attitudes. Given the resources and their training, they were willing to undertake whatever came their way. On behalf of them and myself, I no longer accept that kind of criticism.

Regarding the automation of community information files, the technology has not quite caught up with the need--the expense is just prohibitive at this point. When we got into rural counties, one of the first things the civic organizations asked (they provide almost 50% of the services) was whether these services would be computerized--if so, they planned to be involved.

Ruth Eveland - Cuyahoga County Public Library, Ohio

We are a large, unsophisticated public library system. We are using The Information Bank; for all of its faults it is a way for us to feel we are entering the twentieth century in terms of service. The large attendance at this meeting is an indication that an enormous number of people will be working with computer systems in the future in all sorts of professions.

Ellen Detlefsen

How useful would it be to have Readers Guide on-line in the public library setting?

Ruth Eveland

Personally I would find it interesting. Many people would like to access information through a terminal; others prefer print media. Young people would enjoy using terminals and it would give them some control of output.

Question - University of Pittsburgh

In our institution we are doing bibliographic searches for clinicians, researchers, and graduate and undergraduate students. What is the impact of such computer searching on the educational experience of the student, for whom the process of doing research should be just as important as having the end product of a computer search? What is happening to the traditional role of the academic librarian in providing guides to the literature and in instructing the student?

Martha Williams

The role of the librarian in providing guides to resources is the same. Guidance is provided to both machine-readable resources and "manual" sources.

Thomas Galvin

The question really is directed at whether our main emphasis in the future should be on improving information delivery as an alternative to doing a better job of instructing people to become, to some degree, self-sufficient in the library.

Richard De Gennaro

When the hand-held calculators first were made available, many teachers of mathematics did not want students to use them because the process was made too easy. The newer tools are there, and one must come to terms with them. They are tremendously useful; they can co-exist with the old-fashioned methods of calculation.

Ruth Atwood - University of Louisville

Being with a rather small and poor university, we are very much concerned about the prospect of higher data base prices. Fifteen years ago, in the city of Louisville, there were thirteen subscriptions to Chemical Abstracts; ten years ago there were three; now there are three subscriptions and five additional people using Chemical Abstracts through terminals. In our library, we are using data bases that we cannot afford to subscribe to because of very limited use. But we are spending money that was not in the book or periodical budget through Lockheed and SDC services. Might this usage counteract the trend of increased data base prices?

Roger Summit

The on-line services are bringing a whole new group to the use of secondary services. It has yet to be shown that on-line services are supplanting the abstracting and indexing services. It would be our hope and feeling that the potential community that can use information services is so vast and so untapped that it will be possible for both types of access to coexist: the hard copy as well as the on-line.

Martha Williams

My view is somewhat different: at least two research studies have shown a decrease in the number of hard copy subscriptions as they are being replaced by on-line services. I believe we will reach some point at which subscriptions will cease to drop. None of the major research libraries will give up their subscriptions to the hard copy abstracting and indexing services. Some of the smaller institutions will drop subscriptions, causing some increase in cost of data bases; I believe that will be offset by the increased use of the services on-line. The net result should not be much higher cost for use of on-line services.

Jim Cogswell - University of Pennsylvania

I resent the overtone of Ellen Detlefsen's remarks. These seem to imply that the information community is engaged in purposely denying on-line services to the unserved users. The problems of these groups are very real; concern for them is very real, at least among those I know in my own library and others I talk to at various meetings. Her allusions to the New York Times Information Bank, providing all the news that's fit to printout, implies that the New York Times is maliciously censoring their data base for a sinister purpose. I don't see this.

By this logic, any library that applies any selection criteria in collections development, or in indexing resources, are in on the same kind of plot. Selection is made on the basis of a desire to reach a given user group; the fact that all are not reached does not imply a plot.

I do not believe that those at this conference are unconcerned about the unserved. We come to this conference with some understanding of realities; the reality of on-line services is that they have a relative novelty; they have built-in limitations; they have not inconsiderable cost. We should be able to look forward to the day when a wider range of users can be served. In the meantime, we must deal with a known user population in terms of the collections we have available in our own libraries.

When did Ellen Detlefsen serve in a real-live library, with real-live patrons, under real-live budgetary and staff constraints?

Ellen Detlefsen

Two and one half years ago as chief librarian of the Western Psychiatric Institute and Clinic, one of the country's largest mental health information centers.

Jim Cogswell

Your reality is different from mine.

Ellen Detlefsen

If the concern for the underserved is so great, why are the vendors not providing the missing data bases?

Roger Summit

It is very useful to look at trends; more useful than looking at current status and evaluating on the basis of some absolute standard that one has in one's mind. In 1972-3, there were some 10-15 data bases on-line; today there are more than 75. Regarding the character of the data bases, they tend to be more specialized. This is possible because it becomes cheaper and cheaper to produce data bases as the technology advances. It also becomes economically feasible to mount those specialized data bases that will receive very little access play on-line as the number of on-line users grows, and as cost of storage decreases. So if we look at this trend, it takes very little capital to establish a machine-readable data base today, which can be mounted on-line. Several years ago, I used to say that once we acquire a few more data bases we can return to the business of providing service--but we never reached that point of stability. The potential data bases for loading far exceeds our ability to put them on-line, even though we are processing 15-20 per year at the present time. So if Ms. Detlefsen would be a bit patient, she will see her objectives realized, not simultaneously and concurrently, but one at a time.

Martha Williams

Certainly more data bases are being created for "average" users, e.g., to serve neighborhood information users. But there must be an

economic benefit for a vendor and data base producer--in the private sector.
This is probably an area where the government should be responsible.

We should have data bases available to help, for example, counselors
in welfare agencies who help welfare clients. The clients themselves would
tend not to use data bases.

Keith Doms

I wish to assure Ms. Detlefsen that there are some very important
data bases, of the sort she referred to, being developed locally and regionally, particularly in some of our large metropolitan areas.

I wonder what sort of articulation Roger Summit might envision between very important social services information referral data bases for
southeastern Pennsylvania and the national services (e.g., Lockheed).

Roger Summit

Our service can be viewed: (1) as a public service with public data
bases, where we accept the economic risk of mounting the data base and
offering service on it; and (2) as a private service, with the data base holder
accepting the risk of putting it on-line. The data base to which you refer is
in the second category--such a data base can be mounted for $3,000-$4,000.
The data base holder would be obliged to decide whether the investment is
warranted.

Larry Osborne -Clearfield County Public Library, Pennsylvania

I see an apparent dichotomy between those who consider themselves
information scientists (dealing with quantifiable data) and those who tend to
support emotional stands and traditional library services (without investigation). We are playing the game by different rules and it hurts both types.
There may not be two camps, because for those of us in management both
voices beckon. We should demand better accountability and make explicit
the human benefits that accrue from our services. The real revolution will
come when we can lay out the costs and benefits more effectively.

Maryruth Glogowski - State University College at Buffalo

I'm from a small undergraduate college, with about 10,000 students,
not to be confused with the University at Buffalo.

A population not being served by the on-line revolution is represented by the undergraduate students. Our college recently shifted from an emphasis on "education" to consumer studies, criminal justice, and social services. The needs of our students are not served by the available data bases. For example, MEDLARS is too broad for specific nutrition questions. We do invest in automation in technical services, with costs not passed on to the patron. We receive funds readily for these services, but it is assumed that a fee must be charged for on-line reference services.

Alphonse Trezza

I have heard frequently that if on-line services are provided "free" the use would increase to the point where we couldn't handle it. I would love to see the day that the libraries are so crowded that the volume couldn't be handled. When we reach that day, I can assure you that money will be no problem. Right now, libraries are used 25-35%. We have failed to find out what the user wants. We tell the user what he needs. That is part of our problem. If you really want to try, it is not difficult to find out what the public wants. Our problem is that we are professionals and we know what is needed.

Philip Tompkins - University of Missouri, Kansas City

Some emphasis should be given, in those areas where it is geographically possible, to interdependence among libraries and librarians in the pooling of resources in providing on-line services. We are doing this in our area.

Roger Summit

We are finding an increasing number of user groups developing which are very helpful to all concerned.

Arnulfo Trejo - Graduate Library School, University of Arizona

Ellen Detlefsen's remarks were long overdue. Things are not going that well in our country when we get down to the values, to the ghettos. We make do with what we have; but if we continue with that attitude, we will have what we had in the 1960's--the riots, the fires. One person (a black) wrote that the only reason the libraries were not burned down was because they did not know where they were. I do not wish the data banks to be destroyed; on the contrary, I wish to see them enriched with information

concerned with all the ethnic groups in the country. I hope there will be an
opportunity for you to cooperate with a network we have in mind (for the
Spanish-speaking community).

Cheryl Casper - Kent State University, Ohio

The debate regarding user fees for on-line library services has become a highly emotional one. Most economic goods always have had explicit
price tags, and the role of the economist has been to discuss problems such
as the optimal quantity to be produced or the profit-maximizing price. It is
rare to encounter a situation where the producers of an economic good are
still debating whether or not a price should be charged at all. What is needed
is a set of guidelines or criteria that the library manager can apply in determining whether or not user fees are appropriate in given situations. (This
need does not just apply to on-line library services, but to all library services in general.)

To begin, let me state one favorite economic cliché which was not
voiced at the conference: there is no free lunch. The implication of this
cliché for on-line services is that someone--users, libraries or library
funders such as state, local or the federal government--will ultimately pay
for the economic resources that are absorbed in the production of on-line
services. Whether these costs will be paid for through explicit user fees or
absorbed by the library and ultimately paid for by someone else--most likely
society at large--is at the heart of the fee-for-service debate.

It is very important to stress that the lunch will be paid for by someone. Some of the strongest opponents of user fees--those that emphasize the
importance of equal (i.e., free) access to information--might well change
their minds if they were to understand that the option of having society pay
really means that most of the lunch will be paid for with the tax dollars of
the middle and lower income groups and not by the "have's" that would be
paying most user fees, if they were charged. For example, economists who
have researched the distribution of costs and benefits related to subsidized
higher education have discovered that the majority of the benefits have not
accrued to poor families who might not otherwise be able to afford to send
their children to college.[1] Rather, most of the benefits of state-supported
higher education have gone to families that could afford to pay the full cost.
I suspect that the same finding would apply to the end-users of on-line services.

---

1. See W. Lee Hanson and Burton A. Weisbrod, Benefits, Costs and
Finance of Public Higher Education, Markham Publishing Company:
Chicago, 1969.

Arguments in Favor of User Fees. At least three distinct arguments in support of user fees for on-line services exist:

1. user fees will generate needed revenue;
2. user fees will ration demand;
3. user fees will serve as a measure of value.

While the first argument may appear to be the most cogent to the library manager facing serious budgetary constraints, it is actually a very weak argument by itself. Libraries may well need additional revenue, but that problem alone does not imply that the solution must entail user fees for on-line services. Why not user fees for some other or all library services? Why not get additional revenues in some other manner?

The rationing argument in some situations can be very strong. Roger Summit has cited evidence that suggests that the character of demand is very sensitive to whether or not a user fee is charged, yet not so sensitive to changes in a non-zero fee. Some positive fee--even a nominal one--may have to be charged in order to eliminate waste of library resources. However, for many libraries the rationing problem may not apply. Most librarians are concerned with how to stimulate fuller use of library materials that may be underutilized. Yet, as more potential users discover the attractiveness of on-line services, libraries will have to consider some form of rationing devise; user fees are simple, efficient rationing mechanisms.

The third argument is one that may not be familiar to librarians. Yet, one hears repeatedly librarians making comments such as "We do not know the value of information," "Librarians do not know the worth of library services to users," etc. Problems invariably arise in any cost-benefit study of library services because the benefit side is so uncertain. The major reason why benefits are so difficult to quantify is because price tags have usually not been attached to library services. Like it or not, in our society, price is a measure of value. Under some circumstances it may be a poor measure, but nonetheless the price a willing buyer and seller agree upon in a free market is commonly accepted as a minimum value of the exchanged good or service. By not charging user fees, librarians are denying themselves information about users' evaluations of their services. Rational allocation of library resources requires estimates of the net benefits of library services; these estimates are easier to obtain (and probably more accurate) if the marketplace is used.

Arguments Against User Fees. There are also substantial arguments against the imposition of user fees for on-line services:

1. user fees for library services are non-traditional;
2. in some cases, the costs of imposing and collecting the fees might exceed the revenues generated;

3. on-line services may have some public good properties;
4. user fees may deny users "equal access" to information.

These arguments are used distinctly yet are interrelated. The first argument is basically non-economic in nature. Simply because user fees have not been charged before or are not charged for other library services is not by itself a sufficient argument against the imposition of user fees for on-line services. However, the reason why user fees have not been charged in the past may be primarily due to the suspected public good properties mentioned in the third argument.

Unfortunately, most librarians do not understand what economists mean when they discuss "public goods" or refer to the "public good properties" of information or library services. To the librarian, a public good is simply one that is provided by the public sector--that is, supported or funded by some level of government. In most cases, however, economists use the term "public good" in a more specialized sense. They are referring to economic goods or services that have characteristics such that in order for these goods to be optimally produced and distributed, they must be provided on a collective rather than individual basis. Library services may possess the properties of the public good of economic theory--namely, jointness of supply, external economies, and/or a third property related to public production or subsidy, decreasing average costs.[2] Opponents of user fees would be wise to study the public good literature of economic theory since it contains several strong rationales that could be used to argue against user fees or, if any, only nominal ones.

The fourth argument involving equal or free access was clearly the most emotional one voiced at the conference. In a nation that treasures individual freedoms it has an understandably strong appeal. However, individuals that apply this argument to on-line services must realize, as Carlos Cuadra noted, that they are really asking that all taxpayers underwrite the costs for the benefit of a few. As noted above, the income distributional affects of free on-line services are not likely to be neutral. Is there any reason why on-line services should be free and bread and milk should have price tags? Solely on the basis of equity, the answer must be no. Furthermore, if one is concerned with the problem of equity, there is no reason why

---

2. Jointness of supply is present if, once produced, a given amount of a good or service can be made equally available to all--for example, street lighting. External economies refer to the spill-over benefits that accrue to third parties or society at large as a result of the production or consumption of a good or service--for example, public education.

user fees might not be structured using the "ability to pay" principle. (Imagine, for example, the disadvantaged being given information stamps to take to their local library.)

   Conclusion. The above discussion has detailed some of the many arguments--both pro and con--that have been used in favor of or against user fees for on-line services. Without further investigation of the public good properties of on-line services, the average economist would probably be reluctant to state whether or not user fees should be charged, or if charged, what the optimal fee structure should be.

   There are, of course, many non-economic arguments that enter the picture as well. As an outsider, I can only speculate about the political undercurrents present. Librarians seem very insecure about the value of the services they offer.[3] During the 1973 energy crisis, most of the public felt that the demand for petroleum was inelastic--that is, they thought that no matter how high the price went, the quantity demanded ("needed") would remain constant. Librarians seem to hold a diametric opinion regarding the demand for library services. They appear to believe that demand is highly elastic--that is, if a user fee is charged or if any existing user fee is increased, the quantity of service demanded will fall to virtually zero. Observers of the post-crisis petroleum market found that demand was not as inelastic as was thought; the public did adjust to higher prices. After some experience with user fees, librarians are likely to discover that the demand for library services, especially the demand for on-line services that may have no close substitutes, is also not as elastic as they suspect.

---

3. As noted above, there is good reason for some of this insecurity since librarians receive very little of the feedback provided by the marketplace.

Part Three

TRAINING AND RETRAINING OF LIBRARIANS AND USERS

The mechanical techniques for accessing on-line facilities are quite straightforward; however, full exploitation requires skills in subject matter, and reference interaction, etc. The appropriate interrelationships are explored.

The position paper distributed in advance of the conference is given in Chapter 21. Chapters 22-26 present reactions from the panelists. Chapter 27 presents the discussion at the conference.

Chapter 21

TRAINING AND RETRAINING OF LIBRARIANS AND USERS

Elaine Caruso

Assistant Research Professor
Interdisciplinary Department of Information Science
University of Pittsburgh
Pittsburgh, Pennsylvania

THE PROBLEMS OF THE WOULD-BE USER
OF ON-LINE SEARCH SERVICES

Nature of the Problem. We have discovered that using on-line bibliographical retrieval systems is not something that just anyone among the
hordes of passersby on our evermore crowded streets can walk in, sit down,
and learn to do in a few brief moments. Early enthusiasts developed conversational dialogues which would permit this--we thought. Our present
situation, shaped by the realities of economics and computer technology, and
of human capabilities and interests, is somewhat different from early imagin-
ings.

On-line retrieval systems development, rebuffed in its attempted
seduction of the entire literate community, now expends its energies in woo-
ing the information professional, or, alternatively, in developing more
specialized, more capable services for smaller but more responsive populations. The first approach is exemplified by the ORBIT, B.R.S., and Lockheed Systems; the latter by LEXIS, AGRIS, SCORPIO, among others.
Training in the latter instance is somewhat eased by the intensity of the
intrinsic interest of the more narrowly focussed content and the smaller
size of the potential user population.

When we proposed that "anyone" could learn to use the computer
search techniques, we weren't just saying these systems would be as easy as
the use of printed counterparts, but easier! Those heavy volumes arranged

in date order, grouped by subject, which had to be lugged about, whose supplements could be confusing in their varying time spans, and missing, too, in other people's hands, or just lost!; where items had to be copied, by hand, and where comparisons of entries under intersecting subject aspects was at least tedious, often impossible; all this was to be supplanted by the simple typing of the desired search term or terms, and the output would appear on the typescript before you.

What went wrong? Nothing really. Those volumes of indexes and abstracts were solid stuff, real, and you could hold them in your hands, examine them, and discover for yourself (or rediscover!) the contents, its organization, ways of identifying needed items, its particular values. You could see at a glance, or verify, its organization through time. Now what we're using is machine-sensible tape, data banks and files that we never touch or see in any physical sense, much less "read." You can make analogies from printed counterparts where such exist, but the value of such analogies is limited, for practical purposes, to gaining understanding of the subject content: scope, perspective, geographic coverage. Indexing and points of access, particularly, are apt to be different; and there are machine stored files which have radically diverged from their printed progenitors; e.g., Chemical Condensates, and some which had no such parent: e.g., The Information Bank of the New York Times.

We need to orient ourselves in a new way to the study of this new resource. We need a new approach, not just because the data base files are different in structure and invisible to us, but because use is so different; the strategy for searching a machine stored file is qualitatively and quantitatively different; it is also different in a purely physical, mechanical sense. Searchers of mechanized systems need to think, not just of the best first approach to file contents, but of all possible approaches, and how to combine them in a kind of simultaneous combing of the whole file. One doesn't thread a narrow winding path--except at great expense!

And then too there is the problem of the mechanical system which you use to "read" the files, and to copy off parts in man-readable form; the machine program which locates for you that bit of the file content which you can identify, to it, as being wanted by you. How does one learn about the computer programs which are used to put the magnetic tape issues into the computer system to keep them in order, to organize them for retrieval in the first place.

THE POPULATION OF TRAINEES FOR ON-LINE SYSTEMS

The population of potential trainees, as indicated in our title, consists of students of librarianship, of practicing information professionals, and of "users": "users" being those who put the information to use in their own pursuits or interests: research; teaching; industrial, medical, economic, social...applications. There is little need for distinguishing the student and the practitioners of information science in the development of training programs; while the student tends to have more computer exposure and know-how and the practitioner to know the content and culture of particular subject areas, neither case is consistently true, and the value of this knowledge and experience in the on-line retrieval function is extremely variable. The only real consideration that needs to be made relates to the job role of the practitioner; training should call him away from his work as briefly as possible. The end-user is a more difficult case; this will be elaborated at the close of the next section which describes the currently available aids in gaining access to machine sensible files.

A PART OF THE ANSWER TO THE PROBLEM

As if all this were not enough--or perhaps because it is all too much --there has grown up a new institution which must be dealt with. The growth of the computer information services as retailing businesses, and as information brokers, using the "yellow pages" or "travel agent" approaches, is a response to our obvious but not carefully defined or understood need.

The information services which have developed have taken varying approaches to the problem of facilitating the use of the available data bases; but all perform certain similar services:

1. Bringing together or creating available files; discovering and obtaining and maintaining them on a continuing basis;
2. Storing them in a central computer system, structuring and organizing them into a more or less coherent data base;
3. Providing a user oriented conversational computer dialog for retrieving parts of these files, selectively, on an individual question/user basis;
4. Devising a distribution system consisting of telecommunication and accounting systems: to get the service to wherever the user is, and to allow him to contribute to its support and development, in some proportionate share according with the use he makes of the system.

Much of the contribution of the search service approach could be classed as educational: in addition to the overt effort which results in scheduled workshops and seminars for the users of the service, there is the less visible but very important effect on the suppliers of the files. The institution which generates the files recognizes the information service as a most important aid in "selling" the use of the file to libraries, information

systems, and individuals, very few of whom have computer systems, programs, and personnel to purchase the magnetic tapes, store, and search
them. They are thus sensitive to the needs of the search services; matters
of format and inclusion are thus subject to a normalizing force. Additionally,
where educational sessions bring these file vendor representatives together,
there is an opportunity for them to learn from each other; this also tends to
normalize the content and structure of the various files as each tends to
adopt good workable ideas of other suppliers.

BIBLIOGRAPHIC RETRIEVAL OR MORE?

As a librarian one focusses on the process of bringing a complete
document, the full text of a publication, to the hands of a would-be reader;
or else answering a specific "reference" question from an authoritative
source, citing volume and page. Questions requiring much critical reading
of multiple sources are best left in the guided hands of the reader. If the
user or his institution can afford it, the librarian, devoting more time and
effort, can come closer to tailoring the results of the information search to
the needs of the user, matching approach of the author, level of treatment,
perspective of treatment, even language and style and authority to the users
needs; using all the riches of approach possible in an information rich
system.

Of all the kinds of information available in this information conscious
society, we find only two represented in the generally available computer
retrieval arena: bibliographies with or without abstracts, but always with
indexes, and compilations of quantitative or coded data which lends itself to
a high degree of structuring in the computer system. These should be fitted
into the current patterns of information services; they cannot, at present,
replace them. Just a mention of the problem of providing full-text should
settle that issue, despite efforts of the computer retrieval systems to supply
copy by automating the order process (the "electronic mailbox"!). The way
of fitting the computer service into the library service depends on what is
in the computer system, i.e., the data base content, and the way the system
allows that content to be processed.

The first widespread use of computer retrieval systems has been
focussed on bibliographic data bases because of the size of the potential market; and of course the frequent availability of the machine sensible files as
a by-product of efficient printing processes. While these bibliographically
oriented systems are best known, they do not have the field of on-line retrieval entirely to themselves; numeric and graphic files are also available.

There are three rather universal developmental approaches which
are represented by presently available bibliographic retrieval services:

> In most common use today are those systems in which
> the development of the service emphasizes gathering
> together files from many diverse sources and retails
> them to many kinds of users; they take "finished"
> files and relay access to them to known users.

Search services following this approach maintain long lists of data
base files from sources as diverse as the American Psychological Society,
Smithsonian Scientific Information Exchange, Data Courier (ABI), Society
of Automotive Engineers. Upwards of 60 files are offered by Lockheed Retrieval Services (DIALOG), System Development Corporation (ORBIT), and
Bibliographic Retrieval Services (BRS). Their service is sold, sometimes
on a per use, rather than long-term contract, basis, to libraries, information centers, businesses, or even individuals, anywhere that a telephone
communication link can be established to the host computer system. Simplicity of operation is emphasized in these systems, in order to maximize the
number of users. The product delivered by the service is a bibliography,
with or without abstracts. It may be delivered via the telecommunication
link onto the receiving terminal at the user's location, or less expensively
but with some delay, via the mails, from the computer services printer.
Many of the data base files have associated services to provide the on-line
searcher with full text copies of the bibliographic items, on request at the
time of the search; delivery of the copy is by mail, however.

A second kind of approach is that which in the United States is exemplified by Battelle's BASIS and Mead Data Central:

> The development of the service emphasizes the capa-
> bility of the computer technology for organizing and
> storing files and for exploiting them in uniquely capable
> ways; their business consists of finding a user, build-
> ing him a file and providing him with a tailored capa-
> bility for using that file.

Information services taking this course seek users, most often mission-oriented groups or institutions, who have a need for specially tailored
data bases; or whose existing data base is not in machine readable form.
They will create the data base to user specifications, maintain it with updates on their own or the users' computer system. They adapt their existing
retrieval capabilities to the users' needs, or create new programs as required.

Ease of use of these systems is not a primary consideration in designing the user interface; users are presumed to be "dedicated" to the
learning of the system. Factors such as adaptation to the specific user
application or mission and the capability for generating special reports--

analyses, summaries, tabulations (BASIS), or optimization of data base organization for economic full-text search (Mead Data Central)--are more salient selling points.

Some services grew out of an overriding interest in use of the contents of a particular file; here we have The Information Bank of the New York Times, and the original MEDLINE Service:

> The developmental emphasis is on the data base itself, with file generating and accessing software developed for that particular file. Users of the data base must learn its specialized command language and conventions, in addition to the language they have learned in using the more generalized search services.

An existing body of information may justify, by virtue of the intensity and/or frequency of its use, and a more specialized kind of use, the expense of the development of more specialized computer systems, including independent distribution mechanisms. In such cases the computer technology can be more selectively attuned to both specialized data base requirements and to particular user populations. However, the cost of such custom-tailored programs, and their maintenance and development, may not be justified unless highly specialized uses are required. This is indicated by the fact that the National Library of Medicine file finally turned to SDC developed search and file maintenance programs for its medical data base. Presently the NLM file is also available in the BRS system data base, which uses its general purpose programs for searching the file. The Information Bank has adapted its programs for use on more generally available terminals than the originally developed special purpose terminal, to increase the potential user population.

This is not a complete listing of classes of retrieval service approaches, but does include those which are aimed at large scale national and international use. Neither are these mutually exclusive categories, and there is a tendency to converge, as the advantages of the different approaches become apparent, to the several services. While I put BRS, DIALOG, and ORBIT into my first category, no one could deny that they emphasize, individually, the uniqueness and value of their separate file development procedures; while Mead Data Central and BASIS belong in category two, attempts to "market" the custom-tailored files are made wherever proprietary interests do not supervene. Informatics probably fits midway between categories one and two. DIALOG, in its application to the Predicasts data bases, approaches category two, allowing cross-file searching and report generating capabilities.

The Information Bank and the National Library of Medicine files, while falling into category three, that is, the files have specially tailored storage and retrieval software as adjunctive to them, are, as noted, accessible side by side with other search system services on a common terminal at least, or by virtue of their having been adopted into other services' software families.

THE DATA BASES AS AN ASPECT OF THE "PROBLEM"

Our initial statement of the "problem addressed by would-be users of computer retrieval services and magnetic data bases" is only tangentially responded to by the systems just discussed; the nut of the problem remains to be articulated. The "kernel" of course is the data base, which is unreadable in its medium, and is impossible of any kind of summary presentation by the machines and programs offered by the on-line retrieval system.

We have a considerable body of accumulated experience in teaching on-line systems use: local experience as teachers of users in the Campus Based Information System's (CBIS) training classes over the past three years; in formal courses in the Graduate School of Library and Information Sciences since 1970; and the more concentrated experience of fully-trained search intermediaries in the Knowledge Availability System Center's NASA dissemination center. Much experience in user training and system use is reported in journals and at meetings. All point to the ultimate limitation on the effective use of machine stored files: that is, understanding of the content and structure of those files.

In addition to the difficulty of forming any overall visual model of the machine stored data bases, there are two further levels of difficulties which intrude in the user's attempt to assess the resources of the computer service. The first level of difficulty is peculiar to the magnetic files wherever they are used; the second is a function of the files and decisions about augmentation or limiting of the content of the files as they are incorporated into the data base structure of the several services, and of the data base structures and updating policies of the services.

Use of a data base file can be a frustrating experience; one must be prepared to deal with errors and inconsistencies and arbitrary changes in matters as trivial as spelling and as global as the incorporation (or removal) of whole categories of content coverage (See Figures 1, 2). If we had an ideal world, if there existed a useful, universal classification scheme, data base purveyors and users would find life much simpler. If all files reflected consistent, predictable patterns of selection, analysis and organization; of labeling of data elements for carefully defined, mutually exclusive content areas; if all this, then learning general principles or familiarity with one or two files could nicely transfer to other files to be searched. For example, note the sample records, Figure 3.

? EXPANDDISADVANTAGED

Ref	Index-term	Type	Items	RT
E1	DISAD--------------------------------		2	
E2	DISADV -----------------------------		2	
E3	DISADVANTAGED --------------------		1	
E4	DISADVANTAGE --------------------		162	
E5	DISADVANTAGE ENVIRONMENT		1	
E6	-DISADVANTAGED-------------------		10888	1
E7	DISADVANTAGED ADULTS------------		1	
E8	DISADVANTAGED CHILDREN ----------			1
E9	DISADVANTAGED ENVIRONMENT-------------------		213	10
E10	DISADVANTAGED ENVIRONMEN T COGNITIVE DEVELO -------------		1	
E11	DISADVANTAGED GROUPS------------		1395	9
E12	DISADVANTAGED SCHOOLS-----------		83	1
E13	DISADVANTAGED STUDENTS ----------			1
E14	DISADVANTAGED YOUTH-------------		5142	11
E15	DISADVANTAGEDNESS ---------------		4	
E16	DISADVANTAGEDEGE ---------------		1	

Figure 1. Variant forms and misspellings are to be expected whenever uncontrolled indexing is used. This is most true in cases where the computer simply alphabetizes the words from the text of an abstract.

? EE14

Ref	Index-term	Type	Items	RT
R1	-DISADVANTAGED YOUTH--------------		5142	11
R2	CULTURALLY DEPRIVED CHILDREN -----------------------	U		1
R3	DEPRIVED CHILDREN----------------	U		1
R4	DISADVANTAGED CHILDREN ----------	U		1
R5	DISADVANTAGED STUDENTS ----------	U		1
R6	INNER CITY CHILDREN --------------	U		1
R7	SLUM CHILDREN --------------------	U		1
R8	DISADVANTAGED GROUPS------------	B	1395	9
R9	YOUTH----------------------------	B	10599	22
R10	CHILD DEVELOPMENT CENTERS -----------------------	R	116	6
R11	CULTURALLY DISADVANTAGED -------	R	1659	11
R12	STUDY CENTERS --------------------	R	82	10
?				

Figure 2. Note the "purity" of these entries from a listing of humanly generated terms: the thesaurus entries for term E14 of the ERIC file segment shown in Figure 1.

PNI, A Division of Data Courier, Inc.

SAMPLE RECORD

```
AN - 76-06669
TI - W-L (Warner-Lambert)/P-D (Parke-Davis) divestiture plan as
     approved by FTC (Federal Trade Commission).
SO - FDC REPORTS (PINK SHEET) Vol. 38, No. 43, October 25,
     1976, p. 8.
JC - FDC
IT - W-L/P-D divestiture plan; Warner-Lambert; Parke-Davis;
     FTC approved; Federal Trade Commission; sales figure; cough
     remedies; Ambenyl expectorant (Rx); Cosanyl and Cosanyl DM
     (ethical OTC); Drug Monograph; Over the Counter; Throat
     Discs (OTC); Smith Brothers Cough Drops; Nilcol cough syrup;
     thyroid preparations; USP thyroid; United States Pharmacopeia;
     Thyroid Strong; inventories; trademark rights; interim sup-
     plies; labeling rights; therapeutic blood fraction products;
     Normal Serum Albumin; Tetanus Immune Globulin; plasma;
     promotional, ad and sales training material; BuBio Licenses
ST - cy 1969; text of WL/PD diverstiture plan.
```

COMPENDEX, Engineering Index, Inc.

SAMPLE RECORD

```
AN - 76-065501
TI - Building with Steel Sheet Walls Taking into Account the Regu-
     lations Regarding the Protection Against Construction Noise.
OTI - BAUEN MIT STAHLSPUNDWAENDEN UNTER BEACHTUNG
      DER VORSCHRIFTEN ZUM SCHUTZ GEGEN BAULAERM.
AU - Brackemann, Fritz; Wilzek, Reinhold
SO - Baumasch Bautech v 23 n 5 May 1976 p 252-254, 259-266
JC - BMBTAN
CC - 402; 405; 751
IT - CONSTRUCTION INDUSTRY--Noise Abatement
XR - PILES--Driving; BUILDINGS--Construction
ST - Steel Sheet Walls
AB - The efforts to reduce the noise of pile driving to a tolerable
     measure are discussed. Experiences made in the big towns
     of the Federal Republic of Germany and some neighbouring
     countries show however that it was not complained about pile
     driving noise as long as the level of the construction noise
     does not substantially exceed the traffic noise. The authors
     show how the costs involved in the utilization of silent pile
     driving methods can be kept within tolerable limits by the
     selection of adequate methods and equipment. 16 refs. In
     German with English abstract.
```

Figure 3. The choice of output with or without abstracts is quite often made on economic terms, where the output is on-line to the user's terminal. Some files, as the printout of the PNI file indicates, do not include abstracts in the machine searchable form. (Adapted from ORBIT Quick Reference Guide, 1977)

In reality, files are highly individual in many aspects of their creation and organization; historical accidents during the genesis of a particular file, and often of the cultural or intrinsic organization of a discipline, lead to great diversity. Thus we discover that the only way to learn to use a particular file is to investigate that file itself, as fully as possible, using printed descriptions and exploratory searches; and further, to be aware of any attributes of the search service being used which may facilitate or hinder the use of the contents of the file.

The user needs to know how the search service processing of the data base file affects his capability to use that file; particular fields or data elements may be augmented, or, conversely, be inaccessible for direct searching. Policies of updating, of incorporating revision and corrections, can cause another kind of user problem.

While the depth of data base knowledge required of a user varies according to the kind of information need he presents, we now see that simple comprehension or even detailed knowledge of a file isn't adequate for real search competence; there must also be a recognition of variations in the way the search systems restructure those files for incorporation into their own unique data base organizations and of the effect of these differences on the way a user may select and manipulate subsets of the file.

LEARNING TO USE ON-LINE RETRIEVAL

The on-line retrieval systems which offer their services to a diverse public were developed to aid in the task of making the machine readable data bases more usable, not just to small groups with computer systems and technical competence to bring the various taped files together, organize them for efficient searching, and develop the search programs, but to the total information using community as well. As is often the case with man's problem solving efforts, the solution has become a part of the problem. Accessing and using the services requires training, and now the population to be trained includes many individuals to whom computer use is new. They must learn something--how much? of computers, programs, telecommunication networks. Understanding the data base files remains difficult, despite efforts by search service designers to regularize the different formats and data elements.

Today the services have turned much of their advertising effort into the educational area; while the concerned public has become aware of the value of on-line searching, they cannot use it, or reduce the expense of inefficient and ineffective searches, without adequate training. In the tabulation below, we try to identify the various available training activities; strenuous but "stopgap" efforts on the part of those organizations having the most felt need for an informed, skilled user population:

1. Workshops and seminars conducted by the bibliographic search services, e.g., Lockheed Retrieval Services, System Development Corporation, Bibliographic Retrieval Services;
2. Data base generator and supplier, workshops; e.g., SSIE (Smithsonian Scientific Information Exchange), LEXIS, Predicasts, BIOSIS, Chemical Abstracts workshops;
3. Training efforts by information brokers (agencies which serve as an interface between users and the various competing bibliographic search services), e.g., NASIC, NELINET, many major universities;
4. User-organized groups, e.g., Lockheed and ORBIT user groups, unaffiliated user groups such as the Cleveland Area On-Line Users Group;
5. Professional organization efforts, e.g., workshops and sessions scheduled by ASIS special interest groups for information retrieval systems and the User On-Line Interface SIG and workshops sponsored by local chapters of Special Libraries Association and ASIS;
6. Courses and seminars in schools of library and information science as part of the degree curriculum and in "continuing education" efforts.

A common deficiency of the above is that they are planned with only the librarian in mind; advertisement of the training and time and places of offering are all focussed on access by the professional information specialist. Little effort is directed to any training for the student or researcher for whom, originally, the "conversational" language of the search dialogue was designed.

ISSUES OF CONCERN IN USER TRAINING

One unresolved issue in the training of users is whether searches should be made by the user who has the information need or whether the searches should be performed only by specially trained intermediaries. The user, as searcher, knows his real information need; if he is unable to articulate it, he may try his preliminary verbalization in the system, observe results, adjust his statement. In this way, interacting with the titles and abstracts which display for him the current work of others, he can perhaps come to a restatement of his problem or a redefinition of his need. This refinement can be as important and valuable as any specific data gleaned from the literature. Clues, too subtle or obscure for anyone else to note, can lead him to more useful items in the files; and of course he is the final and only source for deciding which discovered items are useful to him.

The trained intermediary, on the other hand, is skilled in eliciting useful, precise statements of the question, in terms appropriate to the search system and to the data base files. He knows what files are available: their contents and idiosyncrasies of organization, the vagaries of data element consistency, and the available vocabulary aids are known by him and accessible to him. He knows how to create effective, efficient logical statements, and can screen excess documents from the output by skilled preliminary judgments of relevance.

The user can go to a terminal close at hand, and make his own search with no delay, no problem of getting to a library location, of finding appropriately trained personnel on duty; his results can be carried right back to his laboratory or desk. There is no necessity for communicating background and explanatory detail to another individual; the psychological and proprietary aspects of privacy are preserved.

The intermediary will be stationed as close to his user population as the economics and foresight of the forces which establish the institution which provides for his (professional) existence can achieve; results of the search can be put into the hands of the user, if he chooses to stand by, immediately. We assume he has not had to stand in a queue for service. The psychological aspects of the interaction are a function of the personalities involved: user and intermediary; they could be a positive as opposed to an inhibiting factor in generating good value in the search. Proprietary privacy is of course respected and observed by the professional searcher.

We have made many unstated assumptions in this comparison; we believe we reflect the current state-of-the-art therein. The assumptions which must be stated, not being so easily justified, are (1) that the user knows how to use the search system and files of value to him, and (2) the trained intermediary is knowledgeable in the subject area of the user's search needs.

Who then should be trained in using on-line searching? The answer, de facto, is that greatest actual use of the services is obtained by training the intermediaries who act as concentrators to funnel questions to the systems. What is the ideal? There are too many variables, but my thought is that as large a pool as possible should be developed, including both classes of users; we need to give time and thought now to reaching as many "end-users" as possible, as early in their careers as we can. A combination of end-user searching, with available recourse to trained specialists, is an easily achievable situation in the present environment. Such a varied pool of users is more likely to provide continuing stimulus both to the improvement of search services and the development of more comprehensive, comprehensible, and useful data bases; additionally the development of the training methods for the less intrinsically committed end-user may lead to improvements in the present training procedures.

TRAINING END-USERS IS A MORE DEMANDING TASK

The end-user presents a different and perhaps more difficult training problem than the information professional. Although the end-user knows what he wants and can be more certain in judging the value of search results than the specialist acting as an intermediary in running searches for him, the end-user has no particular commitment to learning the on-line search as a means of achieving satisfaction of his needs. If required to find answers for himself, he can turn to more familiar sources.

To make the learning of the new resource, the on-line data base, as attractive and rewarding as possible means that we call into play those features of those on-line data bases which were orginally seen as their greatest strength: availability in the intimacy of the laboratory or study without scheduling or traveling limitation: with immediate feedback and guidance in the search process.

To meet the goal of end-user training requires a series of aids which are calculated to achieve specific skills and understandings leading to defined levels of end-user proficiency which are desirable for the end-user, and which we believe to be achievable within the limited amount of time and effort which the end-user can be expected to expend on learning to use this research tool:

1. An end-user can achieve satisfaction in searching on-line data bases when he can use one or two of the more comprehensive existing document retrieval systems, with ease and confidence, to retrieve useful references from the particular data base files which he recognizes as source files for his area of interest.
2. An end-user can be independently competent to use on-line retrieval systems for all of his information needs when he can use one or several of those systems with a high degree of skill and efficiency to retrieve essentially all relevant references from those data base files of greatest utility to himself in his field of inquiry.

The first level of competence is essential to the second; only user perception of the on-line skill as an instrument of great value, and of potentially even greater value, can serve as motivation for that end-user to develop full competence in the on-line search environment.

Not surprisingly these two levels seem to coincide with observed stages in the development of on-line search specialists. Librarians tend to cluster into "beginning" and "advanced" training groups, in the experience of the developers of seminars and workshops. A period of latency, and practice to an estimated eight hours or more on-line, seems to exist between the two stages; and practice is expensive in the operational system, both in actual dollar costs per minute and in the hidden cost of the less efficient search and quite possibly inadequate results of the search.

Some provision needs to be made for practice time which is sufficient to fix the more mechanical aspects of the search process, to allow for more free exploration to round the skills learned. Presently available training suffers from too condensed presentation; perforced by the expense of bringing very expensive personnel out of their place of work to share the equally (or more!) expensive time of the trainer.

Associated with the time pressure of the sessions, in restricting their value to the neophyte, through inadequate practice time, is the fact that any "hands on" training which is given, a few moments perhaps, is often not in the environment where the skill will be used; the mechanical equipment is often not that which the user will have available. End-user type searchers are particularly hurt by the lack of practice; and their less frequent use of the service will further deteriorate their competence. They, more than the specialist intermediary, need a training experience which is available in-house, and which can be returned to at will for refreshment of learning at actual time of need. On the other hand, if we consider that the intermediary also suffers loss of skill through infrequent use, it is again the end-user who suffers, either through higher search costs or less productive searching. This is a serious problem which must be resolved. The project for a "hands-on trainer," described later in this paper, has as one of its goals the amelioration of this problem.

TRAINING OBJECTIVES--WHAT ARE THEY?

A major weakness of many of the training offerings above listed is that there is no training goal stated or implied that is appropriate to the populations being trained; each effort is directed to a part of the overall learning experience or to an aspect of it. The fact is that a trainee wants to learn how to perform his role as information searcher in an environment which includes many bibliographic retrieval services, each of which offers access to multiple files within their separate data bases. In some cases bits and pieces are offered as one or another system or data base is emphasized; the objectives of the sponsor of the training session are tacitly accepted as the goals of the trainees.

Any comparative study of services and data base files must be achieved by the effort of the trainee; it is seldom an objective of a system or data base representative. (However, see Figures 4a, b.)

MODULE 5-NEGOTIATING SEARCH TERMS
≈ ≈

The process of expressing your query as a list or combination of specific words or "search terms" is not easy. Not
only must your choice of terms express your information need
completely in a semantic, conceptual sense, but it must also
match, mechanically, letter for letter, the words stored by the
retrieval system to represent the documents you need.

To help you bring about this match of your conceptions
with the way that they are represented on the retrieval system,
most systems provide appropriate commands. It is usually
possible to browse lists of index terms to seek possible search
terms, to select specific search terms, to discover the correct
forms of terms of which you are unsure, and to allow a very
rapid general search on a basic term. Below are the commands
that allow browsing, term selection, and discovery of correct
forms. They are listed for each system represented in this
training package.

SYSTEM	COMMANDS
= = = = =	= = = = = = =
DIALOG	EXPAND (E)
	SELECT (S)
ORBIT	NEIGHBOR (NBR)
	SS or FIND
SCORPIO	BRWS
	SLCT

Try using these commands as if you were searching the
ERIC data base. Type the name of a system that you want to
practice. After you have finished practicing on one system,
you can try another system by typing its name, or go on to the
rest of this module by typing DONE. Use only the term
DISADVANTAGED to begin your practice of these commands.

Figure 4a. Excerpt from CALP Module 5. Introduction and
guide to part of the contents of a learning and practice module.
See Figure 4b for a partial illustration of practice use of this
module.

```
        Type a system name or DONE
>ORBIT
        You have chosen to practice ORBIT.  Begin by using NBR
with the term DISADVANTAGED.

SS 1/C?
USER:
>NBR DISADVANTAGED
Your command should be enclosed in quotes.


PROG:
POSTINGS                    TERM
      162           DISADVANT  (IT)
        1           DISADVANTAGE ENVIRONMENT  (IT)
    10888           DISADVANTAGED  (IT)
        1           DISADVANTAGED ADULTS  (IT)
      213           DISADVANTAGED ENVIRONMENT  (IT)
UP N OR DOWN N?----HOW MANY TERMS UP OR DOWN?
```

        [ORBIT is asking you if you want to view more of the index.
If not, you would enter NO or NONE. If so, you would enter
UP or DOWN and then the number of terms alphabetically before
or after this list that you want to see. You can go UP or DOWN
as many as 10 terms. Try going down 3.]

```
UP N OR DOWN N?----HOW MANY TERMS UP OR DOWN?
USER:
>DOWN 3

PROG:
POSTINGS                    TERM
        1           DISADVANTAGED ENVIRONMENT
                    COGNITIVE DEVELO  (IT)
     1395           DISADVANTAGED GROUPS  (IT)
       83           DISADVANTAGED SCHOOLS  (IT)
UP N OR DOWN N?----HOW MANY TERMS UP OR DOWN?
```

Figure 4b. Computer assisted learning and practice sequences
to learn how to use the DIALOG, ORBIT, SCORPIO commands
and displays to examine indexes to a data base file. This example illustrates ORBIT's NEIGHBOR command; it is a continuation of the sequence shown in Figure 4a.

Below are the commands, special truncation characters (if any), and command forms for the systems represented on this training package.

SYSTEM	COMMAND	SPECIAL CHAR.	COMMAND FORM
=====	=====	=========	==========
ORBIT	SS	:	SS 1/C?
			USER:
			CRYST:
DIALOG	SELECT S	?	SELECT CRYST?
SCORPIO	SLCT	NONE	SLCT CRYST

Practice truncation on one of the systems by typing the system's name. After you have practiced on that system, you may either type the name of another system and practice truncation on it or type DONE to go on. Use the stem CRYST to practice.

Type a system name or DONE
> ORBIT
You have chosen to practice ORBIT truncation. Use the stem CRYST.

Figure 4c. Excerpt from Computer Assisted Learning and Practice Module 5. Further listing of commands which may be learned, practiced, and/or compared in this module.

Where systems and data base files are brought together for the edification of user populations, the presentations are apt to be brief; there is little possibility of achieving integration or realization of comparable capabilities or sources. User organizations tend to be sensitive to user problems, attempting to patch around or cause curative action to be taken for the most painful of the user-felt difficulties. Ultimately these groups may prove to be very powerful aids to the improvement of the environment of on-line bibliographic searching, but lack the organization and motivation to become a focus for training users.

A more disinterested source of training is needed than can be found in the instances just given; the locus may better be in the training programs within traditional educational institutions. These programs tend, however, to ignore time constraints of practicing professionals. Certainly the end-user whose professional orientation is not toward librarianship or information science is not likely to seek out registration in such courses or workshops.

The failure to provide a coherent, comprehensive learning experience, thus, is seen as the most obvious failure of the existing training scene. Unevenness of treatment to the several aspects of on-line searching, biases introduced by commitment to one or another system as a "first experience," high costs of training sessions plus hidden and overt costs of on-line practice; requirements to be at certain locations and at certain time periods, inflexibility of content, and incapacity to tailor the experience to individual needs, are among the weaknesses identified. The "hands-on trainer," previously alluded to, attempts to address these identified problem areas.

DEVELOPING USER SKILLS TO THE FIRST LEVEL OF COMPETENCE

Our experience and our study of the experience of others leads us to believe that the early training process can be divided into four time sequenced intermediate goals which should bring the user to a desirable first level of skill:

1. Learning to use the mechanical devices: teletypewriter, acoustic coupler, display terminals; accessing remote host computer systems via telecommunication networks;
2. Acquiring confidence and fluency in the conventions of the most-used elements of language of a system and in reading the displays generated by the system;
3. Recognizing searchable fields (data elements such as title words, author names) of the document record, and knowing what files exist which are relevant to his own information needs, and how to identify them within a data base;
4. Becoming competent in the use of logical connectors to broaden or narrow the scope of the search and the size of the retrieved document set.

Further training would lead to greater use of system capabilities, and more skill in making the on-line search less costly, but may not be useful to the beginning user if presented before he has become at ease in this first stage of training.

A further look at the staged sequence of intermediate goals for training the end-user in the effective use of the new information service will serve as a device to clarify the training approach. While we reflect here the specific case of the end-user, intelligent but not committed to the use of this tool for his information seeking, the same statement could apply to any beginning trainee.

Learning to use the communication terminal. Some end-users may be proficient, or at least comfortable, using an ordinary typewriter; others may have used the teletypewriter for various computer processes. Even these may never have attempted to establish a computer linkage using telephone lines or data communication networks. Practice, in varying amounts, is needed by almost every trainee to establish competence in use of the communication equipment.

The procedures for establishing communication with a remote computer system are almost never taught in the abbreviated training sessions most frequently offered; the process is too trivial, and in fact has no special identification with any particular bibliographic retrieval service; the network is after all a common carrier. User manuals for the services give lists of telephone numbers and tables of codes to be used, but such practice during the brief, competitively achieved hands-on sessions is ignored. (See Figures 5 and 6.)

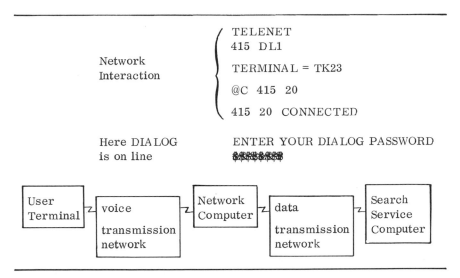

Network
Interaction

TELENET
415 DL1

TERMINAL = TK23

@C 415 20

415 20 CONNECTED

Here DIALOG
is on line

ENTER YOUR DIALOG PASSWORD
●●●●●●●●

| User Terminal | voice transmission network | Network Computer | data transmission network | Search Service Computer |

Figure 5. Visible record at user terminal of interaction between the user and a commercial data transmission network. The purpose: to link user terminal to distant computer, via local telephone lines and less expensive network.

(User has been shown a list of terminal identifier codes
and instructed to use TELENET protocol to link to
DIALOG)

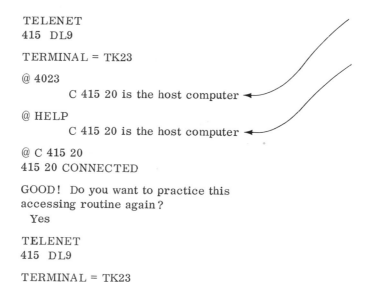

```
TELENET
415  DL9

TERMINAL = TK23

@ 4023
        C 415 20 is the host computer

@ HELP
              C 415 20 is the host computer

@ C 415 20
415 20 CONNECTED

GOOD!  Do you want to practice this
accessing routine again?
  Yes

TELENET
415  DL9

TERMINAL = TK23

@ C 415 20
415 20 CONNECTED

GOOD!
```

Figure 6.   Excerpt from training program sequence in which
the user-trainee becomes familiar with network (TYMNET and
TELENET) access to DIALOG and ORBIT. When the user-
trainee fails to enter an expected response or asks for help,
he is given the correct entry and a brief explanation of it (see
arrows in the illustration).

Nevertheless this is an unavoidable preliminary to the on-line search.
The beginning user is likely to find himself on his own resources to get the
connection from his terminal to the search system computer established.

Learning to use the terminal to access the remote system is a good
instance, because it is brief and easily isolated, to use in explaining much
of the difficulty which plagues new users. The process is trivial in the

written description and not complex. However, when the new user sits down to a terminal and there is no indication from the system as to what he is expected to do, if anything, and the exchange is cryptic, both network generated prompts and his own responses having little or no mnemonic value, the effect may be a "turnoff" of the user, and a turning off of the terminal. When the user may not really know if it is a network processor or a computer processor he is interacting with, or has no conscious operating awareness of any separateness or multiplicity in the communication system, the user may spend frustrating moments in what is, to his purposes, an irrelevant preliminary exchange.

SUMMARY STATEMENT--EXISTING TRAINING PROGRAMS

With all of the noted objections, as stated, we are yet dependent on the agencies listed above for most of our learning about on-line systems use at the present time. While expensive, they offer the considerable virtues of brevity and portability; they can and do come to you. They keep users, services, and data base developers in intimate, face-to-face communication. Unless you are already a subscriber to the services, however, it may be difficult to discover where and when such sessions will be scheduled. The two new journals, ONLINE and On-Line Review, should be consulted, both for their educational and informational content per se and for scheduled training sessions of service and data base suppliers.

A LOOK TO THE FUTURE

The National Science Foundation funded project underway here at the University of Pittsburgh may soon bring some relief to the individual trying to make use of the tremendous potential of those on-line information resources: Under the rubric "Training Modules for Scientific and Technical Information Services," but more affectionately, "Hands-On On-Line in a Multi-System Multi-Data Base Trainer," we are creating a learning environment for users. *

The training program includes emulations of the most-used retrieval services and a large number of the files which are available through those services. The emulators look just like the operational services and may be used to gain interactive facility, to become skilled in the dialogue with the retrieval system--without long distance communication charges or the expense of practice searching on full-scale data bases. With the several

---

*NSF Grant DSI 76-09538, Training Modules for S. T. I. Services, D. E. Caruso, Principal Investigator.

systems available, "side-by-side" as it were, there is also the opportunity
to compare their functioning on identical subsets of a data base.

The training program includes supportive practice and learning sequences for the command languages of the retrieval services also. One of
the real problems of learning to use the search services is that so many
errors which you may make in using them are not diagnosed by the system.
For instance, if you get no results when you ask for articles on "SOLAR
ENERGY," it may mean that there is nothing in the file on the subject. It
may also mean that this particular file, as structured by the service you are
using, does not include multi-word terms in the searchable index; thus, only
a combination of terms, "SOLAR" and "ENERGY," separately entered, will
find your information. The supportive programs, used with the emulators
for each service, combine to spotlight these otherwise undiscoverable errors
of searching; in the computer assisted learning and practice programs the
errors are recognized and diagnosed; the training emulators allow the testing of the techniques.

The training program is undergoing test uses at the present time;
when complete it will be made accessible either by remote terminals or for
implementation on other computer systems. When the training program
becomes fully available, we believe the need for commercially inspired
workshops and seminars will become less pressing. Indeed we strongly feel
that the burden of these sessions, here and elsewhere in the United States
and abroad, is becoming too heavy for the services and data base suppliers
to sustain, as they have done in the past. If (when?) acceptable solutions to
the "fee problem" are found, we can expect to see use rates, and numbers
of users, climb: the Congressional Reference Service recently reported
that its on-line services logged its first million transaction month in March
1977; SCORPIO alone averages 1,350 searches daily.

Chapter 22

TRAINING AND RETRAINING: REACTION

Sally Bachelder Stanley

Vice President
The Information Bank
New York, New York

When I began to prepare for this conference, I very diligently se-
questered myself in my office, asked my secretary to hold all my calls and,
with pen in hand, began to read Dr. Caruso's paper (Chapter 21). I jotted
down copious notes in the margins and madly underlined sentences that I
felt leant themselves to some sort of a reaction. After all, I thought to myself, I have to prepare a formal response, so I had better find some nice,
"meaty" passages I can react to with fire and conviction! However, as I
made my way slowly through the paper, I found to my consternation that as
I made a note of some "serious" omission on Dr. Caruso's part, she very
neatly covered that "omission" in the next sentence. As I underlined a statement that I felt was too narrow, she expanded upon it in the next paragraph.
By the fifth page, I abandoned my pen; it really wasn't helping me at all. I
continued reading the paper, and, at its conclusion, could find no statement
whose counterpoint I felt compelled to defend, or any information that seemed
to need correcting. "What now?" I thought to myself; what kind of a reaction
can I prepare when I'm basically in agreement with all of the points raised?

As I mulled over the paper in the following days and reviewed my
experiences in training on-line users, one thought came to me that has continually surfaced in my work that was not specifically covered by Dr. Caruso.
Though implied throughout her paper, one very important comment ought to
be made concerning the value inherent in the training itself--the consideration of training not as a lesson or two to achieve mastery of some mechanical skills, or computer skills, or reference skills, but as the key to the full
utilization of a data base. One must consider training not merely as a step
that must be taken before the "final reward" is achieved, but as a basic element of that final reward.

I have been working with The Information Bank, an on-line current events-oriented data base, for over five years. My first exposure to the system was here at the University of Pittsburgh. As a graduate library school student, it was my job to train other students in the operation of the system. After graduation, I went to work for The Information Bank as an on-line instructor. Eventually, I moved up into sales, and now into management. During all of this, I have had the opportunity to train many different kinds of users and to sell The Information Bank in many different markets. I believe I speak from experience then when I say that we cannot assume people value the training function itself and the new abilities it provides.

I have one story that clearly illustrates this point: I made a formal presentation to a large Fortune 500 company recently, outlining the new information services The Information Bank could provide to that company. After all of the applications were discussed and reviewed by the executives in attendance, the decision was made to subscribe to the service and some $20,000 was allocated out of next year's budget to cover the cost of full service. Now, I believe that $20,000 represents a substantial investment on the part of the organization, so I was quite surprised when, after the contract was signed, the executive in charge told me that he would send his secretary over some afternoon next week to "learn how to work it"! The training was obviously viewed as a relatively unimportant chore that had to be done before all of the benefits the system had to offer could be realized. I had made the mistake of not selling the value of the training as well as the value of the service, because you can't have the latter without the former. I don't think that executive understood that his $20,000 investment rested in his secretary's ability to manipulate the system.

While Dr. Caruso comments on the problem of training users not fully committed to the resource, we must also recognize the problem of people committed to the resource but not the training. This attitude, while more prevalent among non-librarians than librarians, does not altogether disappear in the library community. It is exemplified by the librarian who already subscribes to one or two other on-line systems and figures, "what the heck?" I might as well add another. He or she signs up for training, and the lack of value given to this activity can be seen in the following situations (all of these little vignettes are taken from actual experiences; the names have been omitted to protect the innocent!):

1. When the trainer arrives, we find that the User Guide sent on ahead hasn't even been removed from its envelope, or
2. the person to be trained also has to cover the reference desk that morning, or
3. the person has just recently received training in another on-line system and doesn't fully understand that one yet but is charging on ahead, or

4. the on-line practice time given to a new user by The Information Bank during the start-up phase isn't even used: "I've been too busy with other things to practice." Also,
5. the user really had no intention of using the data base in an on-going fashion in the first place but expects the training to stand them in good stead three months later when they decide to make a stab at running a search.

It's always very discouraging to me when I hear of these situations. As a sales representative, I have come to the conclusion that I must _sell_ people on the value of the training itself. My response to the business executive is to request that an associate who is _research-oriented_ receive instruction, and that he/she be allowed more than one afternoon to learn! My response to the librarian who is acquiring data bases for infrequent use is to ask that they _not_ try to search on their own but refer those questions appropriate to the data base to another library that has some solid searching experience.

When I see a new Information Bank client who has not used up their practice time and did not give our trainers their full and undivided attention during training, I know I'm looking at a problem account. There is no possible way the value of the data base can be realized if the training program is not viewed as _basic_ to that value. As I said before, you can't have one without the other; you can't expect to derive the full benefits of on-line searching if you don't fully exploit all training opportunities offered to you. It's not just learning which button to push. As Dr. Caruso pointed out, the _use_ of data bases is fundamentally different from the use of printed indexes, so there is much more to learn and absorb than simply the mechanical skills. The investment of time and money that must be made in _training_ has to be recognized and accepted as being as important as the cost of the on-line usage itself.

Establishing the value of the training program is a fundamental concern of _all_ of the on-line systems, regardless of the nature of the data bases themselves. Each data base, however, brings to a trainer its own idiosyncrasies to cause more headaches, and Dr. Caruso has mentioned some of them: inconsistent content coverage, erratic labeling of data elements, infrequent updates, etc. The Information Bank is not immune to these weaknesses, and our trainers have to cope with the difficulties presented to them by an enigmatic abstract or an inscrutable scope note. As a _general_ information data base, however, we find ourselves training a fair number of non-librarians: paralegal assistants, speechwriters, executive trainees, secretaries, even some file clerks. The problems inherent in this situation are infrequently discussed at professional library gatherings. As Dr. Caruso pointed out, many of the on-line training programs are planned with only the librarian in mind, and the ever growing body of non-librarians coming in

contact with on-line systems is left in the lurch. I thought I would share
some of the problems encountered by our training staff that, as professional
librarians, we might not otherwise consider.

One interesting fact regarding the training of a non-librarian is that
it takes place in a "non-library." In other words, The Information Bank
often stands alone as an available information resource. This means that
when a question arises no decision must be made as to the appropriate resource to use. If it sounds at all feasible, it will be run through The Bank.
This presents quite a training challenge, because to make a data base produce information that it really isn't designed to produce requires a lot of
manipulation for minimal output. Try explaining the rationale of multiple
modifiers in a nested logic statement to retrieve many documents, only a
few of which are relevant!

Another training problem presented to us by non-librarians is that
research is not their primary function. If they should become skilled in the
use of the system and the word gets around that they know how to use "that
new machine," they could be overloaded by this new responsibility to the
detriment of their other duties. Talk about a deterrant to learning! It's to
the benefit of the assistant not to learn. After all, the assistant reasons, if
training is considered to be the mastery of key strokes and the assistant has
done that but is still getting poor search results, it's "obviously" the fault
of the system. Exit one system and enter one assistant who "knew it would
all be a problem right from the start."

One measure of a system's performance is the ratio of precision to
recall: the percentage of relevant information retrieved to the total amount
retrieved. A librarian is interested in knowing also what percentage of the
total amount of relevant information their present retrieval represents. In
other words, how much have I missed? Oftentimes, a librarian will run a
search a number of times to try and extract all possible relevant documents
from the system. Many non-librarians will not do this, and it represents
an over dependence on a single search statement as the measure of system
effectiveness. It is a very important lesson for non-librarians to learn that
what you retrieve (or don't retrieve) is the product of your search statement
and does not necessarily represent the best answer the system has for your
question. Many novice users will take a "no answer to this inquiry" response from the system to mean that it has no relevant documents available.
Imagine the frustration of a new user who, through faulty search strategy
construction, gets this response a number of times; he/she must wonder if
the system contains any documents at all! This is a very basic lesson for
non-librarians to learn.

Another problem that we run into is the paralegal or executive trainee
who realizes that he/she has been singled out to receive system instruction.

Because they are not librarians, their selection to learn the system sometimes has career implications for them, and the pressure to learn is intense.
This can be compounded by their superior's demand of immediate mastery
of the system, i.e., they want relevant retrieval right away with a minimum
amount of search time. Even though the student may be fully committed to
learning, the pressure environment in which they must operate is counter-
productive to that learning.

This demand for immediate acquisition of on-line searching skills is
indicative of that very basic training problem we all confront that I discussed
at the outset: the inability of many people to view on-line training as a highly
valuable activity. As on-line teaching methodologies are refined and improved, I would hope that the professionalism with which they are approached
is also enhanced. While we must guard against the development of system
training programs geared only to librarians, we must avoid the temptation
to develop programs that attempt to reduce the importance of the lessons
being transmitted.

Let's make on-line instruction as easy as we can to reach as wide an
audience as possible, but let's not downplay its importance to the audience.

Chapter 23

SOME COMMENTS ON THE "TRAINING AND RETRAINING
OF LIBRARIANS AND USERS"

Judith Wanger

Vice-President
Cuadra Associates, Inc.
Santa Monica, California
(At the time of the conference, Ms. Wanger was at the
SDC Search Service, System Development Corporation)

Elaine Caruso has given us much to think about regarding the challenge of training for on-line use. She has identified a number of problems and issues; she has also posed one possible solution to some of these problems, from her perspective. The value of a conference such as this one is that it gives us the opportunity to share our perceptions of problems, issues, and possible solutions. These perceptions will clearly reflect our roles and levels of involvement in the on-line world over the past several years and may reveal some major differences of opinion. My own perspective is as Manager of User Services and Training and my ten years at SDC.

I concur, in general, with Elaine's premise that the face-to-face workshop cannot be all things to all users and that it cannot be the sole medium for training. However, my perceptions and interpretations of yesterday and today, as well as the promise of tomorrow, will differ in several ways from Elaine's. I would like to discuss four major areas that she touched on and, as well, respond to some of her specific observations.

FOCUS ON BIBLIOGRAPHIC DATA BASES

First, with regard to her contention that the on-line service organizations are focusing on bibliographic data bases because of the potential size of the market, I have a different perception. The focus on bibliographic data bases is partly an accident of history. For example, we at SDC are in the on-line service business today because in the mid-1960's we were developing

a storage and retrieval system technology for time-sharing computers.
These activities happened to dovetail with growing efforts to put bibliographic
data in machine-readable form. For many reasons, bibliographic control
over the published literature--particularly over non-changing textual material, such as the journal article--has, as you all know, traditionally out-
distanced, and still does outdistance, control of data bank-type data bases,
of handbooks and directories, and of other more dynamic and volatile information. The historical happenstance, therefore, was that the original technology of storage and retrieval systems, which was designed to provide
access to records with fairly fixed element definitions and to files that remained fairly static, matched up very well with a particular type of informa-
tion--bibliographic information.

    Incidentally, I must observe that, even now, a number of data bases
available on-line are not truly bibliographic. The Smithsonian Science Information Exchange data base of current research is not a true bibliographic
file; neither is the World Patent Index, the GRANTS data base, or some of
the PREDICASTS files. However, our field does not yet have a vocabulary to
distinguish the various kinds of data bases that are available through the on-
line services. Anyone who has tried to do a comprehensive search on this
subject in a multi-disciplinary file, such as NTIS, knows exactly what I
mean.

    In the meantime, the major on-line services are indeed focusing on
the bibliographic-type data base and on the intermediary-type searcher. In
doing so, we are learning quite a bit, in a living laboratory, about what we
need to do to get to the next stages of development and how to move toward
an expanded base of users and data bases. This brings me then to a discussion of the end-user versus the intermediary.

THE END-USER VS. THE INTERMEDIARY IN TRAINING

    First, I must contribute one more piece of history from our perspec-
tive. The original ORBIT system of the middle 1960's was not designed for
either an information intermediary or an end-user. The SDC designers were
trying to improve the characteristics of a man-machine interface (where
"man" was a non-programmer person) from the experiences we had in designing radar defense systems in the 1950's. In the early 1970's, when we
were using ORBIT in an experimental context with the National Library of
Medicine, one of the clearly stated goals was to enable end-users to use the
system effectively. However, the design of the interface was optimized for
the novice intermediary.

    I think that for some purposes, and particularly for purposes of
training and system design, it is not useful, and may even be counterpro-

ductive, to characterize system users in terms of end-users versus intermediaries. We fully recognize and give credence to the distinction for purposes of marketing, because the individuals' work environments are quite
different, and the ways in which we identify and reach them are quite different. However, today we are focusing on training of users and not on marketing.

The limitations in using the dichotomy of end-user versus intermediary become clear when we characterize a group of individuals who attend one
of our new-user training workshops. Incidentally, we do set goals for all of
our training workshops (a topic which I will explore later), but we also attempt to tailor our sessions for the particular group in attendance. To tailor
a session, we must take into account characteristics such as: 1) the data
bases or general discipline of interest to the individuals; 2) their level of
previous experience with on-line systems; 3) their readiness to begin using
the system (e.g., familiarity with the terminal; familiarity with the printed
tools); 4) their attitudes and abilities (e.g., willingness to use a "machine";
degree of initiative); and 5) their work environment (e.g., Are they the only
searcher or one of many? Will they be a "frequent" or "infrequent" user of
the system?).

We obtain some of this information prior to the workshop; we learn
the rest when we talk to them at the workshop and see them at the terminal
for the first time.

When you think about some of these characteristics, you realize that
any given individual will be somewhere on the continuum between the extremes of each characteristic. It is an absolute fallacy to believe that any
random group of librarians will necessarily be more ready, more frequent
users of a system, more willing and eager, or even more knowledgeable
about corresponding printed tools and literature-searching principles than
any random group of subject information specialists or end-users. In fact,
for any three groups of librarians, information specialists, and end-users,
the differences within a group are likely to be as large as those between the
groups.

We have found that an individual's attitudes and general abilities may
contribute even more to the development of searching skills than his background or previous experience. For example, if someone is eager to learn
and has a systematic, organized approach to thinking about a research problem, he or she may become a more successful searcher than one who is, by
training, a librarian, but who does not have those attitudes and abilities.

We also believe that what happens after the initial training is an even
more important factor in the development of successful searchers. Particularly important are their levels of involvement in the searching activity and
their levels of investment in the ongoing process of learning.

Let's look at both of these stages of learning. First, at the outset, let me say that we see a positive contribution being made by some of the training that is not provided by the on-line suppliers: the emulation system at the University of Denver and at the University of Pittsburgh, as well as the simulation-type system developed by Dr. Lundeen at the University of Hawaii, other library school programs, and the person-to-person program of individuals who are training their colleagues. However, we must also raise this important point: that those individuals who assume a training responsibility are also assuming a moral responsibility for keeping themselves, their material, and their systems current. For instance, many of the ORBIT examples in Elaine's paper will be obsolete within a few months with the advent of the ORBIT IV system features. Will each of the trainers and training systems accurately reflect the most current system? Will these individuals and organizations have the continuing funds and motivation to invest in modifying their system and materials or procedures in a timely fashion? If not, they may unwittingly be doing a great disservice to their colleagues, students, and clients.

THE NEW-USER TRAINING WORKSHOP
IN A TOTAL INSTRUCTIONAL PROGRAM

For the short term, particularly because of the dynamic nature of our industry, we believe that training workshops, especially those sponsored by on-line suppliers, will continue to be the major means of providing initial training. On-line suppliers have the continuing interest and the resources to reach out to users in all corners of the United States and elsewhere in the world.

Quite apart from the question of who does the training, the workshop is still only one medium, and even now it exists within the context of a broad instructional program, particularly needed to support the ongoing learning process. Our instructional program has a number of components carefully designed to be mutually supporting. These include:

- New-user, advanced-user, and data base workshops
- Action desks with toll-free lines so users can get help as it
  is needed
- The ORBIT user manual and data base supplements
- The ORBIT quick-reference guide
- Newsletters
- Educational rates for institutions of higher education
- Practice time
- An on-line facility for sending us comments and questions
- On-line explanations and tutorials

These nine user service components are important and essential elements in our service. The reason is that all of these elements support the instructional process but also interact and point up needs in other service areas. For example, the kinds of questions we receive at our Action Desk help us to determine what needs to be conveyed in the newsletter, or where explanations in the user manuals need to be improved, or what shifts of emphasis might be needed in our training sessions. And what we see in the training sessions feeds back in the same way to other components, including --and this is probably most important of all--helping us to identify the ways in which our system can be improved to meet the behavior patterns of users.

The instructional support arm of our service is, in effect, the "sensing network" of our total service. For example, the needs we have sensed contributed, along with data from the On-line Impact Study we conducted, to the design of several important new capabilities: the standardization of element names across all of the data bases; the standardization of the way we handle subject-related searching across data bases to facilitate cross-file searching; and some new ORBIT features that will facilitate multiple-system use.

The goals of our new-user training workshop--probably of others as well--are to help users feel as comfortable as possible about interacting with the system, to learn principles involved in data base searching, and, in general, to learn enough about these principles and processes to continue their own learning. Specific content goals include:

- Introduction to the terminology and the technology of the service;
- System language and protocols, which includes the logging-in process;
- Search strategy development, including Boolean logic;
- Learning how to learn about a data base;
- Cost-effective searching techniques; and
- Trouble shooting.

For most sessions, we cannot--and we state this explicitly to attendees--teach in depth about each of the data bases in a new-user training session.

The user must rely on several additional means to learn more about particular data bases: 1) reading the user manuals and other tools available for those particular files; 2) attending data base workshops sponsored either by on-line suppliers or data base suppliers; 3) making full use of the user assistance provided, at no charge, by on-line suppliers (e.g., SDC's Action Desk toll-free lines) and by many data base suppliers; and 4) equally important as these, learning from and sharing with other searchers.

THE RETRAINING COMPONENT OF TRAINING

One area that we cannot do a great deal about in our instructional program is the reshaping of attitudes and basic approaches toward literature searching by machine, and this is my final topic.

There seems to be no evidence that any widespread revolution in thinking is taking place. On the contrary, we know that the on-line services are being used by many intermediary searchers in the same manner that batch and manual searches were being done. The traditional manual literature search is a one-person activity with invisible thought processes taking place while the searcher pores over one or more printed indexes. The introduction of on-line searching has not dramatically changed some parts of this picture. Reference interviews are still being held over the telephone. Users requirements are still being expressed on a piece of paper delivered to a searcher. The process of thinking through the strategy and interacting with the system is still mostly the lonely activity of the searcher.

Probably no more than 25% of the searchers have end-users by their side when they do the search. The data supporting this statement are derived partly from our on-line study, but also reflect more recent data from the National Library of Medicine. And yet... McGill University did a study in which they required end-users to sit with the searcher. After the study, 50% of the end-users said that their presence was necessary; another 47% said that it was desirable. In the British Library Study, to be published soon, we understand that, when user satisfaction was reviewed, it was highest when they had been present at the search.

To me, this kind of retraining of thinking, including thinking about the ideal searcher/user relationship, represents a much greater challenge than teaching someone to learn the mechanical procedures for a machine search.

We emphatically do not agree with Elaine that the on-line systems have, themselves, become a part of the problem. On-line systems are being learned; they are being used. They will also become even more easy to use and even more effective in retrieving a wider variety of information. Therefore, it will be a mistake for the information specialists who have interested themselves in the on-line services to focus only on today's smaller problems and to overemphasize the mechanical aspects of the systems. It would be far more useful to have their help on some of the greater challenges, of defining new searcher/user relationships, and of better characterizing the relationship of search strategy approaches and user/intermediary relationships to different kinds of organizations, users, and user needs.

The traditional approach, for example, may be most appropriate in certain circumstances. The side-by-side approach may be best for other kinds of searchers, for other kinds of users. The use of dual-terminal searching, where an end-user in a remote location watches at his or her own terminal while the searcher is at the master terminal doing the searching, may be most appropriate for other kinds of institutions and circumstances.

There are many models to explore and yet more to be defined. I hope that we will not dwell on the new-user and initial training as the whole definition of training needs. There is an entire continuum of training and education needs to be met, and most of these needs will need to be met from within the community of practitioners. This is where the rethinking and retraining for optimizing the use of on-line technology--taking full advantage of the opportunities it offers--must take place if we are to meet the true promise of tomorrow.

Chapter 24

TRAINING FOR THE WHOLE ON-LINE REVOLUTION

Susan K. Martin

Head, Library Systems Office
University of California-Berkeley
Berkeley, California

I am a confessed science fiction addict, with the habit still going
strong. This summer I read an older work of Robert Silverberg entitled
Recalled to Life; the plot focusses on the discovery of a process for re-
storing life to people who had died less than 36 hours previously. Much of
the novel revolves around the social consequences of this new process and
the attitudes displayed by the world's population upon learning of the life-
restoration technique. Negative attitudes prevailed, and only within the
Moon-based colony did enthusiasm abound. The explanation was twofold:
the Moon colonists lived constantly with the threat of accidental death in a
sparsely populated area, and (more significantly) they were intimately
associated with a wide variety of new technologies and were not afraid of
trying yet another one.

If I may generalize this example, the science fiction description of
societal attitudes toward technological innovation seemed to have some
bearing on the real-life attitudes toward the topic we are discussing this
week. Apprehensions about technological developments, raised and perhaps
unrealistic expectations of the potential of technology, and the need to deal
with widely varying levels of experience all enter into the question of training
librarians and users to learn the intricacies of our developing systems, despite the confidence and enthusiasm of the attendees at this conference.

What are some of the major issues? Some have been addressed in
Elaine Caruso's presentation. I would like to focus on additional particular
aspects of training in the use of on-line systems: the question of intermediary vs. end-user; the relationship of on-line reference to on-line technical

processing systems; user expectations; training for the negative aspects; and funding and political issues.

THE INTERMEDIARY VERSUS THE END-USER

As did all the speakers, Dr. Caruso has drawn the distinction between the information professional intermediary and the end-user, identifying the more considerable efforts required to provide end-users with the needed skills for on-line searching. There is no question that training for system use must differ with the system user. The mechanisms listed in the position paper as being available for intermediaries, such as service bureau documentation, training programs and professional society training sessions, are widely accessible to information professionals; we can refine existing approaches to training these intermediaries, but my sense is that technical training of searchers presents few problems at this time.

Although I believe that significant hands-on use of on-line systems by end-users is years away, we do need to begin teaching end-users more now about how our information systems work and what services are available to them. Especially in large research libraries, we have not yet mastered even the technique of training our clientele to use the card catalog. How then can we expect to train them to use on-line systems as well? We can train them to use only on-line systems, but they will then be lacking the important background knowledge of the bibliographic tools used locally, regionally, and nationally. The link between the card catalog and the on-line information system must be made; since the Library of Congress has announced its intention to close its card catalog in favor of a machine-based catalog in 1980, it behooves us to begin orienting our patrons toward a machine-based environment in which the card catalog plays an important role but is by no means the only tool to be consulted.

Many librarians are openly or secretly wary of future developments, and they expect their patrons to be similarly timorous. As a result, they worry a great deal about the political impact of the closing of the catalog within the institution and about the introduction of machine-based reference services into their libraries. According to experiences in various libraries throughout the country, users are pleased with increased access available in their libraries; training and orientation for change will have to aim more at the needs of the information professional than at the end-user--at least initially.

Nonetheless, user training and orientation are important for the successful implementation of technological innovations. Let us examine the difference between intermediary and end-user training as it affects the library's operation. Intermediaries are likely to be staff members, located at the library 30 or 40 hours a week, knowledgeable in the use of existing bibliographic tools, and readily available to take classes or workshops in the use of on-line systems. Intermediary training costs the library money, but these costs do not represent large budgetary reallocations (although the use of the on-line systems may require reallocation of funds). End-user training, as described vaguely in the professional literature, is sporadic, one-on-one, and difficult to arrange. The program being developed here at Pittsburgh described in Dr. Caruso's paper is an exception, and one which promises considerable improvement in our approach to end-user training. Libraries must answer the following questions: who will train? who will be trained? where will the funds come from? how do we reach all the patrons who might wish to learn the use of on-line systems? At Berkeley, we have made successful steps in the direction of library instruction for students and have now held faculty seminars for over 150 faculty members, orienting them to basic principles of library use. A natural follow-up in the future might be specific training in the use of on-line systems.

The ability to completely train the end-user will be required at the point that card catalogs are closed, machine-readable catalogs abound, and links exist between the data in the library catalogs and the data bases that we have been discussing this week.

TECHNICAL PROCESSING SYSTEMS

Over the next few years, we will find that we are making an unnatural distinction between on-line technical processing systems, such as OCLC or BALLOTS, and on-line reference systems. Indeed, nearly two years ago a subcommittee of a CLR-based committee on national bibliographic control was constituted to work on the problems involved in bringing together the library bibliographic data with the abstracting and indexing data. Our profession has made this distinction in developing the manual and automated systems; we continue to make the distinction when we discuss the systems, but the user who is looking for information on a specific topic, or all the works of a certain author, does not differentiate between books, reports, and journal articles. He or she wants everything relevant. And location information is essential. Why do we discuss OCLC and BALLOTS as unrelated to data base services? We are beginning to place terminals which access these systems in public areas, allowing end-users to complement their use of the card catalog. User training should incorporate the concepts common to all on-line bibliographic systems in order to allow patrons to understand and use these systems most effectively. I look forward to the time (far in the future, I am afraid) when the bibliographic data produced by the Library of Congress will be linked automatically to records produced by data base proprietors. At that time, we shall serve our users better and training will be easier!

USER EXPECTATIONS

Several of the position papers referred to problems or issues raised by user expectations. Librarian, searcher, or end-user--the problem is the same: everyone is different. As Silverberg described in his book, a gamut of emotions and expectations can be found regarding this relatively new technology. Why is this important? Because any attempt at training, whether it be of intermediaries or end-users, must take into account the wide range of reaction to the on-line systems. Gentle defusing of overly high expectations is just as necessary as gradual persuasion of the skeptics that the system is indeed useful for certain purposes. Individual or group training should be geared to carefully explain the nature and goals of the system, and trainers should additionally be instructed in techniques for identifying attitudes of very high or very low expectation so that remedial action can be taken. We are in our infancy in public use of on-line systems; we will need political support and, as you all know, a satisfied user can be very helpful in furthering the success of the system.

User expectations which must be addressed directly and comprehensively are those which relate to the juxtaposition of manual and machine-based tools. The position paper on the impact on clientele indicated concern that users might use machine-based systems to the total exclusion of the manual tools. To ignore the relationship between the various sets of tools is to perform incomplete training. Likewise, the users must be made aware of the relationship between the data they see on the CRT screen and the collection which is available in the local library. Until we are able to provide the direct link between library bibliographic information and the data bases, we and the end-users will be faced with a multiple-step, often tedious, process of retrieving the material after the citation has been found. In the technical processing systems, a similar phenomenon occurs: users must be trained to realize that although they see it on the screen their library does not necessarily own it.

Training must incorporate the skills necessary to match data with documents. How difficult is it to obtain the material? It depends, of course, on the nature of the collection and the cooperative arrangements held by each library, among other factors. Our bibliographic systems and procedures are extremely complex and becoming more so by the month. While the complexities of document retrieval do not need to be incorporated in a training program for data base use, librarians and trainers must be constantly aware of the pitfalls presented to users.

TRAINING FOR THE NEGATIVES

One rule of thumb for the instructor is always to present ideas in a positive way, to derive the most benefit for the learner. This is all well and good; however, our systems have a few negative points to cope with, as we have heard this week. We must train for the negatives in a positive way. Let us look at two examples which have been described.

Bibliographic data bases represent a mass of confusing entries, a variety of styles, many classification systems, and a welter of subject headings. Professionals have to spend many hours mastering the similarities and differences sufficiently to be able to serve the end-users; how can we expect the end-user to comprehend the confusion, much less understand why we did it this way? Well, the end-user has one advantage over the information professional: in most cases, he or she is working on a specific problem with specific terminology. Even in an interdisciplinary field, the sophisticated user may be able to learn the various systems, classification schemes, and thesauri employed to describe his area of interest. I see no easy way in which we can describe these problems and inconsistencies in a positive manner. It seems to me that the best technique in training is to describe the problem, suggest solutions to typical obstacles, and be completely frank with the end-user, as opposed to letting the user discover alone and with horror that our bibliographic "system" isn't well organized.

Technical problems were referred to earlier primarily in the context of the intermediary. Any system user (intermediary or end-user) should be trained to ask certain basic questions when a piece of equipment fails to operate, or garbage appears to be spewing from the terminal, and should be provided with the appropriate basic routines for solving the problem. Not all questions can be addressed, of course, and this is the negative message which must be conveyed during training. Naturally, if something can go wrong, it will. However, there should be a telephone number to call for assistance.

Incidentally, I composed this paper using the text-editing capabilities of a Datapoint 1100 minicomputer, of which the Berkeley library has several. I don't use the Datapoint very often and found myself in exactly the position that we have been discussing: I had forgotten almost everything about the text-editor and needed retraining. My past training, however, had included sufficient information about Datapoint concepts and equipment that I was able to reason my way through with appropriate documentation. Of course, a Datapoint programmer was sitting at his desk in the next room--my equivalent of a telephone number in case of an emergency.

FUNDING AND FINAGLING

"Although training does involve a financial commitment, a commentary on training should not focus heavily on funding." Right? Wrong! You have heard from others of concern with "free or fee" information. The spectre of user charges and weak library budgets are problems for all of us. I believe that two events must occur before our situation can begin to stabilize: 1) libraries must look at their existing programs and budgets and make reasonable reallocations wherever possible when new programs such as machine-based reference are desired, and 2) librarians must become politically more sophisticated in order to compete with myriad other functions which require funding from the same pots. The first event--reallocation of funds--will be necessary to provide justification to our funding agencies that we are acting in a responsible fashion vis-à-vis library programs. Political sophistication--the second event--is a new concept for most librarians. As I mentioned earlier, one approach is to inform the end-user of the nature of the problem. If enough users are satisfied with the service, they may be able to provide assistance in lobbying for additional funds. If you do not have enough users, then your service has not passed the market test; it might be inappropriate for you to ask for additional funding.

Many factors must be put together to form a package sufficiently strong to persuade an administration to provide more funds. Training is truly a part of this package. So are public relations, marketing of the service, and a wisely administered overall budget. Librarians do need to train themselves and others in the use of machine-based systems, but they also must train their public and their administrators to understand that the rapidly changing technological environment applies to the library and information sector as well as to the private sector--business and industry. We assume too much; we assume that non-librarians understand that the library environment is changing. Some do understand; most do not. For most non-librarians, a librarian is still the library assistant who checks out books. The White House Conference and the preceding statewide conferences would provide an ideal setting to begin to educate the public and obtain support for funding of programs for increased access to information. Those of you who are involved in the state conferences might consider an effort to place this item on the agenda, such that it will be on the agenda of the White House Conference in 1979. The on-line revolution will be expensive for our society as a whole; we want to ascertain that users understand the issues so that they can make a reasonable choice.

How many of you have done searches for your congressman? I have a good friend who works in the policy development office at the Office of Education. Last year a librarian did some on-line searching for him; he was stunned at the capabilities of the system and at the size of the combined data base available to him. His reaction was a good learning experience for me. Training involves more than use of the system. Indeed, use of the system may be our easiest task. It seems to me that we must train society to the value of information if our society is to buy and fund these services.

Chapter 25

TRAINING AND RETRAINING OF LIBRARIANS
AND USERS: REACTION

Anthony A. Martin

Director
Carnegie Library of Pittsburgh
Pittsburgh, Pennsylvania

The paper presented by Elaine Caruso really "hits home" with its obvious understanding of the ideals and the realities of training in the use of information retrieval systems with all their potential and problems. However, the presentation was slanted towards the academic researcher in the university environment. The public library is a different situation with its own set of unique problems and solutions.

Carnegie Library of Pittsburgh has been enchanted by the concept of faster, better, more efficient service to the user through computerization. For the past several years, we have investigated ways to better serve the patron through the automation of library procedures and information retrieval. Our experience has been limited; yet we were the first public library in the United States to participate in the computerized cataloging services offered through the Ohio College Center, we served as the contractor for the Commonwealth of Pennsylvania in the development and installation of an on-line computerized registration and circulation system for the Library for the Blind and Physically Handicapped in Pittsburgh and Philadelphia, and most recently we contracted for service from The Information Bank. I will react to Elaine Caruso's paper with respect to The Information Bank experience only.

Before choosing The Information Bank, we did investigate the various available data bases, including the three different types outlined in the paper. We studied each data base from the point of view primarily of what data it

contained and how that data related to our clientele. Besides the constraint
of user needs, we also had the traditional limitations of time, energy, money,
and staff.

In investigating the various data bases and the mechanics for accessing them, we did discover a "normalization" of the various techniques and
equipment. There were many similarities of techniques and equipment, as
well as differences that made each data base valuable in its own right, including such items as fields covered, file structure, access points, and ease
of use. Reassured with the possibility of access to other data bases using
similar equipment and techniques, we proceeded with The Information Bank.
Once the decision was made to make The Information Bank available to our
users in the library, we were in the position described in the paper--"Who
would be the actual users of the system and how would they be trained?"

Perhaps the most obvious decision was the first--the professional
librarians would be the actual users of the system and would be the intermediaries between the end-user and the system. It would have been an impossible task to have the end-user the initial user of the system without our
staff knowing and using the system firsthand.

A well-trained intermediary must be available in-house to assist the
end-user in the system. Our first goal then was to adequately train our
librarians in the complex use of the system and to give them a sufficient
understanding of the make-up and use of the data base.

Perhaps, in the near future, some end-users might be efficient
enough to use the system under the supervision of an intermediary. In the
public library environment, there is not a specific clientele as there is in the
academic environment. In effect, anyone within our service area can have
access to the system. To attempt to train all these potential users at this
time is almost impossible, because they differ in educational background,
level of training, and need for the system. There is such a diversity of user
that training must begin with the most qualified, or at least the most easily
trainable, individual.

The two basic assumptions made in the paper concerning the user and
the trained intermediary are not really valid in the case of the public library.
The user generally does not know how to use the search system, and the
trained intermediary is not necessarily knowledgeable in the field of the
user's search needs. The patron generally has a question that requires an
answer, and he does not care in which files the answer is found. He generally approaches the first librarian available, regardless of her subject area
specialty.

It is then the librarian's (or searcher's) decision as to which file should be approached and a negotiation of the question is begun between the patron and the searcher. At this point, problems concerning the user's knowledge of the system and the librarian's background are resolved.

Our main aim was to train our librarians to become trainers of the rest of the staff and those few members of the public who would have a serious and continuing interest in computerized searching. Initially, our librarians wanted to examine the data base as they would the printed index. They were all familiar with the printed indexes and were experienced reference librarians. The major problem, as discussed by Elaine Caruso, was "How do they get to know the data base?"

The suggestion that they "learn about the computer programs which are used to put the magnetic tape issues into the computer system" seems unnecessary. There is really no benefit, in an analogy with the printed index, to know the physical make-up and composition techniques used in compiling the printed indexes. The real need is to know the file content, and not how it got there.

The data base can be examined, although not totally "read" as might be the ideal. Some of the files can be "dumped" for examination. There are available printed lists of terms used along with cross-references and other thesaurus items. Results of various searches can be examined to determine the file structure and the various interrelationships between the various files, along with the results of searches using different logical connectors.

As suggested in the paper, the primary way of knowing a data base is to investigate the field itself by using printed descriptions and exploratory searches. Unfortunately, such printed descriptions were not available to us with The Information Bank in the format, quantity, or quality we felt necessary for complete and adequate training of our staff.

What was needed (but never obtained) as a primary instruction tool for our librarians was an in-depth description of the system, the building of the data base, the extent of coverage, the structure of the files, the methods of standardization with other data bases and the methods of updating the fields. In defense of the data base vendor, this type of information is also sorely needed in the understanding of a printed index. It is generally not available there either.

However, as Elaine Caruso put it, "Simple comprehension or even detailed knowledge of a file isn't adequate for real search competence." There must also be an understanding of the variations in the way the system handles the various files in their own data base and how the user may select and manipulate these files.

To help reinforce our knowledge of this data base, as well as other data bases, our staff did attend various workshops and seminars on on-line systems. These helped our staff obtain an understanding of the data base and its use. Unfortunately, this understanding was not sufficient.

Before initiating service to our patrons, our staff did receive a one-day training session from The Information Bank. Unfortunately, Elaine Caruso's description of the existing training scene describes accurately this one-day, quickie training session. As Elaine Caruso stated--"The failure to provide a coherent, comprehensive learning experience, thus, is seen as the most obvious failure of the existing training scene. Unevenness of treatment to the several aspects of on-line searching, biases introduced by commitment to one or another system as a 'first experience,' high costs of training sessions, plus high expense of on-line practice; requirement to be at certain locations and at certain time periods, inflexibility of content, and incapacity to tailor the experience to individual needs, are among other weaknesses identified."

To this, I say "Amen." Although this condition can be explained in terms of the cost involved in providing an ideal training program, it is still unfortunate that this condition exists. It would be far better to spend more staff time and project money to start the project off with the proper training of the user than to attempt to save money initially and then waste money and time later as the user flounders at the terminal. This waste of money is indicated in the paper by the description of the frustrated user attempting to simply log-in and finding little or no help from the system.

A solution to our particular training problem would have been a comprehensive presentation to our librarians concerning the system, how it works, and why it works. A training session covering several days would have been ideal, particularly if it were preceded by a detailed explanation of the data base, its structure, function, updating procedures, and limitations. The hands-on training should have been conducted under the watchful eye of the trainer for several days, handling real questions that were perhaps previously fielded by librarians using traditional manual methods. Such an extended training session would give the trainees a solid feeling for the data base as well as confidence in using the files for information retrieval.

A detailed evaluation of both the manual and automated method, in terms of results obtained, is critical to understanding the system. Such an evaluation would also prove helpful in justifying the existence of an information retrieval system within a particular institution. Obviously, this is an expensive proposition but really worth the money and time.

This type of training program would enhance the possibility of the user going from the "beginner" stage to the "advanced" stage. With the training our librarians received, they did reach the first level of training and are now prone to the "period of latency" between the two stages referred to in the paper. This "period of latency" is the result of a lack of confidence on the part of the librarian to use the system successfully. A proper training session would instill that necessary confidence in the librarian.

The period of latency may not be the clear-cut void of not using the system as implied in the paper but rather an extended period of very limited use. The searcher is reluctant to use the system that she does not fully understand and feels more comfortable answering the question through more traditional methods. There is a concern on the part of the "half-trained" librarian using the system with the patron looking on and watching the searcher struggle through the mechanical operation of the system and perhaps flip-flopping through decisions involved in the logic construction.

As indicated in Elaine Caruso's presentation, this lack of practice particularly hurts the end-user. The competence of the searcher is deteriorated and the search is less productive than it really should be. Elaine Caruso states that "this is a serious problem which must be resolved." It will be resolved through a substantial training session for the intermediary, giving that individual a firm foundation in the data base and its use. This will automatically lead to increased usage on the part of the intermediary and therefore greater competency and greater efficiency. Each search therefore becomes more productive and less costly.

This is particularly critical in a public library situation. At the very beginning we charged a user fee for conducting searches in The Information Bank beyond a certain minimum time as stipulated in our contract with the State Library. The State Library assumed that the cost of operating an information retrieval system could really only be justified by charging a user fee. However, our staff becomes particularly concerned about charging for a search that might well be fruitless or perhaps more costly because of an inefficient search. There is enough inherent delay and inefficiency in understanding the patron's real question. This should not be compounded by inefficient searching at the terminal.

Once the staff received its background information concerning the data base and its structure, and its limited training, our primary concern was increasing the proficiency of the searchers. Realizing that, as Elaine Caruso so accurately points out, "the strategy for searching a machine stored field is qualitatively and quantitatively different," all efforts have been made to raise the level of competency among our searchers.

Through training and regular use, the searchers on our staff have developed the time-sequenced skills outlined in the paper:

1. Learning to use the mechanical devises
2. Acquiring confidence and fluency in the conventions of the most-used elements of language of a system
3. Recognizing searchable fields
4. Becoming competent in the use of logical connectors

We are attempting to continue the training of our librarians to raise this level of competency. Unfortunately, our methods are limited by time, staff, and available expertise. Through constant monitoring of the use of the system, we can guide the searchers to a more efficient use of the system --when to use it, and when not to, and how to use it. Through participation in workshops and seminars held by various professional and educational organizations, we can share experiences with other users and thereby broaden our knowledge of the system, its potentials and problems.

And perhaps the most important method of training (at least at this point in the training process) is the "user-group" formed basically by the four librarians we have trained. A half-day general discussion of their particular problems and concerns, among themselves, has proved an extremely worthwhile endeavor. Hopefully, such a "user group" meeting and discussion could be extended in the type of institution involved and give all concerned a better understanding of the problems involved in information retrieval.

At this point it is impossible for us to consider what Elaine Caruso calls the "easily achievable situation in the present environment" of the combination of end-user searching, with available resources to trained specialists. Our clientele is simply too diverse to train in the use of the system, and to make the system available to the end-user in the "intimacy of the laboratory or study" is also impossible under the present structure.

Hopefully we can aim in this direction, although I believe we will never reach that point simply because we are a public library serving a large population of diverse interests, backgrounds, and inclinations. If we cannot go as far as the ideal, then where do we go and how do we get there? We can approach the end-user through a more efficient, solid training program to train our librarians, who in turn would be trainers of other librarians, and they in turn would train those end-users who really want to use the system.

In our original proposal to the State Library, the Carnegie Library of Pittsburgh and the Free Library of Philadelphia (two of the four State Regional Resource Libraries) wanted to develop statewide specialized information services through the use of computerized data bases. The University of Pittsburgh Graduate School of Library and Information Sciences was approached and the teaching/research staff developed an intensive program to provide in-depth system and data base training for Carnegie Library of

Pittsburgh and Free Library of Philadelphia staff and the staffs of the other two Regional Resource Libraries. An intermediate level of training was outlined for the staff of the twenty-five District Center Libraries, while administrators and staff of other public, academic and special libraries would be involved through an orientation program.

The in-depth training program was to be comprised of eight phases:

		# Session	Hours / Session	Training Hours / Librarian
1.	Orientation	1	3	3
2.	Systems	1	2	2
3.	Strategy Writing	2	1	2
4.	Data Base Characteristics	2	3	6
5.	Hands-on Session/Supervised	10	4	12 1/2
6.	Review and Evaluation	2	3	6
7.	Search Strategy Formulation	2	3	6
8.	Teaching Laboratory	1	4	4
				41 1/2

The intermediate program:

		# Session	Hours / Session	Training Hours / Librarian
1.	Orientation	1	3	3
2.	System and Data Base Characteristics	1	3	3
3.	Hands-on Demonstration	1	4	2
4.	Search	1	3	3
				11

The orientation program for the administrators was to be covered in one three-hour session.

This idea died aborning when the State Library rejected the proposal. However, the University of Pittsburgh refined the program and secured funding through the Buhl Foundation. This new expanded training program was announced on Monday by Allen Kent as the "On-line bibliographic and information systems--a training center for librarians and information specialists."

Elaine Caruso outlined in the section entitled "Training Modules for Scientific and Technical Information" an emulation project which, combined with the "On-Line Training Center" concept, would provide a good, solid experience for the user at a minimum cost. It provides a vehicle for training without the inhibiting concern about the cost of searching some of the expensive data bases. It can be employed without an investment in equipment. Under certain conditions, it can be done in your own institution at minimal costs.

Although we will continue to have training by the vendor and our own "user group" training, along with professionally conducted workshops and seminars, participation in the University of Pittsburgh's emulation project and training center would greatly benefit our librarians. I would further propose that network staff and library school faculty cooperate more fully in this training venture.

Proper initial training and continued training through such training centers would bring better results for the information retrieval dollar and make the user and intermediary more comfortable in the environment of data base searching. Such a situation can only lead to one conclusion--providing the user with the correct information in the most efficient manner at the time the user wants and needs the information. This is a result that we will all be happy with. And it is this result that makes meetings, discussions and planning all worthwhile.

Chapter 26

WHO SHOULD BE TRAINED?

Elizabeth E. Duncan

Office of Communications Programs
University of Pittsburgh
Pittsburgh, Pennsylvania

It is generally acknowledged that a searcher of mechanized information retrieval systems acquires skill through practice. This is the reason
for the free search time given the new user of large commercial systems
and offered to all users each time a new data base is added. For the past
five years, I have been involved in teaching faculty, staff and students at the
University of Pittsburgh to do mechanized searching. I know firsthand the
time and labor involved in writing good manuals, providing search programs
with useful help messages, and developing effective instruction for individuals
and groups. I also know firsthand that the manuals, the help messages and
the instructional plans are of little or no value if the trainees do not get on
the system and use it and use it and use it.

Dr. Caruso cites Roger Summit's belief that it takes eight hours of
on-line experience to familiarize a searcher with the DIALOG system. Kemp
of the National Agriculture Library told me he estimates it takes about thirty
hours to produce a skilled AGRICOLA searcher. I am not prepared to say
how much practice is necessary; in my experience, the road to skill is longer
for some than for others. Controlled study of novice users will probably produce some useful rules of thumb. (Such a study is a part of Dr. Caruso's
work.) Meanwhile, there is no doubt whatever that trainees will develop
search skills in relationship to the time they spend in practice, and the wise
developer of training modules will make practice as available as possible and
for a nominal fee. I have great hopes for Dr. Caruso's approach for the
development of user skills, but I know it is not the panacea for all our problems. Too frequently the end-user, the person who really wants the information, is not using the system himself. As a result, most searches are being

done for him (her) either by a librarian or an information specialist. Any
searcher who has interviewed an end-user to determine what he wants knows
the patience, the skill, and the intimate knowledge of available systems and
data bases that are required to bring together the real questions and the
possible answers.

Now what happens in a large public library system where only one
library has a terminal and trained searchers? Must the user go to the
searcher, no matter what the geographical distance? How, or how much,
do you teach a non-searcher to render him capable of making an effective
referral? Are we inviting a situation reminiscent of the old parlor game
where you whisper a message quickly into your neighbor's ear, he passes it
on in the same manner, and by the time the message gets back to you it is
unrecognizable? Of course, we might avoid many of these difficulties if we
simply did not tell the fellow in the boondocks that he is entitled to the library
system's services.

To the best of my knowledge, no one has an adjusted training program
to meet the needs of special groups. Whether a searcher is going to serve
the patrons of a public library, a special library, a college or a university
library, all take the same basic training program. Yet I find it hard to
believe that these searchers will end up using the systems and the data bases
in the same manner. At the University of Pittsburgh where we have "The
Information Bank, " we do many more broad-subject searches and many fewer
personal name searches than the typical special library. It may be this very
heterogeneity of interest and searching experience of the attendees that makes
the advanced training sessions so difficult. I am at least confident that such
differences contribute to the extensive practice needed before a high level of
searcher competence is developed.

There are some who believe our salvation lies in STANDARDIZATION
--of systems, of indexing vocabulary, etc. With such standardization, the
end-user would surely become the searcher, for a routine once learned could
be used over and over again regardless of changing information needs. But
I think we will wait in vain for standardization of bibliographic data bases;
there is just too much of Lewis Carroll's Humpty-Dumpty in all of us. I
recently saw a note about a study done on the overlap of articles abstracted
for Biological Abstracts and Chemical Abstracts. Although the study identified a significant number of articles that were included in both publications,
it found that an abstract in Chemical Abstracts was oriented toward the chem-
ist while an abstract for the identical article in Biological Abstracts was
quite different, being oriented toward the biologist. I doubt if the results of
the study will be any surprise to people familiar with both fields.

I do know there is considerable research underway to enable a
searcher to input one strategy and successfully search multiple data bases.

I, for one, doubt if this approach can succeed. I am willing even to accept that standardization and/or equivalency of indexing language just is not in our future. There is, however, lots of standardization that is long overdue. For example, I find it very irritating if a data base supplier inputs some authors' names: last name, space and two initials and other authors' names with a comma after the last name followed by a space and two initials. Such a difference is hardly noticed by the human eye but to the computer those last names are two entirely different words. There are a lot of these "little" irritants: misspellings, unique abbreviations, etc. This is another reason I want to see the end-user doing his own searches. I don't think John Q. Public is going to be as tolerant of unnecessary variations occurring in a magnetic data base because in the printed version, usually the developer's primary reason for creating the magnetic tape, such variations are less important.

All the foregoing leads to my final and main reason for wanting to train the end-user to do his own searches. I want to increase greatly the user population. We have a powerful new tool in the computer, but we are still inputting the information using all the old methods of bibliographic identi- fication. I am hoping for someone who, using mechanized retrieval, can develop a whole new approach to the information problems.

To expand on this just a little (frankly, I cannot expand on it very much; although I think about it a lot, I fear much of my thinking is fuzzy), I am sure that you are all well aware that except for ISI's citation indexes everyone is using variations of the same approach. Now I happen to like citation indexing, although it might surprise Eugene Garfield to know one of the reasons I like it. That is, that to be used really successfully, the end- user has to be actively involved. Oh, true, you can do a form of subject searching with the title, but to really benefit from citation indexing the end- user had better know some articles that are relevant to his information prob- lem. With my accolades to citation searching, I do not mean that I think this approach is the answer to computer searching. Citation indexes are likewise very visually oriented, although their massive size makes a computer a great convenience. But a computer is a lot more than a convenience; I am not sure we realize this yet.

Chapter 27

TRAINING AND RETRAINING: DISCUSSION

The discussion which follows has been transcribed from tape recordings, summarized and edited. Comments and questions have been attributed
to speakers when their identity was provided. The editors of these proceedings take responsibility for any errors in fact or interpretation resulting
from this process, since it was not feasible to provide proofs to discussants
for checking.

Jim Sanders - University of Maryland

What are the differences in training end-users vs. librarians? What
changes in technology are needed to permit data bases to be directed toward
end-users? Is it the role of the library or information center to train the
end-users?

Judith Wanger

Differences in training should be based on differences in people and
not necessarily in terms of whether trainees are end-users or librarians.
In corporate settings, we have had the opportunity to train chemists. The
ones we've trained grew up on "Chemical Abstracts" in printed form. Their
main objective in learning to search our system was to be able to use "Chemical Abstracts" on-line. They viewed the system and the data bases as one.
The main difference in the training session was that we were able to make
the system and the data base appear to be like one, rather than the system
being a mechanism for getting at multiple data bases that have differences,
with a requirement to learn those differences. But if those individuals had
not grown up with "Chemical Abstracts" and did not come to us with a background in understanding the searching process, we probably would have
started at a completely different point, which sometimes happens with a group
of librarians who have not experienced traditional literature searching.

Users are helping us to design the future generations of systems. We
hear from users and listen very hard. We believe it will be necessary to
move in two directions at the same time: (1) When we first introduced the
service, everyone was a new user; now we have users with up to seven years
of experience (or more)--what the latter need from a system is more "transparency" (a less visible system, fewer prompts, less feedback) so that they
can do what they already want to do;   (2) the infrequent searcher (whether
end-user or librarian) needs a "tailored" amount of feedback and more help
on-line. For this type of user, the system must have more tutorials built in.
Also, more intelligent programs are needed to detect the searcher's intent.
These are the major changes I see in terms of protocols.

Anthony Martin

The largest law firm in Pittsburgh has the LEXIS system. I was in-
vited to view an excellent film designed for the end-user. Lawyers fresh out
of school were in the audience; I later saw them at the terminal, and when I
examined the log, I noted regular usage by perhaps a dozen lawyers a day.
In consulting the librarian, I learned that these users do not seek help or
training from the librarian. The senior staff of the firm are end-users of
The Information Bank, with practically no training.

Tricia McKeown - University of Texas, Health Science Center Library, Dallas

The systems have ignored training for the search interview and negotiation process, which is vital, especially if the requestor will not be present
during the search.

The intermediary should be told to emphasize more the limitations of
the data base, the time limits, the types of material included. One of the
great advantages of having an intermediary conduct a search is that additional
manual sources can be suggested that might answer the question better or
provide additional information.

Novice searchers could benefit by visiting an established searching
center after initial training, observing or using their own code to practice
on-line.

Standards should be developed for selecting good prospects for training. Also, tests or self-evaluation programs should be developed to assess
the effects of training.

I disagree with Dr. Duncan who indicates the end-user should conduct
the search. As the systems are now constituted, without very much help for

the user, the power of those data bases with complex vocabularies and other search aids cannot be exploited by the majority of users. For those who require comprehensive search results, and as long as the cost of a search is related to connect time, I believe that a properly trained, experienced search intermediary would do a better and less expensive job.

Elizabeth Duncan

I believe there is no stimulus to learn as good as the motivation to want to find information. And the end-user does have that type of motivation.

I would like to add to the discussion of fees by pointing out that search services were first introduced in government and special libraries. The fee controversy seems to have emerged only when they were introduced in college and public libraries. The special libraries considered these routinely as another necessary service with necessary expenses. If we look at the traditions of the college and public libraries, the staff is trained to assist the user; but the user is encouraged to do for himself. We place copying machines in libraries for the benefit of the end-user, and we haven't been bothered that the user is obliged to pay for copies. If the end-user sits at a terminal, does his own search, and if it costs money, can we not perceive this as with the fee for photocopying?

Judith Wanger

Regarding training for question negotiation, Pauline Atherton, Syracuse University, is doing work in this area, using media such as videotape.

Elaine Caruso

Reference interview-question negotiation is an established area of study in its own right, not particularized to on-line searches. However, the pre-search interview has been discussed in the literature.

Gaya Agrawal - Robert Morris College, Pittsburgh

Current training programs are full of jargon which is not comprehensible to end-users. Simpler language should be used if the training is to be effective.

Judith Wanger

We have experience in training people with no background in library or information science. The essence of the knowledge we must transmit is the same as when training librarians; changes are made in the manner of presentation to accommodate to the level of trainee knowledge of the terminology of the field.

Ruth Eveland - Cuyahoga County Public Library, Ohio

We are a system of 26 branches, with The Information Bank service available by referral to one location. Training for referral is currently being accomplished through "road shows," with the terminal being set up at each branch. Local librarians invite potential local users; considerable interest has developed.

Penny Worley - Houston Academy of Medicine, Texas

What are the characteristics of the ideal intermediary ?

Judith Wanger

The primary characteristic is desire to learn, to receive training.

Edmund Blau - Applied Physics Laboratory, Johns Hopkins University, Maryland

How can we involve middle and upper levels of management in the educational process--to teach them what on-line services can do for their staff ?

Judith Wanger

Some of our subscribers are providing selective dissemination services to their executives on their pet topics. This is the best way to exhibit capabilities.

Dick Miller - Northeast Ohio Universities College of Medicine

Are there any methods of quality control or testing that can be used with searchers ?

Elizabeth Duncan

There has been some work on monitoring usage: Lockheed monitoring public library usage under an NSF grant; David Penniman (formerly of Battelle) monitored people who used BASIS-70. We are currently monitoring at the University of Pittsburgh to determine how users are reacting to a change in program.

Mary Eidleman - Dundaulk Community College, Baltimore

I have observed some parallels between the development of on-line and community service information services. Training has been a problem in both; defusing the emotional reactions has been a factor. Word of mouth publicity has been the most effective means of educating the user.

George Summers - Loma Linda University, California

There seems to be an assumption that anyone can be trained as a searcher. I do not believe this to be the case. We should develop an aptitude test to screen out those who, by attitude or skill potential, will never make it.

I have also discovered from users that quality of search output differs considerably. Perhaps a certification program should be established for searchers, with a proficiency test administered to measure level of performance--with a minimum set for certification.

Elaine Caruso

Two points have been raised which deserve response: (1) that training programs might become obsolete very quickly due to continuing changes in the programs of the commercial services, and (2) that too much attention is being given to the more mechanical aspects of the interactive dialogue.

To the first point: granted that only the system programmer will always be on top of the latest changes in each system and any teacher, human or computer, will need updating when changes are made. In our machine teacher, the on-line trainer, we anticipate the problem in two ways: by making the programs modular for easy changes and additions and by using the most basic commands which exhibit a greater degree of stability.

As to the second point, I think it only seems that way; because a user can't "use his head" for the higher functions when he is preoccupied with

motor operations--where to put his fingers! That is why we think the trainer
is so valuable; it allows not only ample inexpensive practice time to fix
skills, but also great freedom to explore and experiment with system capabilities for accepting (and satisfying!) conceptualized information needs.

Part Four

CLOSING SUMMARY

Chapter 28

CLOSING SUMMARY

Thomas J. Galvin

Dean
Graduate School of Library
and Information Sciences
University of Pittsburgh
Pittsburgh, Pennsylvania

The synthesis, I suspect, for most of us will come days or even weeks after we've left this conference and had the opportunity to reflect on the meaning of the things we've said to one another here about on-line systems, about their significance for libraries, about the problems they present that must be addressed and resolved, and most important of all, about the opportunities they provide to enrich and enhance access to information.

I would like to take these few last moments simply to try to quickly review some of the key questions about the potential of on-line systems that were raised on the first afternoon of the conference and to propose at least some tentative answers to those questions, based on what has been said during these three days.

First, does the availability of on-line bibliographic and information systems really constitute a "revolution" in the character and quality of the library and information services that we can offer our users? The answer would seem to be--potentially, "yes"! The on-line capability, linked to the power of the computer to organize, search, combine, and rearrange knowledge records in a manner that vastly extends and augments the capacities of both human intellect and traditional, manual indexing systems, constitutes an enormously powerful technological advance. Perhaps most significant of all is the capacity to "negotiate" the reference question in an on-line, real-time interactive multiple-access-point mode. This holds the most exciting potential for a true qualitative leap forward of major proportions in information transfer.

Yet, the answer to the question--is the on-line technology truly
<u>revolutionary</u> in its impact?--can, at this point, only be a qualified "yes,"
or, rather, an optimistic "Yes, if..."

Yes, <u>if</u> we can control the power of this new technology so that it can
be brought to bear directly on user needs. As Joe Shubert reminded us on
Monday afternoon, we need to understand that there is a very important
difference between real information transfer and information overload (or,
as we sometimes less politely characterize it, <u>information dump</u>!). Like
the proverbial sorcerer's apprentice, the computer terminal has the capacity
to bury the information seeker under a mountain of printout, so that the result is not enlightenment, but despair. We function in a world increasingly
populated by clients who are data rich but information poor. Whether the
on-line technology serves ultimately to make that problem more or less
severe will depend chiefly on our individual and collective ability, first to
understand, next to master, and ultimately to direct its power to the most
useful ends.

One key to understanding is education and training, as Dr. Caruso's
position paper and presentation make evident. We have identified at this
conference several very significant aspects of the training problem. First,
we have, I think, established that most of the consumers of on-line technology will, for the foreseeable future, require the assistance of a highly
skilled, highly sensitive intermediary in order to exploit the capabilities of
the systems most effectively. Second, we have made clear that those individuals whom Paul Peters and Ellen Detlefsen have characterized as
"searchers"--"the person who sits at the computer terminal, operates its
keyboard, and reads its display"--have no alternative but to become thoroughly familiar with both content and method. Sam Wolpert sounded the
warning on Monday afternoon--"librarians have two alternatives; they can
move up and become information specialists, or they can move out."

I believe that we must also identify the training needs of those who
will <u>not</u> sit at the terminals and operate the keyboards, but who will remain
--for some time to come--the primary points of contact--whether behind a
reference desk in a school library/media center, at the other end of a telephone in the public library, in the classroom of a community college--
between on-line systems and potential users. As Elaine Caruso and the
panel suggested this morning, they must be thoroughly grounded in what
might be termed "on-line appreciation," so that they can achieve the ability
to select, from among the full range of available manual and automated systems, the response mode that is most closely tailored to the precise informational need of the client. Not all questions are best answered by going to
the terminal. Most important of all, we must look to the training of those
--to follow the Peters-Detelfsen taxonomy--who are the "service managers"
and the ultimate "decision-makers," for they will, in the last analysis,

determine the kind, character, and depth of service to be offered to library users and information seekers.

The training problem is complex. It includes not merely the mastery of keyboard skills (which falls in the cognitive domain of learning), but the far more difficult task of behavior and attitude modification. A whole range of basic operating assumptions about alphabetical and numerical arrays, search procedures, and the ultimate retrievability of specific pieces of data --assumptions that are so powerful in governing both librarian and user behavior that they often remain unstated--and even unrecognized by those whose behavior they govern--need to be unearthed, brought up to daylight, examined, modified, and in many instances, simply discarded as inappropriate in the light of technological advancements.

Next, we come to the equally complex issue of user orientation and training. We recognize at once that we must deal with a highly diverse and differentiated array of user education needs. Here, we stand on shaky ground indeed. We assume that the objective should be to make at least some frequent system users self-sufficient, if they are to derive maximum benefit from the interactive capability of the on-line mode. Yet we come squarely up against the blank wall of the very primative current state of our understanding of the processes of human behavior in its information seeking mode. We simply do not know enough about those intellectual processes by which data (that is, something external to the individual) is converted into information, which is internalized and useful as a basis for action, decision-making or attitude modification.

One thing is, however, clear, and that is the linkage between train-ing, on the one hand, and the combination of cost-efficiency and user-effec-tiveness on the other. This brings me to the third major set of problems considered at this conference. The issue of the identification, determination and allocation of costs was obviously a major item on everybody's hidden or overt conference agenda. As must have been evident from the intensity of the dialogue on this question--who pays? and for what? and how many times? --feelings are strong and tend to cluster at the two extremes of the issue. The truth may well lie somewhere in between, perhaps in some combination of public subsidy to assure at least a minimum level of guaranteed effective access to the best information delivery capability that modern technology can offer, plus a fee structure geared to the value of the information to the client and the client's capacity and willingness to pay for it.

Two things seem clear to me in this otherwise murky picture. First, the funding problem must be addressed, thrashed ut and resolved, for Lee Burchinal is surely correct in predicting that it will loom larger and larger in an increasingly capital-intensive social and economic order. Second, the question must ultimately be addressed and resolved, not by special interest groups (producers, vendors, librarians), but as an issue of public policy through the orderly, consultative processes of a democratic society. The electorate must ultimately determine what price it is collectively willing to pay to assure effective equal access to information for all. Our task, as professionals, is not to solve the problem for the citizenry, but to elucidate the issues in language that society can understand. Let me suggest that the forthcoming White House Conference on Libraries and Information Services, scheduled for the Fall of 1979, and the intervening Governor's Conferences at the state level, offer a perfect arena for elucidation and public debate of this and many related aspects of a national information policy.

Finally, and to conclude on a point of near-unanimous agreement, we identified a clear need to incorporate on-line systems into the larger context of existing library and information technologies. Specifically, we saw the importance of achieving an optimal mix between manual and mechanized indexing systems, of relating the developing on-line bibliographic and information technology to existing library-oriented networks (such as OCLC and BALLOTS) so as to achieve a coordinated, multilevel document and information delivery system, and of reconsidering the present allocation of the monies we control between local acquisition of books and journals on the one hand and the purchase of access to the contents of centralized, remote data bases on the other.

So, to summarize the highlights of the conference in eight words:
                    potential--enormous
                    training--essential
                    funding--uncertain
                    integration--mandatory

In closing, I would like to express our sincere thanks to the more than seven hundred people who made this conference possible. First, to the authors of the position papers and to the panelists who provided us with a rich, if occasionally spicy, diet of substance embellished with just the right touch of rhetoric to sustain our interest and to elucidate the issues. Next, to my colleagues from the University of Pittsburgh who worked so hard to make this conference run so smoothly. I am grateful and proud to be associated with a group of people--faculty and staff--who can manage a conference the size of this one so smoothly and so unobtrusively. A very special word of appreciation is due to our many student volunteers. Without your help we couldn't possibly have done it nearly as well as we did--in fact, we couldn't have done it at all. You all receive "A's" for your efforts--and more important, may you all get jobs! Finally, the greatest thanks go to all our participants. Whatever success this conference has enjoyed is because you came, you stayed, and, above all, you participated.

Appendix

CONFERENCE EVALUATION

James M. Matarazzo,[1] Evalyn Clough,[2] and James G. Williams[3]

INTRODUCTION

Those who attended the 1977 Pittsburgh Conference on the ON-LINE Revolution in Libraries were asked to complete questionnaires prior to the first session and following the last session. The results were analyzed to determine changes in perception and attitudes, as one means of evaluating the conference.

The evaluation was made by using a modified dialectic instrument and a pre/post methodology. The purposes of the evaluation were: (1) to determine the nature and strength of ideas regarding the on-line revolution in libraries held by attendees upon arrival at the conference; (2) to determine the major problems and advantages of on-line systems as perceived by the participants prior to the conference; and (3) to determine how the conference was received by those who attended and whether the conference had any influence on their thinking. The questionnaire shown in Attachment A was administered in an attempt to elicit how attendees felt and thought about the potential of on-line systems upon arrival, and what problems and advantages they foresaw with the adoption of on-line systems and technology. Administration of the post-conference questionnaire (Attachment C) was an attempt to investigate these same feelings and thoughts as well as the impact

[1]Assistant Dean for Student Affairs and Associate Professor, School of Library Science, Simmons College, Boston, Massachusetts
[2]Assistant to the Dean and Lecturer, Graduate School of Library and Information Sciences, University of Pittsburgh, Pittsburgh, Pennsylvania
[3]Associate Professor, Interdisciplinary Department of Information Science, University of Pittsburgh, Pittsburgh, Pennsylvania

of the speakers and comments of the other attendees at the close of the conference. The number of participants from each state and foreign country as well as the position held by the attendees was collected and is reported in Attachment B.

METHODOLOGY

On the first day of the conference before any of the speakers had been heard, the 725 attendees were asked, but not required, to complete the questionnaire in Attachment A. This same procedure was used on the last day of the conference after the last speaker, using the questionnaire found in Attachment C. The pre-conference questionnaire was completed by 53.2% of the attendees and the post-conference questionnaire was completed by 32.1% of the attendees. Those questions which asked for a simple scaled response were tallied by possible response category. The questions that required an indication of problems or advantages, as well as arguments for or against, were content analyzed. The results of the content analysis produced a number of major factors with sub-categories or variables that summarized problems and advantages, as well as arguments for and against on-line systems. A frequency count of the occurrence of the sub-categories was made, and they are listed by frequency of occurrence. This ranking is based on the assumption that the frequency is indicative of a commonality of importance to the attendees. It should be emphasized, however, that both the major factors and sub-categories within them were derived from the written responses of the participants and were not based on prior definitions or classifications.

INITIAL EVALUATION

Those who attended the Pittsburgh Conference on the On-Line Revolution in Libraries, as is clear from the response reported in Question 2 of Attachment A, came with a strong bias that these systems would have a significant impact on the quality of library service. While the respondents were nearly unanimous about the impact of these systems, the problems libraries would encounter incorporating the new technologies successfully were isolated and are summarized below.

Question 2: Very briefly, what do you see as the major problems for libraries and information centers in the successful adoption of on-line technology and systems?

The additional costs of these systems were among the most serious problems noted by the respondents. Specific cost areas included equipment, line charges and user fees to be paid by the libraries to the vendors. These dollar factors were frequently pointed out by respondents who noted stable or declining budgets as well as some difficulty in maintaining traditional services and resources at present and anticipated levels of funding.

The education and retraining of library staff members to utilize new systems also appeared to be a serious problem to the attendees on this initial questionnaire. While training, and where and how it would be obtained, was mentioned frequently, so was the need to change attitudes on the part of the library staff members, administrators, and users. It was noted that attitudes would have to be changed prior to the acquisition of equipment and the proposals for funding. Similarly, the need to market or sell these new services aggressively was considered essential by a smaller but articulate group of respondents.

A large number of respondents saw the standardization of protocols for these systems as something the vendors should attempt. Respondents clearly wanted to learn and use one set of conventions to access all data bases rather than face the variety of conventions presently available. The quality of the input in these systems also raises some concerns among eleven respondents, while a small number noted issues of the man-machine inter-face, browsing, retrospective indexes, delays in response time, duplication of coverage and the lack of enough data bases in the social sciences and the humanities.

The issue of equality of access to data bases was pointed out as a problem by sixteen respondents in the initial questionnaire who referred to the fact that the costs of searches would certainly inhibit the use of these services by a rather large segment of the population. The problems peculiar to developing countries, ranging from inadequate telephone service to unre-liable sources of electric power, were also noted, as were issues of proprietary rights, privacy of information and the control of information by a few vendors.

A number of respondents also stated that they would need more staff to make use of the new technology. Several warned that if forced to use these systems, they would have to take staff away from traditional services. Three respondents pointed out that only one user can be served at one time with these systems and an even smaller number wondered what impact the new technologies and new on-line services would have on the employment of librarians.

Seven respondents to the initial questionnaire called for research on the interrelationship between manual and on-line searching, on models for justifying on-line services and on options for training, terminals and the number of searches. Several of these noted the lack of a research base for the whole subject of on-line technology and systems.

Question 3: Very briefly, what do you see as the major advantages for
             libraries and information centers in the successful adoption of
             on-line technology and systems ?

    The speed of these systems, the comprehensiveness of the searches,
the multidimensional aspects of these searches and their accuracy were
among the major advantages cited by respondents. Similarly, better service
to users and the cost effectiveness of systems as well as the prospect of
sharing resources by means of these systems were noted.

    A number of attendees also noted that the use and operation of on-line
systems was considered by them to be a professional task and/or a challenge.
And several indicated that the image of the librarian and the library would be
improved by the introduction and use of on-line technology.

    While responses to this question on major advantages were grouped
under five major factors, the category of "Products and Services" yielded
the largest number of comments by attendees. It is clear, then, from these
responses that those who attended the on-line conference felt that the technology and systems to be explored at the conference would lead to better
patron service and considered this the major advantage.

                          FINAL EVALUATION

    After the conference, attendees were again asked to indicate their
view on the actual or potential impact of on-line systems. Once again, as
can be seen in Question 1 in Attachment C, respondents reflected a strong
conviction that on-line systems would have a positive impact on libraries
and information centers. While respondents arrived and left with this
opinion, they had little difficulty in identifying the major problems in adapting
on-line technology and systems to their particular settings in this final evaluation.

Question 2: At this point, what do you personally see as the major problem
             for libraries and information centers in the successful adoption
             of on-line technology and systems ?

    On the post-conference questionnaire, cost was identified as the
major problem in the successful adoption of on-line systems. A single call
for "national funding of public libraries" was also made by one of the
respondents as a solution to this problem.

    The education and training of library staff members also continued to
be seen as a service problem by the respondents to this final questionnaire,
as did the issue of users and the need to promote the services to users.

In the category of "System Development and Use," a smaller number of respondents pointed to a need for quality control for data bases, for standardization of protocols and for expansion of the subject coverage of these services. Respondents also pointed to a need for administrative support in order to establish on-line systems in libraries. While several attendees pointed to a lack of leadership, three respondents asked if there was a need for these types of services. Additional research was called for in three areas: cost benefit models, the subject of on-line itself, and understanding of user needs.

Question 3: At this point, what do you personally see as the major advantage for libraries and information centers in the adoption of on-line technology?

A large number of respondents pointed out that these services provide for comprehensiveness and speed which could lead to an enhanced quality of reference service to users. Several also noted the ability to search data bases in a multidimensional mode, the currency of data bases, and system versatility as major advantages.

A still smaller number identified the "Public Relations" value of these new systems which would allow their operation to offer a new service and improve their image and that of the library. Indeed, a still smaller group of respondents actually saw an economic benefit from the new technology which would produce income, increase staff, and allow for the elimination of printed indexes and abstracts.

Question 4: What was the most powerful argument you heard during the conference that would lead you to disagree with the notion that on-line technology represents a revolution for libraries and information centers?

Question 5: What was the most powerful argument you heard during the conference that would lead you to agree with the notion that on-line technology represents a revolution for libraries and information centers?

Combining the responses to these two questions, the most powerful argument heard against the notion that on-line represents a revolution in libraries and information centers was the suggestion that the whole process of introduction and reactions to these systems was in fact evolutionary rather than revolutionary. This was in turn followed by Mr. De Gennaro's remarks and the fact that other so-called revolutions have come and gone.

On the other hand, arguments advanced to support the notion that on-line represented a revolution were scattered over a large number of responses. The largest group of respondents felt that no one had advanced an argument which would allow them to agree that on-line represented a revolution. Growth in use, Dr. Licklider's remarks, the newness of the approach, the availability of technology, the 725 attendees, and Professor Kent's paper were each cited by several respondents as support for the revolution.

Question 6: Was the conference influential in affecting your attitude about on-line information systems?

As noted in the initial polling, most of the conference attendees were already convinced of the positive impact on-line information systems and technology would have on libraries and information centers. Most respondents who circled "somewhat influenced," "very little influenced," or "not at all" noted on their questionnaires that the conference reinforced the attitudes with which they came.

Question 7: How would you rate the overall effectiveness of this conference in conveying information?

Most respondents considered the conference "extremely," "significantly," and "somewhat" effective in conveying information. Conference attendees' suggestions, as well as their encouragement for future conferences, are contained in Part B of the last question. While respondents wanted small discussion groups, and more audience participation as a planned segment of future conferences, they praised the conference, the speakers, the papers and the panels.

ANALYSIS

Tabulation of the responses gives evidence that the majority of participants believe that on-line systems and technology would have a very positive effect on library and information center service. While this is not surprising in a self-selecting group, there was little room for change in a favorable direction from the pre- to the post-questionnaire.

Question 2 requested that attendees give their view as to the major problems libraries and information centers will encounter in successfully adopting on-line systems and technology. In the pre-conference questionnaire, the major factors noted by respondents as problems were "Economic," "Educational," and "System Development and Use." From the post-conference questionnaire responses, it can be seen the "Economic" and "Educational" problems remained most important; the problems of "System Development and Use" received a proportionally much smaller vote.

Within the sub-categories on Question 2, a large number of respondents noted the problems of attitudes of staff and the importance of selling the service in the pre-conference questionnaire. However, the identification of attitudes and the importance of selling the service decrease dramatically as problems on the post-conference questionnaire. One can infer, then, that the conference influenced the attendees to the extent that they were confident that attitudes can be changed and that the services can be effectively marketed.

One of the major problems noted in the pre-conference questionnaire was the need to standardize protocols. In the post-conference questionnaire, the drop in this sub-category was dramatic. The conference also must have influenced the attendees at least to the extent that this issue was diminished, as were all of the issues under the factor "Social/Political."

Question 3 was asked in an attempt to ascertain the advantages of adopting the on-line technologies. In the pre-conference questionnaire response, the major category was clearly "Products and Services." The sub-categories which delineate the specific advantages included: speed, comprehensiveness of search, multidiminsional aspects of the search, accuracy of information, better service to users and amassing of information. This category in the post-conference responses continued to be paramount. Within the sub-categories, there is a remarkable similarity in rank order and in frequency of citation. The exception is, however, that the comprehensiveness of the search replaces speed as the single most cited advantage on the post-conference questionnaire.

The major problems perceived by conference attendees prior to the start of the conference centered on the costs of these services, the training of staff to use these services, and the standardization of protocols. At the end of the conference costs and training remained as central problems, but concern for problems relating to system development, operation, and use was dramatically reduced.

The advantages of on-line systems and technology were clearly grouped under "Products and Services" and remained so at the close of the conference with only minor changes in order and frequency of citation.

The completed post-conference questionnaires provided data on the most powerful arguments heard for and against the notion that on-line technology represented a revolution for libraries and information centers. Although there were not as many responses as for other questions, those that were made seem to reject the idea of a revolution and view the trend as evolutionary. However, the responses to these questions with reference to specific papers and/or speakers cited as sources of arguments did affirm the impact of those who participated in the conference program.

Research was mentioned by several participants as a factor in both the pre and post questionnaires. It appears very clear the results of research would help in the decision-making process and would be most useful to those who wish to acquire these systems and technologies for their libraries and information centers.

CONCLUSIONS AND RECOMMENDATIONS

As demonstrated in Attachment B, the conference was attended by a widely diverse group of participants from all over the United States as well as a number of attendees from Hong Kong, Canada, Nicaragua, Nigeria, and Switzerland. They arrived at the conference feeling that on-line systems and technology would have a positive impact upon these operations but that the problems posed by costs, education, and systems were great. At the conference, they found the costs and the problems of education were real and yet to be solved, but that system problems they envisioned were much less than first perceived. They came believing that attitudes would be difficult to change and that they would have to market aggressively whatever systems they could afford. They left the conference less concerned about attitudes and the problems of marketing.

A small number pointed out that research on the forms of cost benefit models, on the on-line concept itself, and on models to justify implementation of these systems would be extremely useful. Thus, in order to provide an approach to the problems of costs, research studies ought to proceed along these lines and the results ought to be monitored by all concerned.

Finally, the problems of retraining staff to use these systems ought to receive priority at locations other than the University of Pittsburgh. Once opportunities for such retraining are available on a broad base, then the problems of how to find these activities and how to allow staff the choice to avail themselves of such training will be forced toward solution. Therefore, the training experiments at the University of Pittsburgh Graduate School of Library and Information Sciences under Dr. Caruso ought to be monitored closely and possibly replicated in other geographic locations as a service to those already employed in libraries and information centers.

The compilers of the Conference Evaluation Appendix wish to acknowledge the contributions of Ms. Kate Purcell and Ms. Pauline Bean, who made the initial tabulation of questionnaire responses; Mrs. Eleanor Dym and Mr. Kevin Whitfield, who provided computer assistance; and the students of the Graduate School of Library and Information Sciences who distributed the questionnaires and served as conference aides.

Attachment A

PRE-CONFERENCE EVALUATION OF THE
ON-LINE REVOLUTION IN LIBRARIES

Question 1: At this point in time, before the conference begins, what is your own view of the actual or potential impact on the quality of library and information services of on-line information systems? Please circle the appropriate number below which best represents how you feel. For example, if you think on-line systems are having or will have a slight positive impact, you would circle the number 3, etc.

Very Significant Positive Impact	Significant Positive Impact	Slight Positive Impact	Neutral	Slight Negative Impact	Significant Negative Impact	Very Significant Negative Impact
156	201	20	7	2	0	0

Question 2: Very briefly, what do you see as the major problems for libraries and information centers in the successful adoption of on-line technology and systems?

ADMINISTRATIVE/MANAGERIAL

8 Need for more staff
6 Staff time away from traditional services
3 Number of users that can be served at one time
2 Impact on employment of librarian
2 Vendor cooperation and support
1 Need for these systems in a small college library
1 Impact on job classification
1 Change in the role of the librarian
1 Lack of cooperative efforts by types of libraries
1 Reluctance to think about systems and procedures

1 Effect of the increase by outside users
1 Role of librarians as subject specialists
1 Time
1 Space
1 Too many on-line systems
1 Information on matching data bases and types of libraries
1 Vandalism of equipment

ECONOMIC

246 Costs
2 Cost of converting manual files on-line
1 Impact on the publishing industry

Question 2 (cont.)

EDUCATIONAL

142 Training/re-education of library staff
61 Attitudes of library staff, administrators, and users
22 Selling the value of these services to potential users

RESEARCH

3 Interrelationship between manual and on-line searching
2 Models for the justification of on-line services
2 Options for training, terminals and number of searches

SOCIAL/POLITICAL

16 Equality of access to data bases
6 Problems of developing countries
3 Proprietary rights
2 Privacy of information
2 Control of information by a few
1 Lack of Canadian content
1 Children treated as second-class citizens with these systems
1 Government subsidies to private vendors to develop data bases
1 Polarization on the free vs. fee issue
1 Exploitation by vendors

SYSTEM DEVELOPMENT, OPERATION AND USE

65 Standardization of protocols
11 Quality control of input to data bases
7 Man-machine interface
6 Browsing
4 Conversion of retrospective indexes to on-line
4 Delays in response time
4 Duplications of coverage
4 Lack of number of data bases in the social sciences & humanities
2 Relevance of data bases
2 Currency of data bases
2 Reliability of citations
2 No guarantee that all important literature has been searched
2 Reference interview
2 Need more data bases
1 Need to develop on-line data bases for service rather than publishing
1 Impact of in-house computers
1 Inconsistent indexing
1 Adaptation of present system to take advantage of new efficiencies
1 Hardware design
1 Indexing incomplete
1 Access to telecommunications
1 Purpose of data base design
1 Technological development
1 Accuracy of data bases

NO RESPONSE 17

Question 3: Very briefly, what do you see as the major advantages for libraries and information centers in the adoption of on-line technology?

ADMINISTRATIVE/MANAGERIAL

18 Enhances opportunities for resource sharing
11 Provides management information
7 Proper emphasis on reference function

7 Allows for a literature search service
4 Enhances opportunity for networking
4 Increases and encourages the sharing of research results

Question 3 (cont.)

ADMINISTRATIVE/
  MANAGERIAL (cont.)

2 Potential for use
1 Requires interface with all segments of information industry
1 Requires careful comprehensive
   planning
1 Will bring revolution under control
1 Cause a review of service
   objectives
1 Exploitive control
1 Low cost of telephone connect time

ECONOMIC

35 Cost effective
1 Cheaper than printed copy
1 Will put libraries on a "pay as you
   go" basis

OPERATIONS

24 A professional task--a challenge
9 Acquisitions information
6 Cataloging information
6 Librarian's time freed for other
   projects
4 Current awareness applications
1 Less in-house indexing
1 More fun
1 Possible use by students
1 More efficient referral systems
1 Versatile
1 Assists ILL with location of
   documents
1 Transferability of technology to
   document delivery

PRODUCTS AND SERVICES

168 Speed
96 Comprehensive search of the
    literature
58 Multidimensional searching
37 Accuracy of information
28 Better service to users
20 Increased access to information
12 More current information than
    print sources
6 Ease of use
6 Printed bibliography
4 Saves user time
4 Direct use by end-user
3 Availability of multiple data bases
2 Improved bibliographic control
2 Actual data on file
2 Wider dissemination of
   information
2 Multiple users on same file
1 Expanded coverage
1 More effective than manual
   searching
1 Standardization of bibliographic
   resources

PUBLIC RELATIONS

8 Improves the image of the library
3 A means of attracting the new
   user
3 Improves the image of the
   librarian
1 Increases rapport with user

NO RESPONSE 19

Attachment B

GEOGRAPHIC ORIGINS AND POSITIONS HELD BY PARTICIPANTS

I. Number of Participants from State/Foreign Country Based on Registration
   Data Base

States:

Alabama	3	Missouri	4
Arizona	3	Mississippi	3
California	15	North Carolina	18
Colorado	13	New York	43
Connecticut	11	New Jersey	18
Delaware	1	Ohio	48
District of Columbia	35	Oklahoma	1
Florida	6	Pennsylvania	291
Georgia	5	Rhode Island	2
Illinois	23	South Carolina	1
Iowa	3	Tennessee	6
Indiana	4	Texas	13
Kansas	2	Utah	3
Kentucky	4	Vermont	1
Maine	1	Virginia	11
Maryland	28	Wisconsin	11
Massachusetts	15	Washington	5
Michigan	18	West Virginia	3
Minnesota	3	Wyoming	2

Foreign Countries:

Canada	43	Nigeria	1
Hong Kong	1	Switzerland	2
Nicaragua	1		

Participants came from 37 states, the District of Columbia, and 5
foreign countries.

II. Title Held by Participants Based on Initial Questionnaire

Acquisitions Librarian	1	Government Publications	
Acting (Interim) Director	1	Librarian	1
Administrative Services		Head, Bibliography Section	2
Librarian	1	Head, Data Preparation and	
Advisory Services Manager	1	Files Maintenance Unit,	
Army Librarian	2	Geography & Map	
Assistant Director	22	Division, LC	1
Assistant Librarian	14	Head, Education, Theology,	
Assistant Professor	9	Philosophy, Religion	
Associate Director	9	Department	1
Associate Librarian	1	Head, Educational Refer-	
Business Librarian	1	ence Center	1
Canadian Government		Head, Extension Services	2
Librarian	3	Head, Government Publi-	
Cataloguer	8	cations	1
Chair, Data Base Coordin-		Head, Information	
ating Committee	1	Exchange Center	1
Chair, Library Science		Head, Information	
Department	2	Processing Group	1
Chemistry Librarian	1	Head, Library Systems	
Chief, Education Librarian	1	Office	2
Chief of Planning and		Head, Librarian/Director	39
Development	1	Head, Reader's Services	2
Circulation Technician	2	Head, Reference	14
Coordinator, Media Center	1	Head, Serials Division	1
Coordinator of Department	14	Head, Technical Informa-	
Coordinator of Libraries	4	tion	1
Corporation Librarian	3	Information Analyst	1
Data Services Librarian	5	Information Center	2
Dean, Graduate School of		Information Chemist	1
Library Service	4	Information Industry	1
Deputy Manager	1	Information Retrieval	
Director, Computer Services	1	Specialist	1
Director, Information		Information Science	
Retrieval Center	1	Librarian	1
Director of Learning		Information Services	
Resources	4	Consultant	1
Director, Technical Services		Information Services	
Center	2	Librarian	3
Editor	1	Information Specialist	5
Education Librarian	1	Interlibrary Loan Librarian	2
Free-lance Librarian	1	Law Librarian	1
General Manager	2	Lecturer	4

II. (cont.)

Librarian	17	Professor	2
Librarian Analyst	1	Program Officer	1
Librarian, Health Service		Public Services Librarian	7
Library	2	Readers' Services Librarian	1
Library Consultant	4	Reference Librarian	36
Library, Cooperative		Research Librarian	2
Librarian	2	Reserve Book Librarian	1
Library, Instruction		Science Librarian	2
Librarian	1	Social Science Librarian	4
Library, Project Coordinator	2	Social Work Librarian	1
Library Service Manager	1	Student	19
Literature Chemist	1	Student Center Librarian	1
Manager, Corporate Library	3	Supervisor, Cataloguing	
Media Consultant	1	Section	1
Media Specialist	3	Supervisor, Search Section	1
Medical School Librarian	1	Systems Analyst	3
Methods Analyst	1	Systems/Programmer	
OB and Gynecology Depart-		Data Processing	1
ment, Librarian	1	Technical Information	
Periodicals Librarian	1	Specialist	1
Pharmaceutical Company		Technical Services	
Librarian	1	Librarian	6
President	2	University Librarian	11

Attachment C

POST-CONFERENCE EVALUATION OF THE
ON-LINE REVOLUTION IN LIBRARIES

Question 1: At this point in time, what is your own view of the actual or potential impact on the quality of library and information services of on-line information systems? Please circle the appropriate number below which best represents how you feel at the conclusion of this conference.

Very Significant Positive Impact	Significant Positive Impact	Slight Positive Impact	Neutral	Slight Negative Impact	Significant Negative Impact	Very Significant Negative Impact
71	125	23	1	2	1	0

Question 2: At this point, what do you personally see as the major problem for libraries and information centers in the successful adoption of on-line technology and systems?

ADMINISTRATIVE/MANAGERIAL

12 Administrative support
4 Lack of leadership
3 Is there a need for this service
2 Document delivery
2 Need to establish priorities
1 Perceived need
1 Choosing the right system
1 Formulating objectives for use
1 Consultants
1 Integration with traditional methods
1 Based on concept of resource sharing
1 Useful only in an academic community

ECONOMIC

158 Costs
1 Shift to a capital intensive transfer system
1 National funding for public libraries

EDUCATIONAL

67 Training/re-education of library staff
6 Selling the service to users
4 Attitude of users
3 Attitude of librarians
3 Conservatism of librarians
2 Acceptance by staff

288   MATARAZZO, CLOUGH, WILLIAMS

Question 2 (cont.)

EDUCATIONAL (cont.)

1 Confusion over equipment
1 Community support
1 Can librarians be accepted as
   information intermediaries
1 Changing the work habits of users
1 Need for positive attitudes by
   librarians

RESEARCH

6 Need for cost/benefit models
1 Lack of research basis on on-line
1 On understanding user needs

SOCIAL/POLITICAL

5 Access by others than elite

SYSTEM DEVELOPMENT,
  OPERATION AND USE

5 Quality control
4 Standardization of protocols
4 Limited subject coverage
1 Insufficient library/information
   center impact on technology
   development
1 Making needs known to vendors
1 Communication between librarian
   and user
1 Retrospective coverage
1 Emphasis should be on use, not
   technology

NO RESPONSE 9

Question 3: At this point, what do you personally see as the major advantage
            for libraries and information centers in the adoption of on-line
            technology? Please write it in below.

ADMINISTRATIVE/MANAGERIAL

7 More efficient
7 Ease of resource sharing
3 Eliminates tedious tasks
3 Management feedback
2 Necessary for research
2 Opportunity for librarians
1 Forces rethinking of service goals
1 Communication with other librarians
1 Needed for library to retain viability
   as an information source
1 Inevitable
1 Staff freed for other assignments
1 Brings libraries to full cycle of
   information delivery
1 Cooperation is enforced
1 Increase use of library

ECONOMIC

2 Produces income
1 Gain additional staff
1 Pay as you use
1 Need it to survive
1 Reduction of staff
1 Do not have to purchase
   expensive resource
1 Elimination of printed indexes
   and abstracts
1 Long-term cost benefits

PRODUCTS AND SERVICES

96 Comprehensiveness
81 Speed
54 Enhanced quality of reference
    service

Question 3 (cont.)

PRODUCTS AND SERVICES (cont.)

9 Multidimensional access
5 Currency of data
4 Versatility
3 Added dimension of information service
1 Eliminate redundancy in technical processes
1 Better bibliographic control
1 Technical service applications
1 Flexibility of the search
1 Users will see it as the only valid search
1 On-line delivers what it promises
1 Saves time for the user
1 Free of human error
1 Not strictly printed data
1 Manipulation of information

1 Ease of use
1 More personalized information service
1 Another source of information

PUBLIC RELATIONS

5 A new (different) service
5 Image of library improved
2 Service to small elite user groups
2 Value to user
2 Attract new clientele
1 Image of the librarian improved
1 A sign of leadership in the information area

NOT SURE   1
NO RESPONSE   12

Question 4: What was the most powerful argument you heard during the conference that would lead you to disagree with the notion that on-line technology represents a "revolution" for libraries and information centers ?

39 Evolutionary rather than revolutionary
23 De Gennaro's remarks
11 Other so-called revolutions have come and gone
10 None
8 Detlefsen's remarks
7 Licklider's remarks
4 Just another step
4 Small portion of population served
3 Lorenz's remarks
2 For public library not enough subjects in data bases
2 Nothing has changed
1 Martin's remarks

1 Summit's statement
1 Drake's remarks
1 For the elite
1 Lack of leadership
1 Need more money
1 Need more staff
1 Old systems intact
1 The talking has not stopped
1 Training
1 Microforms
1 Appreciation is slow to show
1 Effect on the unemployment of librarians
1 Prices are stable
1 Merely a change in approach

Question 4 (cont.)

1 Savings possible with manual   1 The cost vs. the benefits
  systems   1 The revolution lacks a broad base
1 It's a loss leader to attract people 1 The revolution is unimportant
  to the library   1 A bandwagon not a revolution
1 Does not cover all subjects   1 Service mission is not affected

                                        NO RESPONSE 63

Question 5: What was the most powerful argument you heard during the con-
            ference that would lead you to <u>agree</u> with the notion that on-line
            technology represents a "revolution" for libraries and informa-
            tion centers?

17 None heard   1 Changing role of librarians
12 Growth in use   1 Basic change of procedure
 7 Licklider's remarks   1 Rejection of cost models
 7 Newness of approach   1 Power and usefulness of
 6 The technology is available   librarians
 5 700+ attendees   1 More competition
 4 Kent's paper   1 Union of A & I's catalogs and
 4 Failure to adopt new technologies   findings aids
 4 A new dimension for service   1 Will spread to school and public
 3 Burchinal's paper   libraries
 3 User payment   1 Decrease in prices
 3 It works   1 Doms' remarks
 3 Critical mass of information   1 Detlefsen's remarks
 3 LC's on-line catalog   1 Schiller's remarks
 2 Rethinking of service objectives   1 Cuadra's remarks
 2 Evolution   1 De Gennaro's remarks
 2 Speakers   1 White House Conference leadership
 2 Williams' remarks   1 Publication of articles on demand
 2 Trezza's remarks   1 Number of searches
 2 Growth in use of data bases   1 Computer does the drudge work
 2 Required aptitude for technology   1 Better, faster service to users
 2 Proliferation of data bases   1 Promise of document delivery
 2 Applications to all phases of   1 Success rates
   librarianship   1 Future costs
 2 Lorenz's remarks   1 Bibliographic access
 2 Drake's remarks   1 Non-library use
 1 Participation of vendors   1 <u>Readers Guide</u> on-line
 1 Multidimensional search

                                        NO RESPONSE 23

Question 6: Was the conference influential in affecting your attitude about
on-line information systems?

Extremely Influenced Me	Significantly Influenced Me	Somewhat Influenced Me	Influenced Me Very Little	Not At All
5	60	77	47	24

Note: Most respondents who circled "somewhat influenced," "very little
influenced" and "not at all" noted that they were already in favor of
on-line systems and that the conference served to reinforce their
attitude.

Question 7: How would you rate the effectiveness of this conference in
conveying information?

Extremely Effective	Significantly Effective	Somewhat Effective	Very Little	Not At All
34	105	50	17	3

Please share with us any comments you would care to offer about
the conference or your thoughts about on-line information systems
in libraries.

A--On "On-Line"

2 On-line is essential
1 Access is critical
1 Problem of paid service overstated
1 Need training centers at other locations than Pitt
1 Not everyone needs on-line
1 Aptitude test for on-line operators
1 Enhanced image of library
1 Practical models for application
1 Model for proper data base selection
1 Impact on the printed indexes
1 Standardization
1 When will monographs be indexed?

B--On the Conference

30 Well planned
23 Provide for small discussion groups

B--On the Conference (cont.)

14 More audience participation
10 Limit registration
 9 Speakers were excellent
 8 More practical information
 6 Informative conference
 6 Excellent papers
 5 Smaller panels
 5 More breaks during the conference
 5 More specifics
 4 Maps of the city of Pittsburgh
 3 Excellent conference
 3 Too general
 3 More research presentations
 3 More vendor material should be available
 3 Reports on studies done abroad
 2 Demonstrations by vendors
 2 Excellent panels
 2 Publish the proceedings
 2 More on public libraries
 2 Best conference ever attended
 2 Politics of the problems discussed too much
 2 Stimulating conference
 2 Present more solutions
 2 Adjust location of "no smoking area"
 1 Vary format of presentations
 1 Provide for more contact with vendors
 1 Speakers should attend whole conference and be available
 1 More debate
 1 Great conference
 1 Bring divergent views into context
 1 Poor lighting
 1 Tour of Pitt
 1 A follow-up conference
 1 Conference too long
 1 More industrial librarians should have attended

INDEX

293